Terrorism's War with America

Terrorism's War with America

A History

DENNIS PISZKIEWICZ

PRAEGER

Westport, Connecticut
London

Library of Congress Cataloging-in-Publication Data

Piszkiewicz, Dennis.
    Terrorism's war with America: a history / Dennis Piszkiewicz.
        p.   cm.
    Includes bibliographical references and index.
    ISBN 0–275–97952–0 (alk. paper)
    1. Terrorism—United States—History—20th century. 2. Terrorism—
    Prevention—Government policy—United States—History—20th century.
    3. United States—Foreign relations—20th century. 4. Islamic fundamentalism.
    I. Title.
HV6432.P57 2003
303.6'25'0973—dc21   2003042940

British Library Cataloging in Publication Data is available.

Library of Congress Catalog Card Number: 2003042940
ISBN: 0–275–97952–0

First published in 2003

Greenwood Press, 88 Post Road West, Westport, CT 06881
An imprint of Greenwood Publishing Group, Inc.
www.praeger.com

Printed in the United States of America

The paper used in this book complies with the
Permanent Paper Standard issued by the National
Information Standards Organization (Z39.48–1984).

10 9 8 7 6 5 4 3 2 1

For Andrew and Samantha Piszkiewicz.
May the world they inherit be more civilized than ours.

Contents

Photo essay follows chapter 10

Preface

For most Americans, terrorism made the transformation from theoretical threat to frightening reality on September 11, 2001. The murderous and tragic events of that day began the United States' "War on Terrorism." Terrorism's war on America, however, had begun four decades earlier. The historical narrative of this book takes us from those first blundering acts of terrorism and through the intervening years until, on that Tuesday morning, America finally understood that it was a target.

Because the attacks were spaced out over time, they were as easy to forget as the headlines of last week's newspapers. We remember the bombing of the U.S. embassies in Kenya and Tanzania, but we are less likely to remember the slaughters at the U.S. embassy, the marine peacekeeping force barracks, and the U.S. embassy annex in Beirut, Lebanon, in 1983 and 1984. We are less likely still to remember the first airliner hijackings of the late 1950s and early 1960s. In attacks on U.S. citizens and its interests prior to September 11, 2001, terrorists killed at least a thousand people and injured close to ten thousand (see chapter 2). The most deadly attacks, those resulting in the greatest numbers of casualties, did not take place on American soil, however. Perhaps for that reason and because of the fading memory of earlier attacks, Americans were unprepared for the most audacious act of modern terrorism.

If you think you know what terrorism is, if you think everybody agrees on the same definition, think again. According to the U.S. Department of State, in its annual review of terrorism titled *Patterns of Global Terrorism*, "No one definition of terrorism has gained universal acceptance."[1] Even within the U.S. government, different agencies—the Department of State,

Federal Bureau of Investigation (FBI), and Federal Emergency Management Agency—use definitions that differ in significant ways that seem to reflect their perceptions of their missions.[2] Beyond the federal bureaucracy, other governments and political organizations are likely to have their own agendas and often self-serving definition of terrorism. There is truth in the cliché that "one person's terrorist is another's freedom fighter."

Before we abandon reason for moral relativism, let us have a definition. My favorite is that of former secretary of state George Schultz, who has been quoted as saying, "Terrorists practice random violence on as large a scale as possible against civilian populations to make their points or get their way."[3] It is an equal opportunity definition, letting any political group, government, individual, religious group, or criminal organization commit acts of terrorism. Terrorists are enemies of civilization, and regrettably, civilized people have become terrorists by adopting the tactics of terrorists.

Although this book focuses on the experience of the United States with terrorism, it includes relevant experience of others that define the global context. It follows terrorism as it evolved from a disorganized rebel strategy, through its use by nationalists and insurgents and "rogue" states, to its more recent appearance as the battle plan of holy warriors. And of course, it examines what the United States has done—and not done—over the decades before September 11, 2001, to deal with its unconventional enemies in its undeclared war with terrorism.

The events of September 11, 2001, have reminded us that the hijacking of airliners is a basic tactic of terrorism as we know it today. This is where we will begin our journey in chapter 1, with an airliner that has taken off from an American airport and is commandeered by armed men who have a political cause and a plan.

Acknowledgments

Over the past several years, many people have given of their time and support to help me complete this book. I wish to thank Lyn Chevli, Nanette Heiser, Mike Stein, Bruce Boycks, Jack Baldridge, Jerry Baldridge, Eric Knabe, and GiGi Mullins. I thank P.J. Kaylor for her unwavering support despite my antisocial moods. Also, I thank Heather Ruland Staines, my editor, for her faith in this project and for her encouragement.

Chapter 1

Skyjackers

The five men who boarded the Cubana Airlines flight in Miami intended to join Fidel Castro and his guerrillas at their stronghold in the Sierra Maestra Mountains of Cuba's Oriente Province. They believed, no doubt, that their mission would change history, and it did. But their mission ended much sooner than they had planned, and it changed history in ways they neither intended nor expected.

The Vickers Viscount airliner carried a crew of four, with sixteen passengers—nine Cubans and seven U.S. citizens—when it departed the Miami airport in the late afternoon on Sunday, November 1, 1958. Its destination was Varadero, on the north coast of Cuba, approximately two hundred miles to the south. About a half hour into the flight and halfway to its destination, the pilot radioed that the flight would land on schedule.[1]

A man rose from his seat, drew a gun, and pointed it at the passengers. Four other men followed his lead and also drew guns. They then took from their carry-on luggage machine guns and military fatigues, which they immediately put on. The uniforms included the red-and-black armbands worn by members of Castro's 26th of July movement.

With the passengers and the cabin crew under control, some of the men with guns entered the cockpit and demanded that the pilot change course toward Cuba's Oriente Province, the locale of Castro's mountain redoubt. The pilot refused and received a blow to the head for his lack of cooperation.

One of the men in a rebel uniform took the controls of the aircraft. As darkness fell over Cuba, he turned the airliner east, toward Oriente

Province, where he attempted to land at a small, unlighted airstrip. His skills as a pilot were not up to the task. The plane jumped all over the sky; luggage fell from the overhead racks, and passengers were screaming and vomiting. A man in fatigues ran out of the cockpit and braced himself in an open seat. Moments later, the airliner crashed into the dark waters of Nipe Bay.

Rescuers managed to pull three severely injured survivors from the water. The seventeen others on board the airplane were killed.[2]

People with political agendas had been hijacking airplanes for decades before the Cubana Airlines flight from Miami to Varadero reached its deadly conclusion. The first recorded hijacking is that of a small commercial aircraft by Peruvian revolutionaries in 1930. The dissidents had the pilot carry them aloft so that they could bomb Peru with propaganda leaflets.

As the Cold War was cranking up in the late 1940s and early 1950s, political dissidents commandeered aircraft of all types as means of transportation to geographies where the politics were more to their liking. Both the Western countries and the Soviet-dominated states welcomed hijackers seeking asylum. Historical records of these early hijackings are meager, but what has been compiled indicates that they were relatively harmless events. In more than thirty hijackings—none of which involved American aircraft or hijackers—most airplane crews, passengers, and hijackers came through their experiences unharmed, but there were exceptions. In the hijacking of one plane from Bulgaria to Turkey in 1948, the pilot and copilot were injured. In another incident that took place in 1947, a private aircraft was forced to fly from Romania to Turkey. One report of this incident suggests that the hijackers killed an uncooperative crew member; but because of an absence of records, the death could not be confirmed. The hijackings of early Cold War were followed by a period of peace in the skies; there were no reported hijackings of airplanes in the years 1953 through 1957.[3]

The year 1958 marked the return of airplane hijacking—soon to be renamed "skyjacking" and "air piracy"—as a means of achieving political ends, and its emergence as a tactic in international battles. In February and April of that year, airliners were reported to have been hijacked from South Korea, both apparently without casualties. Only one made a successful trip to North Korea. The American press paid little attention to either incident.

On October 22, 1958, Castro's partisans took a Cuban domestic flight, a twin-engine DC-3. Ten days later, the flight from Miami to Varadero crashed after being commandeered by the four inept guerrillas. At the time, observers speculated that it had been taken to interfere with transportation of troops to Oriente Province, the stronghold of Fidel Castro's rebel forces.[4] Then five days after that, another Cubana DC-3 with twenty-five passengers was hijacked. It landed in territory controlled by Fidel

Castro's rebels. Within a three-week period, the rebels had taken from Cuba's domestic airline, Cubana, nearly a quarter of its aircraft. In doing so, they helped cut communication between the eastern and western parts of the island, and they acquired the aircraft they needed to begin their own air transportation service.[5]

Hijacking three commercial aircraft—one of them from a flight from Miami—was part of the guerrilla war against Cuba's Batista regime. The people on board, especially those who died on the flight that originated in Miami, were the victims of the revolution. The term *terrorism* had not yet come to be associated with the hijacking of aircraft. Nevertheless, terrorism was an integral part of the Cuban revolution.

Batista and his thugs were first to use terrorist methods. The rebels learned quickly, but hard as they tried, they failed to match the bloody outrages committed by their enemy. Batista's police and Military Intelligence Service were notoriously brutal. They used torture as much for their enjoyment as to get information. They killed suspected rebels and left their corpses on busy sidewalks as lessons for those who would oppose Batista's corrupt regime. The rebels went beyond the hit-and-run raids basic to guerrilla warfare. They left bombs where people congregated, in Havana's gambling casinos and movie theaters. One report claimed that the rebels sometimes planted as many as a hundred bombs in a night. They kidnapped U.S. sailors on shore leave, employees of U.S. companies, and tourists.[6] Raul Castro, Fidel's brother, was given credit for taking forty-seven U.S. citizens hostage in the summer of 1958[7] and for executing thirty alleged informers.[6]

The hijacking of airliners by the Cuban rebels was a mixture of showmanship and military action. The rebels' long-term goal may have been international revolution, but their actions were local and unsophisticated. The tactics of modern terrorism were in their infancy. It would take more than a decade and hundreds of incidents before the hijackings would evolve into powerful political statements.

In the early hours of New Year's Day, 1959, Castro's rebels rolled into Havana, and the direction taken by hijacked aircraft changed. That day, supporters of deposed dictator Fulgencio Batista commandeered a Cubana airliner and forced its crew to take it to New York.[8] Hijackers took two more airliners from Cuba to the United States that year. Another aircraft was taken from Cuba to Miami in April 1960, and two more in July 1960.[9] The United States did nothing to discourage what was commonly viewed as the escape of political refugees from a socialist regime—Castro had not yet declared himself to be a communist. North Americans generally accepted the airline hijackers with open arms as political refugees.

By late 1960, Castro had tired of the game of air piracy that his revolution had started two years earlier,[8] especially because U.S. courts were allowing seizure of the hijacked aircraft in repayment of debts owed to

American companies by Cuba.[10] Castro instituted tighter security measures for air transportation in Cuba, including armed guards on commercial flights.[8] The hijacking game, which had no serious casualties since the Miami to Varadero flight of 1958, turned deadly again on October 29, 1960, when nine Cubans commandeered a Cubana DC-3 on a flight from Havana to the Isle of Pines. The armed guard on board resisted. In the fight that followed, four people on board, one of them the pilot, were wounded by gunfire, and the guard was killed. The hijacked DC-3 made an emergency landing at Key West, Florida. The hijackers asked for political asylum and got it. They were not held accountable for killing the guard.[11]

A little over a month later, on December 8, five men attempted to hijack another Cubana flight. They were foiled by Castro's security forces, and in short order, all were executed.[11] In 1961, there was one successful hijacking from Havana to Miami, as well as a bloody, failed attempt to hijack a flight from Havana, in which three people were killed and six others wounded. A few more attempts were made to hijack Cuban aircraft in 1966 and 1971, all ending with violence and failure; but with the exception of these, Castro and his regime had put an end to the hijacking of airliners from Cuba.[12]

As Cuba was ending its problems with air piracy, those of the United States began. On May 1, 1961, fourteen days after the humiliating defeat of the Cuban exile force sponsored by the United States at the Bay of Pigs, a man who identified himself as Elpirata Cofrisi bought a ticket aboard a National Airlines flight that would stop at Marathon, in the Florida Keys, on its way to Key West. Nobody connected the man's name to *El Pirata* ("the pirate") Cofrisi, an eighteenth-century Spanish pirate. The man boarded the plane, and when it took off from Marathon on the second leg of its flight, he entered the cockpit, put a knife to the throat of the pilot, and, pointing a gun at the copilot, ordered the copilot to leave. Cofrisi told the pilot to fly to Havana. The airliner's crew, seven uninvolved passengers, and one hijacker arrived safely in Havana, where Cuban soldiers took the hijacker into custody. Within three hours, the airliner with its crew and remaining passengers were back in the air on their way to Key West.[13]

En route, Cofrisi, whose real name was Antulio Ramirez Ortiz, told the pilot that he was a U.S. citizen of Cuban descent who had served in Korea. He also said that General Rafael Trujillo, dictator of the Dominican Republic, had offered him $100,000 to kill Fidel Castro, and he wanted to tell Castro of the plot against his life. The pilot believed that the hijacker was mentally unbalanced.[13] Cofrisi's claim may not have been as absurd as it sounded, although Trujillo may not have been the one offering money for the hit. At that time, the Central Intelligence Agency (CIA) was plotting to kill the Cuban leader.[14] Trujillo himself was the victim of an assassination less than a month later by killers who had been in contact with the CIA.[15]

The year 1961, it seemed at the time, was a big year for hijacking. Ten aircraft were hijacked worldwide, four from the United States, of which two made it to Cuba.[16] In the years 1962 through 1967, hijackings dipped into the single digits, with at most two airplanes being taken from the United States to Cuba in each of those years. But in 1968, air piracy became an international criminal activity. Thirty-five aircraft were commandeered that year, with twenty of them redirected from the United States to Cuba, although not all of them reached Cuba. In 1969, there were eighty-nine hijackings, and the following year, eighty-four.[17]

These hijacking incidents resulted in remarkably low casualties. The few who were injured or killed were usually the hijackers, although during one incident in 1971, a hijacker shot and killed a passenger.[17] For air travelers, hijacking became a joke, but flight crews were not amused when boarding passengers asked them about the flight time to Havana or what the weather was like there.[18]

Cuba developed a routine for dealing with passengers on hijacked flights that arrived in Havana. Although American pilots disagreed, the Cuban authorities claimed that the runway at Havana's Jose Marti Airport was not long enough to permit the safe take-off of a loaded jet airliner, and the planes were sent home empty. Meanwhile, Cuba treated its reluctant visitors with Caribbean hospitality and a bus ride through the socialist state to Varadero, where they boarded a plane that would take them home. When the aircraft and its passengers had departed, Cuba presented the airlines with the tab for managing the unscheduled flights and hosting the unexpected visitors. The airlines were stuck with bills that ranged from $2,500 to $3,000 per hijacking; they also lost up to $45,000 for every day one of their airliners was not carrying paying passengers.[19]

What set the hijacking of the 1960s apart from those of the early days of the Cold War, the late 1940s and 1950s, was that these later hijackings were widely reported. Cold War refugees trying to find their way to a safer land were not big news, and few details were reported in the print media. But the hijackings from Cuba to the United States and vice versa were part of a major battle of the Cold War: the communists' ascendancy in Cuba and the United States' opposition to it. The disaster of the Bay of Pigs invasion and the Cuban Missile Crisis were not only international news events; they were on the front pages of the morning newspapers, and they were the big stories on the evening television news. So were the hijackings of the airliners, the skirmishes in that undeclared war. In other parts of the world, those with political grievances were bound to take notice and add air piracy to their tactics.

While the United States and other countries in the West were trying— and failing—to deal with skyjacking, people elsewhere in the world were learning to use it to advance their political agenda. Air piracy arrived in the

Middle East on an El Al 707 jetliner intended to go from Rome to Tel Aviv on July 23, 1968. Three Arab men commandeered the plane and had the pilot take it to Algiers, where they released all women, children, and non-Israeli passengers. The hijackers, who identified themselves as members of the Popular Front for the Liberation of Palestine (PFLP), held twelve male Israeli passengers and the crew hostage, and they demanded the release of 1,200 Palestinians held prisoner by Israel.[20] The PFLP hijacked and attacked more aircraft, both of the Israeli carrier El Al and of other nations, in the years that followed. The PFLP conducted its most spectacular hijacking operation on September 6, 1970, when its guerrillas simultaneously commandeered four commercial airliners with the intention of trading the passengers and aircraft for Palestinian guerrillas being held prisoner by Israel. (These incidents are examined in detail in chapter 4.)

Between May 1, 1961, and December 31, 1972, skyjackers commandeered 159 aircraft worldwide. Eighty-five of these aircraft, or 53 percent, were taken from the United States to Cuba. By the end of that period, in 1972, two-thirds of hijacked planes were destined for Cuba.[21] During one period in 1972, skyjackers took a plane every Friday over a seventeen-week period. The last day of the workweek soon acquired the name "Skyjack Friday."[22]

The United States finally took action in early 1973, nearly fifteen years after the first hijacking of an airplane from the United States to Cuba. It required airport operators to search passengers with metal detectors and to search their carry-on baggage. In addition, the government required that armed law enforcement officers be stationed at checkpoints during the boarding of aircraft. Furthermore, the United States, Cuba, and Canada signed an agreement to prosecute hijackers of airplanes and seagoing vessels in their own courts.[23]

By the 1970s, the record of aircraft hijackings was substantial enough to give an insight into motivations. Skyjackers could be sorted into three major categories according to motive: political terrorists, common criminals, and psychologically disturbed people. Political hijackers have shown themselves to be the best organized and most sophisticated. Their goals have been to escape a political regime, to create propaganda for their cause, and to use the hijacking as leverage for the release of political prisoners, who were often other terrorists. Members of the PFLP were an early example of this type. Islamic radicals have in recent decades joined this group. Common criminals have hijacked aircraft to escape from jurisdictions they found hostile. Some, such as the notorious D. B. Cooper, have used the threat of destroying an aircraft as a means of financial extortion. The psychologically disturbed, such as the previously mentioned Elpirata Cofrisi, craved attention at the expense of airlines and air travelers. Individual hijackers such as Cofrisi could fit into one, two, or all of these categories.[24, 25]

BOMBS ON AIRCRAFT

The rise in aircraft hijackings was paralleled by a rise in bombings of aircraft. Bombings have been particularly vicious in that they have often destroyed the targeted aircraft while killing all on board. A few numbers may help the reader understand the growth of the problem. The U.S. Federal Aviation Administration (FAA) reported that worldwide, from 1950 through 1959, there were eight "explosions aboard aircraft." During the 1960s, that number rose to fifteen; in the 1970s, it had reached forty-four. For the first six years of the 1980s, the FAA counted eighteen explosions aboard aircraft.[26] These bombings of aircraft from the 1950s through the 1980s killed more than twenty-nine hundred people and injured hundreds more.[27]

Whereas hijackings are commonly done in public, with publicity often being a motive, bombings are committed clandestinely by anonymous criminals. If the bombings are successful, the evidence of a bomb may disappear with the explosion. One writer estimated that possibly half of all aircraft bombings go undetected because of the loss or scattering of evidence.[28] Furthermore, if the culprit does not take credit, there may be no way of knowing who is responsible. Several bombings of commercial aircraft will be encountered in the chapters to come as the evolution of international terrorism is followed.

FROM SKYJACKING TO KAMIKAZI FLIGHTS

A year passed without an attempted skyjacking. Then, on February 22, 1974, an unemployed salesman named Samuel Byck attempted to board an early-morning Delta Airlines flight from Baltimore-Washington International Airport bound for Atlanta. As the security guard checked passengers with a metal detector, Byck walked behind him and fired three rounds from his .38-caliber revolver into the guard's back. Byck ran to the plane, broke into the cockpit, and told the pilot to "fly this plane out of here." The pilot said he could not do it because the wheels where blocked and he did not have clearance. Byck went to the cabin and brought a woman passenger back into the cockpit. He told the woman, "Help this man fly the plane." Either the pilot or the copilot objected, and Byck shot the pilot in the back and the copilot in the head. He then went back to the cabin, where he grabbed another woman by the hair and dragged her to the cockpit. He made her watch as he fired several more bullets into the pilot and copilot.

By then, an off-duty policeman who was in the terminal had drawn his gun and aimed at Byck. He fired twice; the bullets crashed through the terminal window, through the cockpit window, and into Byck's chest. Byck put his gun to his head and pulled the trigger.

Investigators at the scene found under Byck's body a briefcase containing a gasoline bomb they said was big enough to destroy the DC-9 jetliner. The dead included the security guard, the copilot, and the hijacker, Samuel Byck. Although critically wounded, the pilot survived.[29]

Just hours before going to the airport, Samuel Byck had mailed audiotapes to six public figures, among them syndicated columnist Jack Anderson. On the tape, Byck called his hijacking plan "Operation Pandora's Box," and he summarized its key features by saying, "I will try to get the plane aloft and fly it toward the target area, which will be Washington, D.C. I will shoot the pilot and then in the last few minutes try to steer the plane into the target, which is the White House."[30, 31]

Byck, it was learned later, was a manic-depressive who had once been arrested for threatening President Nixon's life. Byck had failed to execute his plan, but he understood the concept of using a fully fuelled jetliner as a missile to destroy an important building. Over a quarter of a century later, other terrorists would use this tactic successfully against America.

Chapter 2

Who Are the Terrorists?

DOMESTIC TERRORISTS

During the late 1950s and early 1960s, the United States experienced a series of domestic terrorist attacks, although the term *terrorism* was not applied to them at the time. The violence and lynchings of the early part of the twentieth century were the legacy of slavery, which ended in the previous century. The violence was reignited by the emerging civil rights movement and a response to its nonviolence. Racist elements, primarily in the south, used violence to intimidate those advocating civil rights for the ultimate purpose of keeping Negroes—the term of the times—subjugated.

The use of terrorism by racists in America's south reached its peak of viciousness during the early 1960s, with the burning and bombing of churches serving blacks that were focal points for voter-registration drives. One account tallied over five hundred bomb attacks on blacks during the height of the civil rights movement.[1] The following are just some examples. In early September 1962, four churches in Georgia with black congregations were torched.[2] On September 15, a bomb exploded in the church of another black congregation as a Sunday School class was being held. The blast killed four young girls and injured fourteen other people.[3] Whites who were involved in the civil rights movement were also targets of attacks. In June 1964, two white civil rights workers from New York, Michael Schwerner and Andrew Goodman, accompanied by a black worker from Mississippi, James Chaney, were taken into custody by police in Philadelphia, Mississippi, while on their way to join a voter-registration campaign. They disappeared after their release, and two days later their burned-out car was found fifteen miles from Philadelphia. A month and a half later, FBI agents working on a tip from a paid informant found the bodies of the three missing men buried in a new earthen dam just five miles from Philadelphia, Mississippi.[4, 5]

The pressure of federal law enforcement brought about a decrease in racial violence in the South as the 1960s came to an end. In the North, violence and terrorism grew as part of the opposition to the war in Vietnam and other perceived social injustices; but it was no longer ignorant thugs in white robes and hoods who committed the crimes—it was the well-educated children of the affluent. Ironically, both the southern racists and the northern radicals of the left had the same enemy, though not the same values and objectives. They were both outside the mainstream of American thought, and they both attacked what was known at the time as "the establishment" and the federal government. The South had the Ku Klux Klan and White Citizens' Councils; the North and West had the Black Panthers, Symbionese Liberation Army, and, most significant, the Weatherman group. They spouted revolutionary philosophies and agendas, but they had more in common with Bonnie and Clyde than Che and Fidel.

One of the best-known social activist groups of that era was the Students for a Democratic Society (SDS), which was founded in 1962 as a nonviolent action group of college students dedicated to addressing the issues of racism and the threat of nuclear warfare.[6] By the late 1960s, the SDS had grown in membership and found itself dealing with the new issues of the war in Vietnam and what it described as the imperialism of America's government and corporations. Because its members were young, educated, and opinionated, the SDS inevitably began to fragment. The most significant splinter group was the Weatherman faction, which espoused the use of violence to bring about change. Members described themselves as urban guerrillas. Today they would be called terrorists.

During the fifteen-month period from the beginning of 1969 to the beginning of April 1970, the United States experienced 4,330 bombings that killed at least 40 people and injured 384 more. It was easier to count the bodies than it was to tell how many of the attacks were nonpolitical criminal acts, how many were committed by racists and right-wing extremists, and how many were attacks by groups of the radical left such as the Weatherman.[7] To give the violent radicals of the left a name suggests that they were an organized terrorist group, but law enforcement officials and they themselves conceded that they were incapable of concerted action. They were at best disconnected cells with a common enemy.[1]

Organized or not, they caused a lot of destruction and chaos. Their primary targets were offices of major American corporations, especially those in New York. In November 1969, unknown terrorists bombed the headquarters of Chase Manhattan Bank, General Motors, and Standard Oil of New Jersey. Domestic terrorists struck New York again in the early hours of March 12, 1970, when they simultaneously bombed the Socony Mobil Building, the IBM Building, and the General Telephone and Electronics Building. The explosions caused tremendous amounts of damage; but because the bombs were set to go off in the early morning hours, and because the bombers warned the police a half hour before the bombs were to explode, the buildings were evacuated and there were no injuries.[8] The urban guerrillas learned quickly that they did not need explosives to be terrorists. A telephone call could be almost as disruptive. In the two days following the March 12 attacks, New Yorkers had to deal with more than six hundred phony bomb reports, all of which required evacuations and inspections before normal activities could resume.[9]

One of the Weatherman groups showed itself to be more dangerous to itself than to its corporate and government targets. The group had been using as its base a townhouse on Eleventh Street in New York's Greenwich Village. On the afternoon of March 6, 1970, something went wrong in the basement bomb factory. The explosion collapsed the four-story building to street level. Two young women were seen running from the wreckage; one was the daughter of the building's wealthy owner. In the debris, police found the crushed and dismembered bodies of two men and one woman. They also found 57 sticks of dynamite and 140 blasting caps. According to one police official, "There was enough dynamite there to demolish most of the block."[1]

Terrorism and destruction from America's leftist radicals reached its peak in the early hours of August 24, 1970, in Madison, Wisconsin. At 3:40 A.M., city police received an anonymous call warning that a bomb was about to explode at the Army Mathematics Research Center on the University of Wisconsin campus. Two minutes later, outside that facility, a rented van loaded with a bomb made of ammonium nitrate and fuel oil exploded. Police did not have the time to warn those working through the night of the danger. The blast killed one scientist who was in the building and injured four others. It destroyed most of the contents of the building, and according to the University's chancellor, it "ruined the life work of five physics professors and wiped out the Ph.D. theses of two dozen graduate students."

A local underground newspaper reported that it had received a statement from a group calling itself "The New Year's Gang" and claiming responsibility for the bombing. According to the statement, the attack was "part of the worldwide struggle to defeat imperialism." The FBI soon identified four suspects in the bombing: three former students and the younger brother of one of them. The bombers had demonstrated that someone with no more than a few years of college education, with little—if any—expertise with explosives, with limited capital, but with exaggerated self-importance could build an immensely destructive bomb. The truck bomb had arrived in America.[10]

The self-destructive accident in the New York town house and the unplanned but predictable deaths elsewhere eventually led to a decline in the use of bombing and arson as tools of social protest. When the war in Vietnam ended and Richard Nixon was hounded from office, the radical left slumped into decline. Nevertheless, the violent tactics of right-wing racists in the early 1960s and of the radical fringe of the young leftists in the late 1960s and early 1970s were prophetic. America would see their legacies again in Beirut in the 1980s, in New York and Oklahoma City in the mid-1990s, and in New York and Virginia on September 11, 2001.

INTERNATIONAL TERRORISTS

As America's home-grown terrorism went into decline, similar violent revolutionary movements elsewhere grew. Germany had its Baader-Meinhoff Gang, Italy had its Red Brigades, Northern Ireland saw the rise of the Provisional Irish Republican Army, Japan had its own Red Army, Israel dealt with the ever-present Palestinians, and a multitude of other terrorist groups that used violence against civilians to press their political agendas sprang up around the globe. Most were small, and many had goals not directly relevant to American interests; but some, as the following chapters will show, chose to make war on the United States.

During the decades after the first hijackings of commercial aircraft and before the attacks of September 11, 2001, the United States, its interests, and its people have been the object of hundreds of terrorist attacks that have killed over a thousand people and injured thousands more. The vast majority of these terrorist attacks were committed on a small scale: a pipe bomb here, a kidnapped diplomat there, attacks on American embassies— it seems—everywhere. But a small number of incidents of terrorism stand out because of their scale and their psychopathic brutality. A listing of these acts of terror that identifies those responsible gives a quick picture of the scope of terrorism and an insight into who the most dangerous terrorists are. The most egregious incidents of terrorism against the United States and its interests beginning with the ill-fated 1958 hijacking of a Cubana airliner on a flight from Miami and ending with the attacks on the World Trade Center and the Pentagon are listed in appendix 1. (Most of these incidents are discussed in detail in the following chapters, which have references to sources.)

This summary reveals several significant trends. First, the number of major incidents has increased with time over the decades. Specifically, there was one incident in the late 1950s, none in the 1960s, two in the mid-1970s, six in the 1980s, seven during the 1990s, and four during only the first two years of the 2000s. Second, the numbers of those killed and injured has also increased over time to the terrifying—as intended—totals of the attacks of September 11, 2001. Not only do these attacks against America stand above the background of four decades of attacks against America; they exceed in their violence attacks experienced by other countries. No other nation has been the target of single attacks killing and injuring as many people as those against the U.S. embassy in Kenya and against the World Trade Center.

Other significant information found in the listing of appendix 1 concerns the identities of those responsible. The two earliest incidents, the 1958 airliner hijacking and a 1975 bombing in New York, were attributed to Cuban revolutionaries and Puerto Rican nationalists, respectively. Timothy McVeigh and Terry Nichols have been tried and convicted for the 1995 bombing of the Murrah Federal Building in Oklahoma City. The bomb attack at the 1996 Olympics in Atlanta is believed to be the work Eric Robert Rudolph. The remaining fifteen incidents—three-quarters of the major terrorist attacks against the United States—are believed to be the acts of the closely linked radical Arab groups and/or Islamic fundamentalist extremists.

Less than a month after the September 11 attacks on America, the FBI created a "Most Wanted Terrorist List."[11] The names and pertinent information of those on the list are summarized in appendix 2. The individuals on the list have been indicted or accused of being responsible for major terrorist attacks against the United States. It is noteworthy that all twenty-two men—there are no women on the list—can be characterized as Arab or Islamic extremists. Three prominent names on the list are Osama bin Laden, Ayman Al-Zawahiri, and Muhammad Atef (now believed to be deceased), the three top men in the Al Qaeda network. Osama bin Laden has also held a place on the FBI's list of "Ten Most Wanted Fugitives" for several years.[12]

Finally, appendix 3 identifies and gives background information concerning the thirty-six groups designated by the secretary of state as Foreign Terrorist Organizations.[13] There are, of course, many other, lesser terrorist groups that have not earned a position on this list. By now, it should be no surprise to learn that twenty of these groups are controlled by radical Arabs and/or Islamic fundamentalists. Some of these groups have made regular appearances in news reports and have familiar names: Abu Sayef of the Philippines, HAMAS, Hezbollah (a.k.a. Islamic Jihad), the Popular Front for the Liberation of Palestine (PFLP), and Al Qaeda. The non-Arab or non-Islamic groups also include familiar names: the Aum Supreme Truth group of Japan, the Revolutionary Armed Forces of Columbia (FARC), the Sendero Luminoso (Shining Path) group that has ravaged Peru, and the Liberation Tigers of Tamil Eelam—commonly called the Tamil Tigers—of Sri Lanka.[13]

After September 11, the government and the media identified terror-ism—the mega-terrorism that obliterated the World Trade Center, shat-tered a significant part of the Pentagon, and destroyed thousands of lives in a few hours—with radical Arabs and militant Muslims. All nineteen of the September 11 hijackers were Arabs or Muslims or both.[14] Fifteen were citizens of Saudi Arabia.[15] The three summaries in appendixes 1, 2, and 3 support the conclusion that the threat to America has come largely from radical Arabs and militant Muslims, and they demonstrate that the violent acts by these terrorist groups against the United States had been increas-ing for at least two decades. By the end of 2001, other groups with violent intent toward the United States were so overshadowed by Arab and Islamic terrorists that they were all but forgotten.

The chapters that follow focus on the rise of this main line of terrorism for two main reasons: first, during the past decades, it has been responsi-ble for the most vicious attacks on the United States and its interests, and second, in the years ahead, it threatens to be the most dangerous.

Chapter 3

Nationalists, Communists, and Insurgents

Terrorism is probably as old as war itself. Our ancestors made no distinction between warriors and civilians when it came to slaughtering the enemy. Modern humankind considered itself civilized and—at least theoretically—distinguished between combatants and noncombatants. The Geneva Conventions of the nineteenth and twentieth centuries formalized the treatment of combatants and civilians, and those who committed terrorist acts were classified as war criminals. That construct served for dealing with a few dozen major villains of World War II but has had limited utility since then. The terrorists of the second half of the twentieth century and the first years of the twenty-first were not aligned with warring nations; they were free agents fighting in relatively small groups against nations and governments.

From the late 1960s and through the 1970s, the nature of the war by the leftist causes against the established powers of the West changed. Communist-backed insurgencies gradually gave way to international terrorism. The enemy was no longer the Viet Cong or the indigenous communist parties of Central and South America. He had once worn black pajamas and a coolie hat, or he wore fatigues and smoked a cigar. Now the enemy was more likely to be dressed in mufti and carrying an assault rifle or driving a truck loaded with explosives. The names of the new enemy—those that became commonly known and elicited fear and hatred in the West—were no longer Patrice Lumumba, Ho Chi Minh, and Fidel Castro, but Muammar Qaddafi, Saddam Hussein, and Osama bin Laden.

Modern terrorism evolved in the late 1960s. The Western, capitalist countries saw a growing wave of bombings, kidnappings, murders, bank robberies, and thefts of weapons and explosives. The groups taking credit for these crimes went by the names of the Baader-Meinhof Gang in Germany, the Red Brigade in Italy, the Red Army in Japan, and the Weatherman group in the United States. They were all native organizations without contacts with the Soviet Union or involvement with communist insurgencies. What they had in common was their hatred for the established order.[1]

Although the Soviet Union and its State Security Committee (KGB) generally avoided getting involved with these bourgeois Western terrorist groups, the intelligence agencies of its east European satellites were more reckless. The intelligence services of East Germany and Czechoslovakia supported some of these groups, much to the horror of Moscow. When the Italian Red Brigade kidnapped and killed Christian Democrat leader and former Italian prime minister Aldo Moro, the Italian Communist Party took a hard line against the terrorists and lived in fear that it would be learned that Moro's assassins were supported by the Czechoslovak security and intelligence service.[2]

The Palestinians and the Irish Republican Army were different matters. Both were indigenous, left-leaning groups fighting wars of national liberation. If they were not clearly in the communist camp, they were at least fighting enemies of communism, Israel and Great Britain, respectively. The Soviet Union through the KGB supported both groups with weapons and the Palestinians with training.[3]

THE TRICONTINENTAL CONFERENCE

If there is one landmark event that can be identified as the bridge from the old threat of communist insurgencies to the new threat of international terrorism, it is the Tricontinental Conference held in Havana, Cuba, in January 1966. It was attended by 513 delegates from 83 groups, 64 observers, 77 invited guests, and 129 journalists from 35 countries. The purpose of the conference, according to the official Cuban newspaper *Granma,* was to devise "the strategy of the revolutionary movements in their struggle against imperialism, colonialism, and neocolonialism, and especially against Yankee imperialism,... [which] calls for closer military ties and solidarity between the peoples of Asia, Africa, and Latin America."[4]

In welcoming the delegates at the opening session, Fidel Castro declared, lest there be any doubt regarding his agenda, "Any revolutionary movement anywhere in the world can count on Cuba's unconditional support."[5]

Even before the conference began, its organizers identified targets for wars of national liberation as Vietnam, the Dominican Republic, the Congo, the Portuguese colonies, Rhodesia, southern Arabia and Palestine, Laos, Cambodia, South Africa, Korea, Venezuela, Guatemala, Peru, Colombia,

Cyprus, Panama, southwest Africa, and the Indonesian province of North Kalimantan. Conference participants accepted the premise that the primary enemy on every continent was U.S. "imperialism." The conference ended with the creation of the Organization of Solidarity of the Peoples of African, Asian, and Latin America (OSPAAAL), with its secretariat in Havana.[6]

Although the Soviet Union's delegation to the conference had voted in favor of the conference's most revolutionary resolutions, it quickly retreated under the heavy criticism of Latin American governments. It claimed that its delegation was composed of representatives of Soviet social organizations and not the government. The Soviet Union thereby ceded its leadership of world revolution to Cuba and the indigenous rebels who had attended the conference.[7]

Before the year was out, the first guerrilla training camps in Cuba welcomed Third World revolutionaries. These first students moved on to start training camps of their own, which, in the 1970s, were located in liberated Angola and Mozambique, Algeria, and Libya. Instructors came from Cuba, East Germany, North Korea, and for a time, Red China. The Soviet Union also participated by supplying trainers and materiel; but it had little control over the independent-minded revolutionaries who had their own agendas and began to use the skills they had learned in the camps and to earn their reputations as international terrorists.[8]

The quintessential guerrilla warrior Ernesto ("Che") Guevara missed the Tricontinental Conference because he was traveling; but on his return, he weighed in with an epistle. Before reviewing those words, it will help to review his earlier thoughts on war and terrorism. Long before the conference, and not long after the victory of the Cuban revolution over Batista, Guevara had written his handbook on revolution, *Guerrilla Warfare*. In those relatively innocent years, he saw limits to revolutionary action, primarily for practical reasons. In discussing the tactical value of sabotage, he cautioned his followers against the use of terrorism. He wrote, "Sabotage has nothing to do with terrorism; terrorism and personal assaults are entirely different tactics. We sincerely believe that terrorism is of negative value, that it by no means produces the desired effects, that it can turn a people against a revolutionary movement, and that it can bring a loss of lives to its agents out of proportion to what it produces."[9]

He wrote these words before the Bay of Pigs invasion, at the time the United States through the CIA was beginning to hatch plots to kill Fidel Castro—and Guevara, although with lower priority. It was before the Kennedy administration ran its secret war against Cuba, which was code-named Operation Mongoose.[10] By the time of the Tricontinental Conference, Guevara had become more pragmatic about revolution, and his hardened attitude was on display in the April 16, 1967, issue of OSPAAAL's magazine *Tricontinental*. The language used in his article, titled "Create Two, Three...Many Vietnams, That Is the Watchword,"[11] suggests that his idealism was eroding and that he was succumbing to hatred and looking down the road to terrorism:

Hate as a factor in the struggle, intransigent hatred of the enemy...takes one beyond the natural limitations of a human being and converts one into an effective, violent, selective and cold killing machine. Our soldiers must be like that; a people without hate cannot triumph over a brutal enemy.

We must carry the war as far as the enemy carries it: into his home, into his places of recreation, make it total. He must be prevented from having a moment's peace, a moment's quiet outside the barracks and even inside them. Attack him wherever he may be; make him feel like a hunted animal wherever he goes.[11]

Guevara left no doubt about whom he saw as the enemy: "Our every action is a battle cry against imperialism and a call for the unity of peoples against the great enemy of the human race: the United States of North America."[11]

His fatalism regarding the inevitability of death in battle seems to invite "martyrs" to the cause and the choice of death made by suicide bomber decades later: "Wherever death may surprise us, let it be welcome if our battle cry has reached even one receptive ear, if another hand reaches out to take up our arms, and other men come forward to join in our funeral dirge with the rattling of machine guns and with new cries of battle and victory."[11]

Guevara's morbid cry became reality six months later when, as leader of a small rebel band, he was captured by the Bolivian Army and was executed. On that day, Che Guevara ascended from the rank of guerrilla leader to become the patron saint of revolutionary causes.[12]

FROM REVOLUTION TO TERROR

One of the countries identified by the Tricontinental Conference as a target for a war of national liberation, Guatemala, was already a battleground. In 1954, the United States engineered a coup that replaced the leftist, democratically elected government of Jacobo Arbenz with a military dictatorship.[13] Guatemala finally fell into a protracted civil war in 1962 that pitted groups as diverse as the Communist Party and the Catholic Church against the U.S.-backed, authoritarian government.[14] Naturally, the U.S. government and its interests were targets in the battle.

On August 28, 1968, John Gordon Mein, U.S. ambassador to Guatemala, was returning to the embassy after attending a luncheon when his limousine was forced to stop by two cars. Several armed men from the cars ordered the ambassador to get out. Mein ran. The gunmen opened fire. Ambassador Mein died in a barrage of pistol and machine-gun fire. The ambassador's driver was not hurt.

The following day, a procommunist guerrilla group calling itself the Rebel Armed Forces (FAR) issued a statement that said it intended only to kidnap the ambassador in retaliation for the capture of one of its leaders by Guatemalan government forces four days earlier. Now it was too late to exchange prisoners. John Gordon Mein was the first U.S. ambassador to be killed by terrorists at his post. There would be others.[15]

Kidnappers struck again a year later in Rio de Janeiro. Ambassador to Brazil C. Burke Elbrick was returning to the embassy after lunch at home when four armed men stopped his limousine and took him prisoner. The kidnappers left behind Elbrick's Brazilian chauffeur and a note demanding in exchange for the return of the ambassador the release of fifteen political prisoners held by the Brazilian government. The message also stated that "the life and death of the ambassador is in the hands of the dictatorship." It gave the government forty-eight hours to comply, or the kidnappers would "be forced to carry out revolutionary justice and execute Ambassador Elbrick." Two known Brazilian terrorist groups signed the message left by the kidnappers, the National Liberating Action (ALN) and the Revolutionary Movement of October (MR 8). MR 8's name was derived from the date October 8, 1967, the day that Ernesto "Che" Guevara was killed after being captured by the Bolivian Army.

Several hours after the forty-eight-hour deadline had passed, the fifteen prisoners boarded a Brazilian Air Force transport that took them from Rio de Janeiro to Mexico City, where the Mexican government granted political asylum to the fifteen men. The kidnappers released Ambassador Elbrick after those who had been held prisoner by the Brazilian government were safely in Mexico.

After his release, Elbrick thanked the Brazilian government for facilitating his release. He reported that his kidnappers had treated him well, and he described them as "all young, very determined, intelligent fanatics." He also said, "They seemed to ascribe all the troubles and difficulties they saw in Brazil to what they called North American imperialism."[16]

The murder of Ambassador Mein and the kidnapping of Ambassador Elbrick were quickly forgotten. The United States did not notice the beginning of an international terrorist war. It was preoccupied with its unwinnable war in Vietnam and the growing domestic opposition to it.

Chapter 4

The Palestine Liberation Organization and the Popular Front for the Liberation of Palestine

Today the word *terrorism* is inextricably linked with the continual war between the Israelis and the Palestinians. Much of the experience the United States has had with modern terrorism finds its roots in this conflict. The United States has been a supporter of the state of Israel since the day it was founded, and inevitably, many Palestinians and Arabs have taken the position that "the friend of my enemy is also my enemy." Nobody should have been surprised, then, that the United States and its interests would also become targets of those who were at war with Israel.

A pivotal event in that conflict was Israel's defeat of the armed forces of Egypt, Jordan, and Syria in the Six-Day War of 1967. The Palestinians, who until then had reluctantly accepted the leadership of the Arab nations in fighting the battle for their homeland, now turned to their own for leadership. Three years before the humiliating Six-Day War, militant Palestinian groups had joined together under an umbrella organization they named the Palestine Liberation Organization (PLO). The largest and best organized of the Palestinian groups was Al Fatah, which was led by Yasir Arafat; in February 1969, the executive committee of the PLO elected Arafat chairman of its executive committee.[1]

Although Al Fatah and the PLO may have turned out to be the most-enduring Palestinian organizations, another group, the Popular Front for the Liberation of Palestine (PFLP), also a PLO member, was, in the late 1960s and early 1970s, the most militant and daring. The leader of the PFLP was a Palestinian physician, Dr. George Habbash. Like many leaders of groups that were members of the PLO, he was a Christian—the Palestinian movement was Arab and secular. Habbash, who until then had been known mostly for his fiery rhetoric, had some creative ideas about tactics in the war against Israel. When he and the PFLP put them into practice, the word *terrorism* took on its modern meaning.[2]

In 1968, there were thirty-five skyjacking incidents; according to one summary, none resulted in death or serious injury (see chapter 1).[3] They were an annoyance, but most were news for only a day. One of these skyjackings, however, rated more than the usual notice because of its novel circumstances.

On July 23, 1968, a Boeing 707 jet operated by El Al, Israel's national airline, left Rome for Tel Aviv. While still in Italian air space, a band of armed men—either three or five, depending on the witness—commandeered the aircraft. Two of the hijackers took over the cockpit, and one of them replaced the pilot at the controls. In the scuffle, one of the hijackers slugged the navigator with a gun butt. Blood covered the injured man's face, but he was in good enough shape to walk out of the cockpit under his own power.

The hijacker at the controls of the jet turned it toward Algiers and, according to the passengers, brought it to a smooth landing.

The crew, the Israeli passengers, El Al, and Israel had a problem. Algeria had declared war on Israel in the 1967 war between Israel and the Arab states, and when the Six-Day War ended, Algeria had not accepted the cease-fire. The hijacked airliner, its crew, and passengers had been delivered to Israel's declared enemy. Algeria immediately released nineteen passengers who were not Israelis, but it held in custody eleven Israeli passengers and the ten-person crew.[4]

Israel's position became even more awkward when the PFLP claimed credit for the hijacking and issued a statement announcing that it had asked the International Red Cross to mediate the exchange of the Israelis held in Algeria for 1,200 Palestinians held prisoner by Israel. Israel condemned the PFLP action as "airborne piracy."[5]

Soon after the hijacking, Algeria released the Israeli women and children who had been on the plane, but it kept in custody five male passengers and seven male crew members. Five weeks later, Israel and Algeria reached an agreement. The twelve men were sent home, and the airliner was returned. In exchange, Israel released sixteen Palestinians who had been captured and imprisoned before the Six-Day War.[6]

The PFLP had done what no other Palestinian or Arab group had ever done. Even though it did not get the release of the 1,200 Palestinians in Israeli prisons, it had won a battle with Israel. A handful of dedicated men armed with a few handguns, hand grenades, and their own audacity had extracted a concession from Israel: the release of sixteen prisoners. The Palestinians, in pursuit of their own nation, had become a player; and they would play again, but not by anyone else's rules.

In the United States, the hijacking of the El Al plane was quickly forgotten. America had its own problems that absorbed its full attention: the Vietnam War, the recent assassinations of Martin Luther King Jr. and Robert F. Kennedy, rioting in the streets, and a presidential election. Those involved in the hijacking were the Palestinians, Israel, and Algeria. The United States had no national interest in the incident—so it thought.

Arab terrorists first targeted the United States on August 29, 1969, when two Palestinians hijacked an airliner of an American carrier, Trans World Airlines (TWA). Possibly the most fascinating aspect of this incident is that one of the hijackers was a woman named Leila Khaled. She later wrote a memoir, which includes a detailed account of the hijacking and gives an insight into the mind of one terrorist of that time. A noteworthy feature of her autobiography is its overriding theme of Palestinian nationalism. Nowhere does she mention a religious component of her motivation—neither Islam nor Christianity nor Judaism. Her primary moral and political inspiration was Ernesto "Che" Guevara.[7]

Leila Khaled was born in Haifa, but as a result of the Palestinian-Israeli war that led to the formation of the state of Israel, her parents took her to live in Lebanon.[8] She passed her childhood as an exile and prepared for adulthood as a student at the American University of Beirut. At that time, she became associated with the Arab Nationalist Movement; but with the humiliation of the Arab states in 1967's Six-Day War, she, like many of her contemporaries, turned to a more radical path. She joined the PFLP, which used her to teach the use of weapons and the basics of PFLP ideology to teenage recruits. On the subject of a woman actively participating in the activities of a militant group, she remarked, "In our revolution, the woman has just as big a role to play as her male counterpart."[9]

TWA flight 840 departed Los Angeles with planned stops in New York, Rome, and Athens before its planned arrival in Tel Aviv.[10] The new passengers boarding in Rome included a diminutive woman in her early twenties with Mediterranean features that could lead one to think she was Greek, Italian, or Spanish. She wore a white blouse, gray trousers, and a stylish wide-brimmed hat. For reading material, she carried a book titled *My Friend Che*, by Ricardo Rojo, and she had concealed in her purse a pistol and a hand grenade.[10, 11] She was prepared to act that day because she knew that President Richard Nixon was scheduled to address the Zionist Organization of America the same day (he actually sent a letter) and would again pledge the support of his country for the Zionists at the expense of the Palestinian people.[12]

Khaled had a first-class aisle seat. In the aisle seat across from her, she recognized a man she had previously seen only in a photograph, Salim Essawai, who would be her partner in hijacking the Boeing 707 jetliner.[11]

When a flight attendant with lunch trays for the flight crew opened the cockpit door, Essawai sprang to his feet, and Khaled followed him into the cockpit. Khaled did all the talking, possibly because she had better command of English or because she was the designated leader. The crew did as it was told.

Khaled then read a message to the passengers over the intercom. She said, "This is your new captain speaking. The Che Guevara Commando Unit of the Popular Front for the Liberation of Palestine which has taken over command of this TWA flight demands that all passengers on board adhere to the following instructions." She gave them a few instructions to let them know who was in charge. Then she said, "Among you is a passenger responsible for the death and misery of a number of Palestinian men, women and children, on behalf of who we are carrying out this operation to bring this assassin before a revolutionary Palestinian court. The rest of you will be honorable guests of the heroic Palestinian people in a hospitable, friendly country."

The comment about the hijackers being after one passenger was a ruse. Almost everybody calmed down because they thought that the terrorists were after only one person who had committed injustices against the Palestinians. The others would be well cared for, although delayed in their travels.[13]

The airliner flew east, beyond Athens, its next planned stop. Hours after being hijacked, it approached Tel Aviv. It picked up an escort of three Israeli Air Force Mirage jet fighters.

A voice from the airport control tower said, "T.W.A. flight 840, you are cleared for landing."

Leila Khaled said, "Don't you address us as T.W.A. flight. . . . We are the flight of the Palestine liberation force."

The voice from the control tower played along. "Okay, Palestine Liberation Front flight, you are cleared for landing."

Khaled said, "We have kidnapped this American plane because Israel is a colony of America and the Americans are giving the Israelis Phantom planes." The airliner pulled out of the approach pattern, and Khaled said, "Tel Aviv, we are from the Front for the Liberation of Palestine. What can you do about it?"[10]

Israel did nothing.

The hijacked airliner flew north, toward Damascus. As it approached the Syrian border, the three Israeli fighters escorting it turned back, and Syrian aircraft took their place. The airliner was almost out of fuel as it touched down at the new Damascus airport. When the plane came to a stop, its captain alerted the passengers and crew that a bomb aboard the plane was about to explode.[10]

The doors popped open and the inflatable slides deployed. All of the passengers and crew were out in less than three minutes. Khaled walked through the plane looking for any passenger who did not get out; she did not find anybody. Meanwhile, her partner Essawai set the explosives in the cockpit and lit the fuse. Khaled and then Essawai slid down the emergency chute to the tarmac and waited. The expected explosion did not happen. Essawai climbed back up the chute to try again. After he came out the second time, the airliner's cockpit disintegrated in fire and smoke.[14]

The taking of TWA flight 840 caught the United States unprepared. The incident was the first hijacking of a U.S. airliner outside the Western Hemisphere.[15] Secretary of State William P. Rogers issued a statement saying, "We strongly condemn this act of international piracy." He expressed his wish that the government of Syria would immediately release the passengers, the crew, and the aircraft.[16] Then the United States impotently waited for the Syrian government to act.

When the Syrians had sorted out their uninvited guests, they sent home the airliner's crew and those passengers who were not Israelis. They held in custody the two hijackers and six Israelis. Four of the Israelis were released a few days later, leaving two Israelis in custody.[17]

Six weeks after the hijacking, Syria released Leila Khaled and her partner Salim Essawai.[18] Three months after the hijacking, the last two Israelis being held by Syria got to go home. Syria traded them for two of its pilots who had made a navigational error and landed their MiG-17s in Israel and for six Syrian civilians and five soldiers who were also held by Israel. The Israelis flew out of Syria aboard the TWA 707 jetliner on which they had arrived. The bomb damage to the cockpit had been repaired while they waited to be repatriated. The PFLP demonstrated again that terrorism pays, although this skyjacking and the subsequent exchange of prisoners paid Syria rather than the Palestinian cause.[19]

The PFLP struck again a year later. The precipitating event was the impending outbreak of peace. In July 1970, both Egypt's President Nasser and Jordan's King Hussein had agreed to a cease-fire with Israel, an agreement to which the Palestinian nationalist groups did not subscribe.[20, 21] That month, Dr. George Habbash, leader of the PFLP, met with members of its revolutionary council to devise a plan of action to keep the fires of war burning in the Middle East. The result was the most brilliantly organized, audacious, and spectacular act of terrorism the world had seen.[21]

Barely a year after her successful hijacking of a TWA airliner, Leila Khaled was back in Europe on a mission. She was about to board El Al flight 219 departing from Amsterdam's Schiphol Airport bound for New York, with a scheduled departure time of 11:20 A.M. She wore a miniskirt and jacket and looked as innocuous as she did a year earlier when she had hijacked the TWA jetliner from Rome.[22] But she did not look like the old Leila Khaled, a known terrorist, either. She had undergone at least three sessions with a plastic surgeon in Beirut to change the appearance of her face.[23] Her partner on this mission was Patrick J. Arguello, the son of a

Nicaraguan doctor who was born in the United States. Arguello was a graduate of the University of California, Los Angeles and was a resident of Los Angeles. He wore a business suit for that day's activities.[21, 22]

Security screening was rigorous, and the Boeing 707 with 148 passengers on board finally took off at about 1:30 P.M.; Khaled and Arguello were in adjacent seats in the second row of the tourist-class section. About a half hour into the flight, Arguello rose with a small pistol in hand and rushed through the first-class section toward the cockpit. Khaled, who had hidden two hand grenades in her brassiere, pulled the pins, and with one grenade in each hand followed Arguello. An alert El Al flight attendant jumped on Arguello, who pushed him off and fired three times. Several men on board drew handguns. More shots were fired. Arguello was hit. He pulled the pin from a hand grenade and dropped it on the floor. It was a dud. Khaled pushed her way forward, toward the cockpit. Several people jumped on her, and somehow pried the grenades from her hands and safely replaced the pins. A passenger who held her down, a fifty-seven-year old grandfather from the Bronx, remarked later, "She was a gorgeous thing. It was a shame we had to bang her up."[21, 24]

They bound Khaled and Arguello hand and foot with their hands behind their backs using neckties and wire. Then, according to Khaled, an Israeli guard rolled Arguello onto his stomach and fired four shots into his back. Khaled later wrote that after Arguello was shot, she also "expected to join the ranks of our martyrs."

The El Al plane made an emergency landing at London. The Israeli crew was happy to get the injured flight attendant off the plane and into a hospital, but they refused to turn over Khaled and Arguello's body to British authorities. In the tug-of-war over Khaled, one British officer threw her over his shoulder, carried her to the open door, and dropped her into the arms of fellow officers and British custody below.[24]

A second hijacking of an airliner from Amsterdam's Schiphol Airport was under way even as the El Al plane was being attacked. Pan Am flight 840 (not to be confused with TWA flight 840, which Leila Khaled had hijacked to Syria in 1969), a Boeing 747 jumbo jet, was on its way from Amsterdam to London when two men, one with a gun, ordered the pilot to fly south. After some time on that course, the captain said that the plane was low on fuel, and he persuaded the hijackers to let him land in Beirut. As soon as the plane came to a stop, a dozen Palestinian commandos came on board, bringing with them a suitcase and a bag full of dynamite. The hijackers, it appears, intended to go to a makeshift landing strip in Jordan, but those who boarded in Lebanon told them that the jumbo jet, which weighed about 387 tons, could not land safely at the airstrip there.[21] All but one of the commandos got off the airplane, and it took off for Cairo with the crew, passengers, and hijackers on board.[25]

As the hijacked aircraft landed in Cairo, someone announced to the passengers and crew that a fuse leading to the explosives brought on board in Beirut had been lit. The emergency escape chutes were deployed, and all 172 passengers and crew rushed from the plane. Two minutes later, the explosives blew it apart.[21]

Hijackers struck a third time on September 6. In this incident, they commandeered a TWA flight that had left Tel Aviv for New York. After a stop in Frankfurt, PFLP commandos took over and instructed the crew to fly the Boeing 707 to Jordan.[25] By the time it arrived, the sun had set. The airliner's destination was not a conventional airport, and the pilot had to set the plane down on an airstrip laid out between two parallel rows of flaming oilcans and the light from jeep headlights.

The Western media called the Jordanian landing site Dawson Field; Arabs knew it as Ga Khanna. It was a baked-mud desert flat twenty-five miles northeast of Amman. The British Royal Air Force had used it in the 1940s as an air base, and the pilots who had been based there named it after their commander. In those days, it had never had to support the operation of anything as big as a commercial jetliner—and there was little reason to believe that it could.[21]

Soon after the TWA jetliner landed, it was joined by a Swissair DC-8. The new arrival had taken off from Zurich on a flight to New York when hijackers commandeered the flight.[25]

The fact that the coordinated hijackings of four commercial airliners were organized by the PFLP would make one think that its primary target was Israel, but that conclusion would be an oversimplification. Habbash and his followers were playing on the broader, international field. Two of the aircraft hijacked that day, including the one that was destroyed at the Cairo airport, had been operated by American carriers. Half of the crews and probably half of the passengers involved were Americans. The two other hijacked aircraft were on flights to New York. Half of their crews and probably half of the passengers involved were also Americans. If one country was more a target than any other, that country was the United States.

The following day, the two hijacked airliners baked in the 100-degree desert air with all passengers and crew members still on board. The airliners were surrounded by a ring of Palestinian commandos, and the commandos were in turn surrounded by the Jordanian Army with its tanks, jeeps, trucks, and ambulances. The Palestinians told the Jordanians to back off or they would blow up the aircraft. The Jordanian Army took up new positions about two miles distant. The Palestinian commandos then began sorting out the passengers and crew. In their blundering way, they tried to keep the Jews on board the airplanes and release everybody else. The International Red Cross pitched in to help the hostages by delivering food, water, supplies, and portable air conditioning units.[21]

Just when the international focus was on the airstrip in Jordan, the PFLP struck again. On September 9, a British Overseas Airways Corporation (BOAC) VC-10 jet flying from Bombay to London, with 115 passengers and crew on board, was hijacked after a scheduled stop in Bahrain. The hijackers forced it to stop in Beirut, where it picked up a young woman commando and then proceeded to land at Dawson Field.[26]

The PFLP now had three commercial airliners parked on the baked-mud floor of the Jordanian desert. They continued sorting through passengers and crew, releasing many but keeping fifty-four people, Israeli and American Jews, as "prisoners of war."[26] In exchange for the hostages' freedom, they demanded that England, West Germany, and Switzerland release seven Palestinians held for terrorist activities; they also demanded that Israel free more than two thousand Palestinian guerrillas it held.[20]

To illustrate the seriousness of its demands, the PFLP emptied the three airliners of all hostages and commandos and blew the planes up. The spectacular photographs of exploding jetliners graced the front pages of newspapers around the world, but the act had an effect just the opposite of that intended. Western governments, the government of Jordan, and Pope Paul VI condemned the PFLP's actions. The PLO suspended the PFLP's membership in the Palestinian organization. Yasir Arafat, the leader of Al Fatah and chairman of the PLO's Central Committee, denounced the PFLP for its ill treatment of the airliners' passengers and crew and for discrediting the Palestinian movement. The PLO and Arafat had little choice. They had to live with the consequences of Habbash's reckless leadership and the PFLP's actions.[26]

The days of reckoning began for Palestinians on September 16, when King Hussein of Jordan appointed a military government to deal with the commandos.[27] After the war that gave Israel its independence, the people of Palestine found themselves in a diaspora of their own. By 1970, 270,000 Palestinians lived in the Israeli occupied West Bank and 310,000 in the Gaza Strip. Syria was the temporary home of almost 160,000 Palestinians, and Lebanon hosted 175,000 Palestinian refugees. Jordan carried the heaviest load, with 506,000 Palestinians within its borders.[28] These increasingly unwelcome guests had formed a government of their own within Jordan that threatened the stability of the desert kingdom and invited intervention by the nations they offended. The Palestinians, especially the commando groups, had to go.

The Jordanian civil war—as it was called—ended ten days after it started when King Hussein of Jordan, Yasir Arafat for the Palestinians, and diplomats representing the Arab countries signed a cease-fire agreement. With all of the face-saving fluff scraped away, the key features of the agreement emerged: the Palestinian commandos would withdraw from all Jordanian cities and towns and re-deploy along the cease-fire lines with Israel; and all people residing within Jordan, both citizens of Jordan and the Palestinians, would be subject to Jordanian laws.[29] In short, the Palestinians had been beaten and driven to the borders of Jordan. Many of them, especially the guerrillas of the PLO groups, crossed that border and found their way into Lebanon. They would look back on the month of September 1970 with bitterness and speak of it as "Black September."

Although there was no formal agreement on the exchange of prisoners, by September 29 the PFLP released all fifty-four of the hostages it held. It is noteworthy that sixteen of them were nationals of Britain, Germany, and Switzerland, countries that held Palestinian prisoners. The other thirty-eight were Americans.[30]

When all of the fifty-four hostages were safely out of the Middle East, prisoners began flowing back in the other direction. On September 30, Leila Khaled, under guard, boarded a British Royal Air Force Comet airliner for a flight to Munich, where three Palestinian men who had been held in custody by Germany boarded the aircraft. After a short flight to Zurich, three more prisoners, two men and a woman who had been held by the Swiss government, boarded the jet. The British airliner then flew its passengers and their guards to Cairo, where the seven Palestinian commandos were turned over to Egyptian authorities. A week and a half later, the Palestinians boarded another airplane for Damascus, Syria, where they were once again free.[31, 32] The PFLP did not get the release of over two thousand commandos from Israel, which it had demanded.

In the short term, the hijackings were a disaster for the Palestinian cause. For the long term, they demonstrated that a small disciplined group with marginal resources could grab the world's attention and influence the affairs of nations.

PALESTINIAN TERRORISTS AND THE SOVIET UNION

As the Palestinian terrorist groups became organized, the Soviet Union began to support their activities as a means of promoting its own interests in the region. In the 1967 Six-Day War, the American-supported Israeli military had destroyed the Soviet-supported forces of Egypt, Jordan, and Syria; and the Soviets turned to the independent Palestinians to fight an insurgency against Israel. An Israeli agent who had infiltrated Al Fatah learned that the Soviet government was, after the disastrous war, prepared to give Al Fatah what it needed to pose an effective challenge to Israel: arms and training. Men from the Marxist-dominated PFLP, the Israeli agent learned, had already gone to Russia to be trained by the KGB.[33]

The KGB's own files reveal that it had been impressed by the airliner hijackings and attacks that the PFLP made on Israeli businesses. It supplied the PFLP with an arsenal consisting of fifty pistols (ten with silencers), fifty machine guns, five British-made Sterling automatics with silencers, fifty American-made AR-16 automatics, a large supply of ammunition for these guns, fifteen booby-trap mines, and five radio-controlled mines. In return, the Soviet Union expected the PFLP to carry out "special actions" required by the KGB. Other intelligence services of Soviet-bloc countries followed the KGB's example by using or attempting to use terrorist groups for their own political ends.[34]

The Soviet Union also supported other terrorist groups through the KGB. The Irish Republican Army received two machine guns, seventy automatic rifles, ten Walther pistols, and 41,600 cartridges to influence the course of the "troubles" in Northern Ireland. The KGB was also the conduit through which the Soviet Union supplied arms to the Sandinista rebels in Nicaragua, although, much to its irritation, its contributions to the revolutionary cause were overshadowed by those of Cuba.[35, 36]

BLACK SEPTEMBER

The success of the PFLP, led by Dr. George Habbash, in its terrorist attacks challenged the PLO and Yaser Arafat for leadership of the Palestinian people. The PFLP had the headlines and the admiration of Palestinians, and the PLO had to meet the challenge or see itself swept into irrelevance. It chose to create its own militant subgroup to take violent action against the enemies of the Palestinian cause. The first enemy it would deal with would be Jordan, the Arab country that had driven out its own brothers, the Palestinians. The PLO's terrorist group would take its name from the date of their exile from Jordan; it would become known as "Black September." It was in the PLO's interest that Black September be seen as an autonomous entity; therefore, it is uncertain how much control the PLO had over its operations.

Black September drew its first blood in November 1971, when it assassinated Jordan's prime minister, Wasfi Tal, moments after he stepped out of the Sheraton Hotel in Cairo. A group calling itself "The Hand of Black September" claimed responsibility and said it had acted to avenge the Palestinian defeat by Jordan the previous year. Having taken a big step in settling its score with Jordan, Black September turned to the real enemy of the Palestinian people, Israel. In May 1972, it hijacked a Sabena airliner that had taken off from Vienna with the hope of trading it, the passengers, and crew for a hundred Arab guerrillas held by Israel. The hijackers made the mistake of having the pilot fly to Lod Airport in Tel Aviv to make their demand. Israeli paratroopers stormed the plane, killing two hijackers and capturing two others.

Not to be outdone, the PFLP organized an operation it called "Palestine's Revenge." It hired three members of the Japanese Red Army as its surrogates in a suicide attack on Israel. On May 30, 1972, the three terrorists arrived at Tel Aviv's Lod Airport aboard an Air France flight from

Rome. Upon entering the crowded terminal, they started tossing grenades and firing their automatic weapons. They killed twenty-four people and wounded seventy-eight more. Sixteen of the dead were Puerto Rican Catholics who were on a pilgrimage to the Holy Land. The Puerto Rican victims, who accounted for two-thirds of those killed, were citizens of the United States.[37]

Black September took the next turn at committing a terrorist atrocity. On September 5, 1972, a team of eight Black September terrorists climbed over a security fence and broke into the Israeli athletes' quarters at the Olympic Village in Munich, Germany. They killed two Israelis on the spot, took nine as hostages, and demanded the release of 200 Arabs being held in Israeli prisons. When the government of Israel refused to deal with them, the terrorists bullied their way to an airport where, they believed, an airliner waited to take them out of Germany.

Within moments after the two helicopters carrying the terrorists and their prisoners landed at the airport, German police snipers opened fire. An hour later, five of the terrorists were dead and three more were in custody. All nine Israeli athletes were dead. The Black September team had machine-gunned five and killed four others with a grenade tossed into the helicopter that brought them to the airport. The drama and bloodbath in Munich was carried live on television for the world to see, making it history's most publicly seen act of political terrorism up to that point.

Israel reacted immediately by sending seventy-five planes on bombing raids against Palestinian guerrilla bases in Syria and Lebanon. Arab sources reported that the raids killed sixty and injured scores more. Israel claimed to have shot down three Syrian planes, and Syria claimed to have downed two Israeli aircraft.[38]

ISRAEL'S SOLUTION TO TERRORISM

With few options, and all of them bad, Israel turned to a cold-blooded approach for dealing with the leaders of the Arab terrorist groups. The country could not afford another terrorist attack like the Lod Airport and Munich Olympics massacres. Israel's prime minister, Golda Meir, appointed the chief of military intelligence as her special assistant for terrorist affairs, and the government doubled the budget of the Mossad, Israel's equivalent of the CIA. The Israelis began by compiling a list of those Arabs who, according to Israeli intelligence information, had played a significant role in the Munich massacre and other acts of terrorism against Israel. Each name on the list was then approved for assassination by a top-secret committee that was cochaired by Prime Minister Golda Meir.[39]

In the months that followed, the Mossad teams found their targets in Rome, Paris, Cyprus, and Beirut. They killed at least nine of those they had identified as terrorists. The Mossad's most spectacular operation was an assault by a task force in Beirut on April 6, 1973, that killed the head of Black September, Mohammed Yussuf El-Najjar, his deputy, Kemal Adwan, and the chief spokesman of the PLO, Kamal Nasser. In addition, the Israelis killed more than a hundred people alleged to be terrorists, the wife of one intended victim, and a neighbor who got in the way. The Mossad also destroyed Black September's Beirut headquarters and retreated with a large collection of Black September's documents.[40]

By July 1973, the Mossad was on the trail of the last man on the list who had been approved for assassination by the prime minister's secret committee. Ali Hassan Salameh was Black September's chief of operations and the man Israeli intelligence credited with planning the Munich massacre.[41] After it learned that Salameh was to set up a temporary base in Lillehammer, Norway, it began organizing a fifteen-member assassination team. They arrived in Lillehammer on July 21, 1973, and began tailing their suspect. The two hit men caught him at about 10:40 P.M. after he and a woman companion had left a movie theater. They shot him down with their Berettas, jumped into a car, and disappeared into the night.

The Israelis' first mistake had been killing the wrong man. The assassins had gunned down a Moroccan who had been working in Norway as a waiter; his woman companion was his wife. The second mistake was bungling the getaway; six of the team were arrested and later tried as accessories to murder, although the gunmen made successful escapes. By being caught red-handed committing an assassination, the Mossad and Israel lost any future recourse to "plausible denial"; they could no longer claim that in the absence of evidence to the contrary, they were not responsible for the act. As one Israeli intelligence officer put it, if one Palestinian was run over by a bus in Paris, Israel would be accused of his murder. Israel's covert war against terrorists was thereafter restricted to targets in Arab countries.[42]

The Mossad finally caught up with Ali Hassan Salameh in Beirut in January 1979, six and a half years after the Munich massacre. The Mossad's assassins triggered a radio-controlled bomb in Salameh's Chevrolet station wagon that killed him, his four bodyguards, and four passers-by.[43]

Israel had set the precedent for dealing with terrorists, its blunders and innocent victims notwithstanding, by means of assassinations. Although it did target lesser villains, it chose as its primary targets the PLO leadership. In 1982, Israel tried but failed to kill Yasir Arafat in Beirut with letter bombs, aerial bombing, and car bombs. In 1988, the Mossad killed Khalil el-Wazir, a.k.a. Abu Jihad, Arafat's second-in-command and military chief, in a spectacular raid on his residence in Tunisia. Abu Jihad had run terrorist activities in support of the *intifada*, the popular uprising of Palestinians residing in Israel. His assassination elicited mixed reactions in Israel. The commander of Aman, Israeli Military Intelligence, commented, "Anyone directing terrorism is a suitable target for elimination." Government minister Ezer Weizman publicly proclaimed his opposition to Israel using assassination as a tool for dealing with its enemies: "It does not contribute to the fight against terrorism. It distances the peace process and will bring greater hostility. It also makes us more vulnerable around the world."[44]

THE ASSASSINATIONS OF AMERICAN AMBASSADORS

It was perhaps inevitable that the U.S. government would become a target of Arab terrorism. It had been a supporter of Israel since its creation in 1948, and that support inevitably alienated Palestinians. True, Americans had been victims of skyjackings and attacks against Israeli targets, such as the Lod Airport massacre, but it was easy to imagine them as uninvolved people caught in a cross fire rather than as targets of terrorism. That view became harder to accept in the 1970s as American ambassadors to Arab countries and countries with predominantly Islamic populations became targets of terrorists.

The chargé d'affaires of the United States in Sudan, George C. Moore, was about to leave his post, where his colleagues at the Saudi Arabian embassy were hosting a party in his honor on the evening of March 1, 1973. The party crashers arrived at about 7 P.M. Eight men armed with revolvers and machine guns came in a Land Rover sporting diplomatic license plates that had been issued to Al Fatah. With guns blazing, they burst into the embassy and took six people hostage. Their prisoners included the guest of honor, George C. Moore, U.S. Ambassador Cleo A. Noel, Belgian chargé d'affaires Guy Eid, the Japanese and Jordanian chargé d'affaires, and Saudi Ambassador Sheikh Abdullah el-Malhouk, his wife and four children. Ambassador Noel was shot in the ankle, and the Belgian, Eid, was shot in the leg. The gunmen tied up their prisoners and beat the Americans "unmercifully."

A few hours later, the terrorists, believed to be members of Black September, presented their demands to Sudanese officials. They demanded that Jordan release all members of Al Fatah that it held prisoner, that Israel release all Arab women it held, that the United States release Sirhan Sirhan, the man who had murdered Senator Robert Kennedy, and that West Germany release all members of the Baader-Meinhoff Gang that it held, "because they supported the Palestinian cause." If their demands were not met within twenty-four hours, they said, they would kill the six diplomats.

Sudanese troops surrounded the Saudi embassy and contained the terrorists. Jordan refused to comply with the demands. President Nixon said that the United States would "not pay blackmail."

As the twenty-four-hour deadline approached, the terrorists untied the Americans, Noel and Moore, and the Belgian, Eid, and gave them all pen and paper to write their last messages to their loved ones. At about 9:30 P.M. on March 2, the terrorists took the three men to the basement of the Saudi embassy and shot them. Noel and Moore were murdered because of America's perceived support of Zionism and its imperialism. The Belgian was killed—it was believed—because his country had joined with Israel and the United States to build an aircraft factory in Belgium.

After killing their hostages, the terrorists demanded safe passage to an unspecified Arab capitol in exchange for the bodies of the three men they had murdered. Sudanese authorities gave the terrorists until the following morning to surrender. The Black September terrorists gave in to the Sudanese ultimatum. The Sudanese information minister said that they had done so at the urging of Yasir Arafat, who explained to them that they "had no way out."[45]

Although Sudan, a largely Muslim country, had been sympathetic to the Palestinian cause, its president, Mohammed Gaafar el-Nimiery, accused Al Fatah of being responsible for the terrorist attack and demanded that Yasir Arafat denounce Black September and its tactics. President Nixon demanded that "the perpetrators of the crime be brought to justice," and the government of Sudan did bring them to trial for murder.[45] But President Nixon's attention was soon to be focused on other crimes, those commonly lumped together under the name "Watergate," and the accusations that he was responsible for a cover-up. The act of terrorism against the United States was quickly forgotten as the country focused on its internal problems, the crimes committed by officials of its own government.

Lebanon obtained its independence in 1943, but the often-conflicting beliefs of its citizens and its proximity to Israel worked against the small country achieving stability. Although the vast majority of Lebanese people (95 percent) are ethnically Arabs, they belong to a spectrum of antagonistic religious groups. Seventy percent are Muslims, belonging to the Shiite, Sunni, Druze, Isma'ilite, and Alawite sects. Greek Orthodox Christians and Marionite Christians, aligned with the Catholic Church, account for 30 percent.[46] The political instability of Lebanon had been exacerbated by the arrival in the early 1970s of the PLO, which had been driven out of Jordan. In 1975, Lebanon tumbled into civil war, with Lebanese fighting Palestinians and Christians fighting Arabs.

Francis E. Meloy Jr. had been the U.S. ambassador to Lebanon for less than two months, and he was still learning his way around Beirut and its political powers. On June 16, Meloy and his economic counselor, Robert O. Waring, were in the ambassador's chauffeur-driven limousine on their way to the Christian suburb of Hazmiyeh to meet with Lebanon's president-elect, Elias Sarkis. As a safety measure, a car with security guards followed the ambassador's limousine. When the ambassador's car was stopped at the imaginary line that separated Christian and Muslim forces, the security guards were nowhere to be seen.

Not long after, soldiers of the Palestine Liberation Army reported finding the bodies of Ambassador Meloy, Robert O. Waring, and their Lebanese driver at the construction site of the new U.S. embassy.

The following day, an official of the Palestine news agency announced to the press that earlier that day security agents of Al Fatah had arrested three Lebanese men who confessed to the murders. He did not say how the men had been identified as suspects or why they had confessed so quickly. The official announced that the three men did not belong to any known political organization and suggested that they were hit men in the employ of an "outside power." He identified the suspected outside powers as Israel, Syria, Lebanon's Christian Phalangist Party, and the U.S. Central Intelligence Agency, but he did not explain how any of these would benefit from the murders.

The Palestinian spokesman said that Al Fatah would turn over the accused assassins to the Arab League peacekeeping force when it came on duty in Lebanon. For the Palestinians, the case was closed.[47]

On February 14, 1979, Adolph Dubs, U.S. ambassador to Afghanistan, was being driven to the U.S. embassy in Kabul when he was kidnapped by four armed men. They held Dubs hostage in a hotel room as they demanded the release by the Afghan government of several men they described as Islamic "religious leaders." They threatened to kill Dubs if the government did not comply with their demands. Afghan security forces stormed the hotel where Dubs and his kidnappers were in residence. Dubs was killed during the assault, although it is not known if a kidnapper or a member of the Afghan security force fired the fatal shot.[48]

After losing three ambassadors, the United States would lose three embassies in one month.

Chapter 5

The Holy War

TERROR IN TEHRAN

Americans woke on the morning of November 4, 1979, to learn that a mob of Iranian student radicals had stormed the U.S. embassy in Tehran, which they now controlled; they were holding the staff as hostages until the United States returned the Shah to stand trial for his alleged crimes. As is often the case, the breaking news was not the beginning of the story but marked a crisis somewhere closer to the middle.

The beginning, at least insofar as the United States was involved, began in 1952 with a coup. In 1953, the Eisenhower administration and the CIA were concerned that the leader of Iran, Prime Minister Mohammed Mossadegh, was too accommodating to the Iranian Communist Party and that Iran might fall under the domination of the Soviet Union. The CIA, with the support of the British government, covertly orchestrated a coup that removed Mossadegh from power and gave control of the Iranian government to the young Shah.[1]

By the late 1970s, the people of Iran had tired of the Shah, his corrupt regime, foreign companies and the Shah's cronies benefiting from Iran's resources, and the abandonment of traditional Islamic values.[2] Unrest turned into demonstrations and riots in the streets. The Shah and his family left in early 1979, and his most powerful enemy, the Ayatollah Ruhollah Khomeini, returned from exile in France to fill the power vacuum. Muslim clerics led by the ayatollah took control of the Iranian government, which became hostile to the Shah's former patron and protector, the United States. The United States only exacerbated the tense situation when it allowed the Shah to enter the country to be treated for the cancer that had been eating away at his body for six years.[3]

The student demonstration began in the street outside the U.S. embassy compound at 7:30 A.M. on November 4. The demonstrators were loud and ill mannered enough to make the Americans within the compound uneasy. Three hours after the demonstration began, about 450 protesters—some of them carrying clubs and wielding handguns—broke into the embassy and rounded up every American they could find. By the end of the day, they held sixty-six people prisoner, and they were demanding the return of the Shah in exchange for the release of the hostages.[4] The student protesters expected that their "sit-in" at the embassy would last three to five days before the Iranian government would insist that they release the hostages and go back to class. Instead, the government, now dominated by Islamic fundamentalists, supported their demands. The student demonstrators gamely took on the role of jailers.[5] As the mob outside chanted, "Death to America," the mob inside quickly learned the fine points of beating and blindfolding prisoners, solitary confinement, and mock executions.[6]

The politics of Iran was now controlled not by a new paradigm but by an ancient one. Unlike the West, the Islamic East, especially those areas where Shiite Muslims dominated, made no distinction between church and state. Government traced its authority back to the prophet Muhammed. Those in power acted as surrogates for the descendants of Muhammed and his son-in-law, Ali; they would surrender power at the arrival of the Savior. The United States, ignorant of the religious basis of power in ancient and post-Shah Iran, attempted to negotiate with the Iranian government for the release of the hostages, and it got nowhere.[7]

Sixteen days later, another, apparently unrelated, group of Islamic fanatics struck in Saudi Arabia. The political target was not the United States—at least not initially—but the ruling house of Saud. In the early morning hours of November 20, in the holy city of Mecca, a force of 1,000 well-trained and organized men seized control of the Grand Mosque, the holiest shrine of Islam. A similar attack was reported to have taken place that same day on the Prophet's Mosque in Medina, 220 miles north of Mecca. The force that attacked the Grand Mosque in Mecca was led by a man named Mohammed Abdullah al-Kahtani, who claimed to be the Mahdi, the messiah who would establish God's kingdom on earth. Kahtani and his followers intended to return Saudi Arabia to the traditions and practices of earlier times that were, they believed, in harmony with the teachings with the prophet Muhammed. On a practical level, they advocated the overthrow of the Saudi royal family, which, they believed, was succumbing to corrupting Western influences.

Four days after the religious radicals took over the Grand Mosque, the Saudi government sent in its troops. When the shooting was over, several hundred people were dead and wounded, and the Grand Mosque was returned to those who wished only to pray.[8]

The incident in Mecca would have been of little concern to the United States had not a rumor spread through parts of the Middle East that the United States and Israel were responsible for the attack on the Grand Mosque. The Ayatollah Khomeini poured gasoline on the fire with his comments on the mosque seizure, which were broadcast by Iranian radio the day after the attack. "It is not unlikely that criminal U.S. imperialism did this in an attempt to infiltrate the solid ranks of Islam," he said. "Moslems must not let down their guard and should expect this kind of dirty act by American imperialism and international Zionism."[9]

The United States denied the accusation, but it was too late. A Pakistani mob had picked up the chant and stormed the U.S. embassy in Islamabad. Before Pakistani troops could restore order, the mob had set fire to every building in the embassy compound. Two Americans were killed—one shot by a sniper, another killed by the fire. Two Pakistani staff members were also killed. Two members of the mob died in the melee, and fifty more were injured. Eight policemen were also injured. The Pakistani government announced that it deplored the attack on the embassy and said that it would rebuild the fire-gutted embassy.

The Ayatollah Khomeini did not pass up the opportunity to comment. "It is a great joy for us to learn about the uprising in Pakistan against the U.S.A.," he said. "It is good news for our oppressed nation. Borders [between Iran and Pakistan] should not separate hearts. This is not a struggle between the United States and Iran; it is a struggle between Islam and blasphemy."[9]

As the Iran hostage crisis dragged on, U.S. embassies in several other countries with large Muslim populations were the targets of demonstrations. For the most part, their governments managed to maintain order. A notable exception was Libya. On December 2, 1979, a mob of 2,000 people attacked the U.S. embassy in Tripoli. Some of the rioters were reported to be chanting pro-Iranian slogans. The embassy's staff escaped unharmed, but the mob left the lowest two floors of the five-story building in ruins. The Libyan authorities did nothing to stop the rioting mob; in fact, some American officials believed that the Libyan government and its leader Muammar Qaddafi encouraged the rioters. The Libyan government expressed its "regrets" for the damage done at the embassy, but it did not offer to take responsibility for repairs.[10] The United States ended all embassy activities in Libya five months to the day after the riot.[11]

THE HOSTAGE RESCUE MISSION

After the Iran hostage crisis had dragged on for six frustrating months, President Jimmy Carter decided it was time to take action. The military had developed a plan for rescuing the hostages that was to be carried out by the coordinated efforts of army, marine, and air force teams. The army's Delta

Force would do the dirty work of going into Tehran, rescuing the hostages from their captors at the embassy, and taking them to an airstrip where they could be loaded onto a transport plane for the flight out of Iran.

In April 1980, the leaders of the task force explained their plan to President Carter and his National Security Council in the Situation Room at the White House. The leader of the Delta Force group that would rescue the hostages, Colonel Charlie Beckwith, explained the operation step by step: Delta Force would be flown into Iran in helicopters, transfer to trucks for the entry into Tehran, assault the embassy compound at night, overpower the guards, take the hostages to a soccer stadium where they would board helicopters, fly to a landing strip thirty-five miles from Tehran, and transfer to transports for the ride out of Iran.

Carter, who had served as an officer on a nuclear submarine before entering politics, understood the risks of military operations. He asked, "How many casualties do you see here?"

Beckwith explained how some hostages might get shot by their rescuers if by their appearance and actions they seemed to be Iranian guards. "This is going to happen," he said. "I hope it doesn't, but we gotta count on it happening."

Carter said, "I understand. And I accept it."

Undersecretary of State Warren Christopher asked what would happen to the guards.

Beckwith said, "Mr. Christopher, it's our objective to take the guards out."

Christopher said, "What do you mean? Will you shoot them in the shoulder or what?"

"No, sir. We're going to shoot each of them twice, right between the eyes." After convincing the doubters in the room that the men of Delta Force were good enough shots with .45-caliber pistols to do the job, he said he expected to find twenty to twenty-five guards on duty: twenty or twenty-five Iranian casualties.

After more discussion of the details of the operation, someone asked, "Mr. President, my agency now needs to know what your decision will be. Should we move forward and pre-position?"

Carter replied, "It's time for me to summarize. I do not want to undertake this operation, but we have no other recourse. The only way I will call it off now is if the International Red Cross hands back our Americans. There's not going to be just pre-positioning forward. We're going to do this operation."

After the meeting wrapped up, Carter took Colonel Beckwith aside. He told the Delta Force leader, "I want you, before you leave for Iran, to assemble all of your force and when you think it's appropriate give them a message from me. Tell them that in the event this operation fails, for whatever reason, the fault will not be theirs, it will be mine."[12]

The mission to free the hostages, code named Eagle Claw, began at 1800 hours, local time, on April 24, when the first of six C-130 transports left a base on Masirah Island, off the coast of Oman. Their destination was a location designated Desert One, a hard-packed dirt road that would be used as an airstrip about two hundred miles southeast of Tehran. The Delta Force unit and support troops aboard the transports were to be met at Desert One by eight marine RH-53D Sea Stallion helicopters that were to fly in from the carrier *Nimitz*, which was stationed in the Gulf of Oman.

The transports reached their destination and secured the site as planned. The eight helicopters had trouble from the start. Soon after crossing over land and into Iran, they ran into a sandstorm. One of the choppers developed mechanical problems and had to be abandoned. Another helicopter picked up its crew and continued on to Desert One. After flying through the sandstorm, a second helicopter began experiencing problems with its instrumentation. It returned to the *Nimitz*. Only six of the eight helicopters—the minimum needed to conduct the operation—arrived at Desert One, and the last of them arrived an hour and a half behind schedule. Worse still, one of the helicopters had developed hydraulic problems and was deemed unsafe to fly. The operation was behind schedule and no longer had enough helicopters to raid the embassy compound as planned. Colonel Beckwith, the officer in charge on the ground in Iran, decided to scrub the mission.

The scene at Desert One was orderly chaos. Three C-130 transports were parked beside the dirt road with their engines idling, ready to take off. The transports had the dual purpose of carrying troops and equipment and of carrying fuel to refuel the helicopters. Hundreds of men were on the ground moving themselves and equipment between aircraft. The whole scene was lighted by a burning Iranian gasoline tanker truck that had inadvertently been driven by and had been stopped by an antitank weapon. The scene was also being watched by forty-five Iranians who had been on a bus that also stumbled by the rendezvous in the desert.

One of the helicopters began to lift off to reposition itself behind a C-130 where it would top off its fuel tanks. In the swirl of transport backwashes and helicopter downdrafts, it slammed into the transport. Both aircraft were burning, rockets were blasting off into the night sky, and men were running for their lives.

The members of Delta Force and the other men on the ground at Desert One boarded the two remaining transports, and they flew back to Masirah Island in defeat. The enemy had not fired a shot. It did not even know that it had been invaded until the following morning.

Five airmen and three marines died in the disaster in the Iranian desert. The retreating U.S. forces left behind five intact Sea Stallion helicopters and all of their armaments and equipment—a windfall for the enemy in Iran.[13]

After the failed rescue attempt, the hostages remained prisoners and the U.S. government remained paralyzed, but history moved on. The ailing Shah of Iran, who had shuttled around the world like the man without a country that he was, died in Egypt on July 27, 1980. The demand that he return to Iran for trial became moot. Iraq, led by its president of one year, Saddam Hussein, chose to settle a long-standing border dispute by invading Iran in September. Hussein expected victory over the chaotic Iranian government within weeks; the war would last eight years.[14]

The Iran hostage crisis ended not with a bang but with a whimper. U.S. negotiators and their Iranian counterparts reached an agreement that the United States would release frozen Iranian assets, and the Iranians would in turn release the remaining fifty-two hostages. The documents were signed in the early morning of January 20, 1981; at 12:25 P.M. eastern standard time, just minutes after Ronald Reagan took the oath of office to become president, an airplane carrying the hostages left Iran. Iran had humiliated retiring President Carter, and it would not have to deal with the new, and likely forceful, strategies incoming President Reagan would devise to retrieve the hostages.[15]

The rise to power of the Ayatollah Khomeini and the hostage crisis in Iran were landmarks in the rise of the Islamic fundamentalists and the beginning of their holy war against the infidels. But this fundamentalist movement was just a modern manifestation of a centuries-old movement within Sunni Islam, known as Wahhabism. Wahhabism was a conservative, monolithic, and puritanical movement within Islam that dated back to the late eighteenth century. In the early twentieth century, it became the religious and political foundation of Saudi Arabia, the most conservative and repressive of the Arab states. Toward the end of the century, Wahhabism found adherents in the region around Peshwar in Pakistan. When the Soviet Union invaded Afghanistan in late 1979, the Islamic fundamentalists were ideally situated to wage a holy war against the invading infidels just the other side of the Kyhber Pass.[16] After the Soviet Union gave up the war and then collapsed, Wahhabism set up outposts in the newly independent states of central Asia, with an influential presence in Uzbekistan.[17] The Taliban and its Saudi Arabian sponsor, Osama bin Laden, set up shop in postwar Afghanistan. The Israel-Palestine war, which had for three decades been dominated by secular interests, began to show the influence of Islamic fundamentalists, and religion, as it had done innumerable times in history, brought out the worst in its adherents. The Islamic holy war of the late twentieth century was to be fought with terrorism.

Chapter 6

Reagan Takes On Terrorism

Terrorism was a growing problem on the international scene when Ronald Reagan took office as president of the United States. Incidents abounded of airliner hijackings, massacres by armed gunmen, and bombs left to explode in public gathering places. Members of his administration saw the United States as an increasingly likely target, and they were quick to sound the alarm and to identify who they thought was behind international terrorism. Within days of becoming secretary of state, Alexander Haig accused the Soviet Union of financing, equipping, and training terrorists.[1] Two months later, CIA director William Casey was browbeating his staff to dig out the proof that the Soviet Union was the chief sponsor of international terrorism. He had been inspired in this quest by a book by Claire Sterling, *The Terror Network*,[2] which claimed to give hard evidence of Moscow's guilt. Casey's staff and critics of Sterling's book found the evidence unconvincing, but they did not change many minds. Reagan and his administration would operate on the assumption that the Soviet Union and its client states were behind the rise of international terrorism.[3]

From the beginning of his administration, Reagan's managerial style was based on delegating authority. As Casey explained to a reporter, "Reagan just won't permit himself to get bogged down in detail and minutia. He's not a yellow-pad President like Carter or Nixon. He doesn't feel compelled to scribble notes during meeting or control who gets on the White House tennis courts."[4] He would not be second-guessing Casey when it came to dealing with terrorists, which delighted the CIA director.

In the late 1970s, the CIA had taken a deserved beating for its illegal activities, and Casey's first order of business was to rebuild the agency.

He began reestablishing links to the Israeli secret service that had all but disappeared.[5] As the international terrorist threat had grown in the late 1970s and into the 1980s, Israel and its Mossad had unashamedly taken decisive action to subdue it. Casey looked forward to doing likewise, and he began exchanging intelligence with the Mossad and supplying it with funds.[6] Some of the intelligence the CIA gave the Israelis included photographs taken by a CIA spy satellite of a nuclear reactor about ten miles from Baghdad, Iraq. Israel believed that Iraq was using the facility to produce fissionable materials for an atomic bomb. On June 9, 1981, using the reconnaissance photos furnished by the CIA, Israeli warplanes, also obtained from the United States, destroyed Iraq's nuclear capability.[5]

Casey was impressed by Israel's audacity in dealing with the threat from Iraq, and it is likely that its example reinforced his desire to deal aggressively with America's enemies. Unlike Israel, however, Casey believed that the greatest threat of terrorism to America would come not from the Middle East but from North Africa.

MUAMMAR QADDAFI AND THE LIBYAN HIT TEAMS

According to the CIA, incidents of international terrorism doubled during a ten-year period, from 238 incidents in 1971 to 489 in 1981. In 1980, 642 people were killed and 1,078 wounded in terrorist attacks. In June 1981, the CIA also identified a disturbing trend that began two years earlier, in 1979: a large number of terrorist attacks were being sponsored by national governments.[7]

The clear leader among those states sponsoring acts of terrorism was the North African state of Libya. One news report counted at least a dozen Libyan exiles who had been murdered in England, Italy, West Germany, Greece, and Lebanon, presumably by Libyan hit teams.[8] The CIA specifically accused Libya of sending assassination squads to the Middle East, Europe, and the United States to eliminate dissident Libyan expatriates and students.[9]

The government of Libya acted under the autocratic rule of Colonel Muammar Qaddafi. Qaddafi, who was the sole surviving son of a poor Bedouin couple, had found a career in the military. He masterfully developed a network of dissidents in the military and among civilians. In September 1969, as a twenty-seven-year-old captain, he led the bloodless coup that deposed Libya's aging King Idris. Although Qaddafi held no official title, he became Libya's de facto chief of state. Within three years, he had consolidated his power, nationalized the oil industry, and put into place a socialist economic system. In foreign affairs, he verbally assaulted the Western powers as imperialists, promoted Arab nationalism, and gave aid to revolutionary and terrorist groups. During his tenure, he has attracted more international attention and wielded more force than normally warranted for the head of a state with a population of only three million people.[8]

The leaders of the Soviet Union thought they had a prize in Qaddafi. Not only did he support insurgencies, but he had the resources of Libya's oil income to buy armaments from the Soviet Union with hard Western currency. By 1981, Libya had purchased $12 billion worth of Soviet-made armaments, and it hosted about two thousand Soviet military advisers. The Soviet Union was willing to put up with Qaddafi's personal eccentricities, egomania, and political naiveté because he served its purpose of keeping the capitalist countries of the West off balance.[10]

Relations between the United States and Libya had taken a deep dive when, in December 1979, a mob burned the U.S. embassy in Libya. The following spring, the Carter administration expelled four Libyan diplomats because they had threatened dissident Libyan expatriates and students in the United States. Then, in May 1981, the Reagan administration ordered the closing of Libya's embassy, or "people's bureau" as the Libyans called it, because of that country's support of international terrorism.[8] William Casey at the CIA reasoned that if Qaddafi no longer led Libya, that country would no longer sponsor terrorism.

The behind-the-scenes maneuvering of the Reagan administration against Muammar Qaddafi broke into public view in early August 1981. The CIA presented the House Select Committee on Intelligence an aggressive plan for overthrowing Qaddafi's regime in Libya. The plan included the components of "disinformation"—basically, lies intended to embarrass Qaddafi's government—establishment of a "countergovernment" that would challenge the legitimacy of Qaddafi's rule, and a guerrilla campaign within Libya to show indigenous Libyan opposition. What upset members of the House committee the most was the vaguely stated goal of Qaddafi's ultimate removal from power. The members of Congress who read the plan believed that removal of Qaddafi meant his assassination. They considered this a real possibility because in the late 1950s and early 1960s, the CIA had plotted to assassinate several foreign leaders. Most prominent among them were Patrice Lumumba of the Congo and Fidel Castro of Cuba. President Ford had issued an executive order prohibiting assassination by the government or its agencies. The committee responded to the CIA's plan for dealing with Qaddafi by sending a letter directly to President Reagan strongly protesting the plan and its goal.[11] After barely six months as director of Central Intelligence, Casey had lost the confidence of the Congress because of his approval of "harebrained" schemes, and influential leaders on Capitol Hill were calling for his retirement—either voluntarily or otherwise.[12]

The brouhaha was forgotten by the second week of August when, just two months after the CIA formally charged Libya with being the leader of international terrorism, President Reagan personally ordered a challenge to Libya in its own hemisphere. Eight years earlier, Qaddafi had pushed Libya's frontier out into the Mediterranean Sea by claiming the Gulf of Sidra south of thirty-two degrees, thirty minutes north latitude as Libyan territorial waters. The United States had taken the position that Libya was entitled to claim territorial waters up to the internationally recognized twelve miles but had not pressed the issue.

The Sixth Fleet of the U.S. Navy, which patrolled the Mediterranean, planned its annual exercises to include part of the Gulf of Sidra. The exercise began on August 8, 1981, and it was greeted by Libyan aircraft flying into the exercise area as a counterchallenge. Seventy-two sorties by Libyan jets were met by carrier-based F-14 interceptors that ushered them away from the exercise area.

On August 20, two F-14s on patrol picked up on their radar two aircraft approaching them from an air base in Libya and turned to meet them. When they closed on each other, the American pilots identified the Libyan planes as Soviet built Sukhoi-22s, which had technology about a generation behind the F-14s. The American pilots put their planes into a sharp left turn to fly on a course parallel with that of the Libyans. The lead Su-22 also went into a sharp left turn, trying to take a position behind the F-14. Before getting into the best position, the lead Libyan pilot fired a heat-seeking Atoll missile. The F-14 pilot easily dodged it, pulled up behind the second Libyan plane, and then fired a heat-seeking Sidewinder missile. It hit the Su-22 in the tail. The pilot parachuted into the sea where he was picked up by a Libyan ship.

The second F-14 maneuvered into position behind the Libyan fighter that had fired the first air-to-air missile. The F-14's pilot fired a sidewinder missile that flew up the exhaust pipe of the Su-22, blowing up the plane and its pilot. Libya protested the destruction of its two aircraft, but kept a safe distance from U.S. ships and aircraft until the exercise ended.[13]

A few days after the air battle in the Gulf of Sidra, U.S. security people heard that Qaddafi was telling his associates that he intended to have President Reagan assassinated. As a precaution, Reagan began wearing his bullet-proof vest whenever he appeared in public.[14] U.S. intelligence sources also reported that Libya had planned to assassinate the U.S. ambassador to Italy, Maxwell M. Rabb, in October 1981. Security measures were increased to protect Rabb.

In November 1981, Christian A. Chapman, the chargé d'affaires at the U.S. embassy in Paris, was the target of an assassination attempt. As he was leaving home, a gunman fired six shots at him. Having taken cover behind his car, Chapman was unhurt. The would-be assassin escaped. Libya was suspected of being behind the assassination attempt.

Intelligence sources then heard that a Libyan assassin named "Jack" was in the United States and that he was planning to kill President Reagan as the president gave a speech to the National Press Club in Washington on

November 18. Reagan made his appearance in his now-customary bullet-proof vest and accompanied by more security agents than reporters.[15]

During the first few days of December 1981, the FBI and Secret Service were hunting for Libyan hit teams that were, according to the government intelligence sources, sent to the United States to assassinate President Reagan in retaliation for its humiliation in the Gulf of Sidra confrontation. The *New York Times* broke the story on its front page on December 4. According to the article, a government informant had described how he had helped train the assassins in Libya, and he gave details of the assassination plans. The team was to kill the president by shooting down Air Force One with a ground-to-air missile, by destroying the presidential limousine and its passenger with a rocket, or by shooting him at close range with handguns. Should the hit team be unable to kill Reagan, their secondary targets would be his top aides and members of his family. The key informant's information was reported to be supported by information from independent sources.[16]

President Reagan was inclined to have a realistic view of himself as a target, having been shot by a would-be assassin on March 30. Furthermore, the near-fatal attempt on the life of Pope John Paul II by a Turk in May and the assassination of Egyptian president Anwar Sadat by a group of Islamic fundamentalists in the Egyptian Army in October no doubt heightened Reagan's awareness of possible assassination attempts. "As to his [Qaddafi's] threats personally against me, I think in view of the record, you can't dismiss them out of hand," Reagan said. "On the other hand, they're not going to change my life much."[16] Reagan conveniently forgot that the concept of the United States sponsoring the assassination Qaddafi had been kicked around Washington the previous August.[11]

To be on the safe side, however, the Secret Service greatly increased its efforts to protect the president, as well as Vice President George Bush, Secretary of State Alexander Haig, and Secretary of Defense Caspar Weinberger. The Secret Service also brought under its protective umbrella Reagan's top aides—Edwin Meese, James Baker, and Michael Deaver.[17]

Muammar Qaddafi appeared on American television on Sunday, December 6, in an interview with David Brinkley. "We refuse to assassinate any person," Qaddafi said through an interpreter. "It is the behavior of America, preparing to assassinate me, to poison my food. They tried many things to do this."[18]

About the alleged plot to kill Reagan, Qaddafi said, "If they have evidence, we are ready to see this evidence." When asked why Reagan was taking the allegation seriously, he replied, "Because he is silly, he is ignorant."[17]

Then, getting personal, Qaddafi said about Ronald Reagan, "And you will see, Reagan is a liar.... We are ready to make judgment of an investigation, to see the evidence, because we are sure we didn't send any people to kill Reagan or any other people in the world. And we want to see this big lies [*sic*]."[18]

The following day, Reagan spoke publicly about the Libyan leader. "I wouldn't believe a word he says if I were you....We have the evidence and he knows it."[17]

What had been a disagreement between nations became a personal issue, with the two heads of state calling each other liars and accusing each other of being behind assassination plots. The Bedouin of the African desert and the American cowboy faced each other at high noon.

As days passed and the FBI, Secret Service, and CIA, tried to bring the details into tighter focus, the plot began to blur. The first version of the story had a hit team of five assassins—four Arabs and an East German—traveling through Paris on their way to Boston. To catch them on entry, the U.S. Custom Service sent to its offices their names, descriptions, and composite sketches. It also sent a warning of a second group of six assassins allegedly led by the legendary terrorist "Carlos," Ilyich Ramirez-Sanchez. The National Security Council summarized the findings of the intelligence agencies in a forty-page report it sent to top White House aides. In various scenarios, it counted twelve to fourteen assassins. The government agencies did not report any hard evidence of the plots or evidence against the alleged assassins. The press, viewing all the confusion, began to wonder if Libyan hit teams really were stalking President Reagan.[17, 19]

The doubts extended to FBI director William H. Webster, who stated in a televised interview that his agency had not confirmed that a Libyan hit squad had entered the United States. He admitted that the reports could have been planted, and he agreed that he would have been happier if the reports had not been made public.[20]

Years after the event, *New York Times* writer Seymour Hersh looked into the source of the hit-team reports. His unidentified sources claimed that the reports had been brought to the attention of government security agencies by CIA director William Casey. When the raw intercepts on which the story was based were examined, they revealed only "broad mouthings" by Qaddafi but no specific details. One intelligence official commented, "The stuff I saw did not make a substantial case that we had a threat. There was nothing to cause us to react as we have, saying Qaddafi is public enemy No. 1." Another official was more blunt: "The whole thing was a complete fabrication."[21]

No one was ever arrested in connection with the alleged plot, and the story faded away.

THE BATTLE OF BEIRUT

After Yasir Arafat and his PLO were driven out of Jordan in 1970, they moved their headquarters to Beirut, Lebanon. A dozen years later, with

Lebanon deep in its civil war, Arafat was running a PLO state within the state of Lebanon and launching raids into Israel, to the south, at will. On June 6, 1982, Israel moved to protect its northern regions by invading Lebanon. Five weeks later, its tanks and armored personnel carriers rode into Beirut. Israeli forces surrounded the PLO stronghold near Beirut and began a siege that lasted seventy days. The siege ended when the PLO agreed to evacuate Lebanon.

Members of the PLO and Yasir Arafat boarded ships that would take them in groups to Arab countries scattered across the Middle East and North Africa. As he boarded a ship for Tunisia, Arafat told an American reporter, "I'll tell you what this war taught us. It taught us that the real enemy is the United States. It is against you that we must fight. Not because your bombs killed our people but because you have closed your eyes to what is moral and just."[22]

A multinational force consisting of troops from France, Italy, Great Britain, and the United States was formed to keep the peace in the hope of facilitating the emergence of a stable Lebanese government. Israeli and Syrian forces that were in Lebanon to protect their countries' interests were also to be withdrawn.[23]

The first group of U.S. Marines arrived in Lebanon in August 1982.[24] Their numbers ultimately rose to 1,600. Most of the PLO's forces had left by the end of August, but the withdrawals of Israeli and Syrian troops were, at best, partial. The mission of the peacekeepers then fell to the back-up position of supporting the Christian-dominated government led by Amin Gemayel. As the presence of the international peacekeeping forces stretched on in time, they and the countries that sent them increasingly became targets of the warring factions.[25]

Some in the U.S. government were aware of the volatility of the situation and the risk to Americans in Lebanon. Richard Marcinko, the former commander of the navy's counterterrorist unit, SEAL Team Six, has colorfully described his group's clandestine mission to Lebanon to assess the vulnerability of American targets to attacks by terrorists.[26] Marcinko arrived in Beirut in December 1982. As he was leaving the airport to go to the city, he noted, "It looked as if there were a riot going on outside, but it was only the usual bustle, common to Third World airports from Cairo to Karachi. The difference in Lebanon was that here, everybody was armed to the teeth."[27] The city was littered with the ruins of war-damaged buildings, and the sound of exploding bombs was common.

Marcinko and his SEALs had no trouble finding security problems. The Lebanese guards stationed outside the U.S. embassy carried only side arms, and the marines with superior weapons were posted inside the lobby. The barricades outside the embassy were at best decorative. The marine compound at the airport was on an open flat occupying the low ground, and the militias, who had been participants in years of warfare, held a superior position in the hills to the east. The marines were hobbled by rules of engagement that required them to not load their weapons unless they were told to do so by a commissioned officer. They were, however, allowed to return fire if fired upon.

If all this was not bad enough, the SEAL unit doing the assessment of security threats could only guess who might attack the embassy or the marines. Marcinko said of the situation, "From what we could tell, there were roughly two dozen separate armed groups in West Beirut, not counting the MNF [Multinational Force], the Israelis, the Syrians, or us. That included militias, private armies, street gangs, just plain thugs, and dyed-in-the-wool terrorists, so we had a full spectrum from which to choose our bad guys." As one member of the team described it, "It's like the goddamn South Bronx. Every street is another gang's turf."[28]

Before departing Lebanon in January 1983, Marcinko met with an unnamed "senior American official" at the U.S. embassy to share the finding of his antiterrorist team's assessment of the embassy's vulnerability to terrorist attacks. The official said, "This embassy has managed to withstand the Lebanese civil war, which has gone on unabated since 1975. ...The security of this embassy is airtight. That is my position."[29]

The concern for security that had developed in Washington did not travel to Beirut.

The U.S. embassy in Beirut stood on Avenue de Paris, across the street from the Mediterranean Sea. It was an eight-story, salmon-pink, crescent-shaped structure that had once been an apartment building. The inner curve of the crescent faced the street and the sea, and a drive came in from the street along the crescent's inner curve. At 1:05 P.M. on April 8, 1983, a man wearing a leather jacket drove a black delivery van up the drive to the embassy's front entrance. A moment later, a bomb in the van estimated to be made of as much as five hundred pounds of explosives destroyed the van and all traces of its driver. The blast took out the building entrance and columns supporting the upper floors, which then tumbled down on to what had been the main lobby. The resulting fire gutted much of what was left of the embassy and shrouded it in black smoke.

Troops from the French contingent of the peacekeeping force were the first to arrive and give assistance to survivors. Soon thereafter, 200 U.S. Marines arrived to reclaim the embassy as ambulances carried the injured off to hospitals.[30, 31] The site was littered with chunks of the shattered building, scattered papers, broken bodies, and severed limbs. The blast killed at least fifty-seven people and injured another one hundred. Of the dead, sixteen were Americans, and fully half of these were from the CIA's Beirut station.[30]

Ten minutes after the blast, a man called the office of Agencie France-Presse to announce that the attack was "part of the Iranian Revolution's campaign against imperialist targets throughout the world." He said he was a member of the "Islamic Jihad Organization," which later came to be identified with Hezbollah, a Shiite Muslim group believed to be loyal to the Ayotollah Khomeini and supported by Iran.[31] Over the next few days, several other groups, most of which had not been heard of before, claimed responsibility for the attack.[30]

President Reagan's comment reaffirmed the peacekeeping mission of the United States in Lebanon: "This tragedy, however awful, must not distract us from our search for peace in Lebanon and elsewhere. We will never give in to this cowardly type of incident."[30]

President Reagan sent Undersecretary of State Lawrence Eagleburger to Beirut to escort the bodies of the American victims back home. While there, Eagleburger inspected what was left of the shattered embassy. Like many others in government, he had difficulty accepting the new reality of terrorist attacks. "An American embassy is in a country to deal with the people of that country. It is not a fort," he said. "We don't hide behind steel doors or peek out through peepholes.... Under these circumstances it is a constant compromise between absolute security and being able to do one's job."[30]

The marines' uneasy presence in Lebanon was challenged again in the early morning of Sunday, October 23, 1983, when a Mercedes truck raced along the road from Beirut toward the U.S. Marine barracks at the Beirut airport. The four-story building, which was built around a central courtyard, was protected by several checkpoints and sentry posts, a wrought-iron fence, and an improvised barricade. The truck, which was reported to be traveling at sixty miles per hour, flew past the checkpoint and guard posts, evaded the barricade, crashed through sandbag barriers, and slammed into the lobby of the barracks building. The bomb in the truck, believed to contain about two thousand pounds of high-explosive, detonated at 6:20 A.M. It destroyed the truck and its driver, excavated a crater forty feet wide and thirty feet deep, and brought down the entire structure where hundreds of marines still slept. Minutes later, another explosion destroyed a building used as a barracks by French paratroopers who were part of the peacekeeping force.[25, 32]

The final tally showed that 220 marines and 21 members of other U.S. services were killed. It was the Marine Corps' bloodiest day since February 1945, when marines took heavy casualties capturing Iwo Jima. The French lost 58 paratroopers when their quarters were bombed.[33]

President Ronald Reagan said, "I know there are no words to properly express our outrage and the outrage of all Americans at the despicable act. But I think we should all recognize that these deeds make so evident the bestial nature of those who would assume power [in Lebanon] if they could have their way and drive us out of that area." One of his top aides added, "We're convinced that this was done by someone who wants us out, and we're not getting out."[25]

At the other end of Pennsylvania Avenue, members of Congress were questioning the purpose of the marines in Lebanon. "What is our Middle East policy?" asked Senator Charles Mathias. "We need a policy." Congressman David Obey wondered, "What the hell are we supposed to be doing over there? What is the role?" The administration did not have an answer.[25]

In addition to his resolve that American forces would remain in Lebanon, President Reagan was adamant that the guilty be punished. "Those who directed this atrocity must be dealt justice, and they will be," he said. Islamic Jihad, a.k.a. Hezbollah, stepped forward to take responsibility, as it had for the embassy bombing six months earlier. In claiming responsibility, it dared Reagan to act. The Free Islamic Revolutionary Movement also said it had committed the bombing. Possibly because it did not know with certainty the identity of the guilty group, or possibly because it did not want to escalate the violence in Lebanon, the United States did nothing.[34]

Most of the marines left Lebanon the following winter, along with the rest of the multinational peacekeeping force. A group of about eighty stayed on to protect the diplomatic staff until their new offices in what was termed the "annex" were ready for occupancy. In the interim, the embassy staff conducted business out of space borrowed from the British embassy. The U.S. embassy annex was located in Aukar, a suburb on the eastern edge of Beirut. The location was chosen partly because the Lebanese government operated out of east Beirut, but mostly because it was thought to be safer than west Beirut, the former location of the embassy. U.S. military advisors trained a group of Lebanese Christians, who took over the responsibility of guarding the new embassy annex.

The embassy annex was a six-story concrete block at the end of an access road that had restricted access. The road was guarded by a set of concrete blocks, called "dragon's teeth," that jutted out alternately from the right and left side of the roadway, forcing drivers to slow while making serpentine turns as they drove along the entry road. After emerging from the "dragon's teeth," a driver would pass a parking lot on the left and, 100 yards down the road, reach the embassy annex. Workmen were completing final construction details that included installation of a security gate at the beginning of the access road, between the main road and the dragon's teeth. On the morning of October 23, 1984, the security gate lay at the side of the road, waiting to be hung from the gatepost.

At 11:45 A.M., a van drove onto the access road. The driver drew a gun and fired at a guard on duty at the checkpoint. Then he zig-zagged the van through the "dragon's teeth" and accelerated toward the embassy annex.

A bodyguard for the British ambassador, who was visiting his American counterpart, was waiting for his charge when he noticed the commotion at the entrance to the entry road and saw the van approaching. The body-guard described the event after the fact: "I fired about five rounds through the door of the vehicle. I saw the driver fall over. As he fell, he pulled on the wheel and the car swung to the right, hitting a parked vehicle."[35]

The van exploded about thirty feet short of its target, the embassy annex. The blast shattered the front of the building, just as a car bomb had caused the collapse of the front of the embassy in Beirut seventeen months earlier. The explosion dug a crater eight feet deep and twenty-six feet in diameter. It seemed likely that the suicide bomber had intended to drive into the parking garage under the embassy before detonating his 350-pound bomb. If he had, he might have destroyed the entire building and killed everyone in it. The casualties were bad enough: the attack killed twenty-four people and injured ninety others. The U.S. ambassador and his British visitor, who were in the ambassador's fifth-floor office, sustained only minor injuries.

President Reagan described the bombing as a "cowardly terrorist act" and called it "another painful reminder of the persistent threat of terrorism in the world."[35]

The question of responsibility again presented itself. An hour and a half after the bombing, the French news agency Agencie France-Presse received an anonymous phone call. The caller announced, "In the name of God the Almighty, Islamic Jihad [a.k.a. Hezbollah] announces that it is responsible for blowing up a car rigged with explosives, which was driven by one of our suicide commandos. The operation proves that we will carry out our previous promise not to allow a single American to remain on Lebanese soil."[35]

After Islamic Jihad had claimed responsibility for bombing the embassy, the marine barracks, and the embassy annex, it seems reasonable to conclude that that group was responsible. It is not clear what U.S. intelligence agencies knew about Islamic Jihad or Hezbollah at the time of the bombings. Several years later, however, the essential facts were public knowledge. Hezbollah was a Lebanese Shiite militia founded in 1982 by a group of Shiite Muslim clerics who had been educated in Iran. Its objective—both political and religious—was the formation of an Islamic republic in Lebanon. Its members had received training and weapons from the Iranian Revolutionary Guards, who in turn received support from and took orders from the Iranian government.[36] Today, the Department of State considers "Islamic Jihad" and "Hezbollah" to be two names for the same group. (See appendix 3.)

Hezbollah, it was commonly held, received spiritual guidance and military direction from Lebanese clerics, most prominent among them Sheikh Sayyid Mohammed Hussein Fadlallah. Although Hezbollah presented itself as an Islamic militant group, there were those who thought that its real mission was a grab for power and that the clerics were a convenient front. One Shiite insider told journalist Thomas Friedman that "Fadlallah is just a cover. He knows little about operations. The people organizing the kidnappings [and bombings] are totally isolated from ideology. Ideology means nothing to them. They are professionals. It is like a play. There are the actors who recite the lines and there is the director who coordinates everything. Never confuse the actors for the director. This is business."[36]

And what about the suicide bombers, the young men who sacrificed their lives to deliver a blow to the enemies of Islam? They were the foot soldiers, the true believers, who sacrificed all they had for their people and for Allah. But they did not make policy or define strategy or tactics. The suicide bombers followed orders. Hezbollah's founding clerics and their Iranian handlers were in charge, but nobody ever saw one of them driving a stolen truck loaded with explosives through the streets of Beirut on a deadly mission.[36]

WILLIAM CASEY RETALIATES

With the marines out of Lebanon and its civil war winding down, most Americans were inclined to forget the bombing of the embassy, the marine barracks, and the embassy annex. CIA director William Casey was an exception. Not only did Casey feel the humiliation of his country being bested by terrorist thugs, but he felt the loss of CIA assets. In the bombing of the embassy in 1983, the CIA had lost its chief Middle East analyst, Robert Ames, its station chief, Kenneth Haas, and several other CIA employees.[31] Also, in March 1984, the CIA's station chief in Beirut, William Buckley, had been kidnapped; and Islamic Jihad (a.k.a. Hezbollah), had claimed responsibility. It would later be learned that his captors had murdered him.[37]

Casey came to accept that the group calling itself Islamic Jihad and Hezbollah was responsible for the attacks against U.S. facilities and its people in Lebanon and that the United States should strike back against that group. Casey believed that Sheikh Fadlallah was the true leader of the terrorist group and concluded that action against the group should begin with the elimination of Fadlallah. Before taking action against Fadlallah, however, Casey had to devise a strategy to circumvent the provision of Executive Order 12333, issued by President Reagan in 1981, that renewed and expanded the prohibition of U.S. employees and their agents from committing assassinations.[38]

Casey asked his general counsel, Stanley Sporkin, to devise a legal rationale that would sanction action against Fadlallah. Sporkin reasoned that taking action that would result in the death of a terrorist who intended to attack the United States would not be an assassination. It would be "preemptive self-defense." To keep the CIA's actions within the law, Casey would have to base his actions on facts, have the president authorize the action with a finding, and inform the appropriate congressional committees.[37, 39]

Casey believed he had the facts, and he went to work on getting the presidential finding. He enlisted the assistance of the National Security Council's expert on terrorism, Oliver North, to draft the document. North drafted two findings. The first authorized the CIA to recruit and train foreign nationals for the purpose of striking against identified terrorists. The antiterrorist units of foreign nationals would go into action only when the president signed a second finding authorizing the action. President Reagan signed the first finding and reminded Casey of his obligation to notify selected members of Congress about it.[40]

Casey turned his plan to train foreign nationals over to members of his agency, who hired Lebanese men to form three five-man teams. Casey soon learned that although his people were following his direction, they were not enthusiastic about the plan. The agency had been eviscerated after the revelations of the mid-1970s that it had illegally engaged in domestic spying against U.S. citizens and had participated in plots to assassinate several foreign leaders, most notably Fidel Castro. They knew that if something went wrong, it would be they and not the president who would take the blame. The Lebanese men they had recruited made it worse. They were not only prepared but enthusiastic about going out and killing somebody. Casey's subordinates feared that they might not be able to control their antiterrorist teams.[41]

In frustration that his agency was not getting anything done, William Casey turned to a trusted ally, Saudi Arabia's ambassador to the United States, Prince Bandar, for help. In the story reported by Bob Woodward after Casey's death, Bandar put up $3 million to finance an operation and hired an Englishman with commando experience to coordinate the operation. The Englishman in turn worked through the Lebanese intelligence service to hire the operative who would carry out the action against Sheikh Fadlallah.[42]

The operation began on Friday March 8, 1985, as a man parked a pickup truck in front of the high-rise apartment building in the Bir al-Abed suburb of Beirut where Sheikh Fadlallah lived. The man walked away from the truck, telling the Hezbollah militiamen who guarded the area that he was going for help to fix a tire.

Across the street from the truck, worshipers were leaving a mosque after prayers. Sheikh Fadlallah's armored Range Rover arrived, and the pickup truck disintegrated in a ball of flame and debris. The explosion set fire to the apartment building where Fadlallah lived. People trapped in the burning building jumped out of windows, only to die in the burning debris below. People walking on the street were cut to pieces by the blast. A dozen people were trapped in vehicles and burned to death. The explosion and its aftermath killed at least ninety-two people and injured hundreds more.[43] Among the dead were five of Sheikh Fadlallah's bodyguards, but the sheikh was not harmed.[44]

The bombers got away clean, but the Lebanese knew who to blame. They hung a banner across the front of a gutted apartment building—presumably the one where Sheikh Fadlallah lived—that read, "Made in U.S.A." Fadlallah made the droll observation, "They sent me a letter, and I got the message."[43]

When news of the bombing in Beirut arrived at CIA headquarters in Langley, Virginia, William Casey called together his deputy director and assistant deputy director of operations to try to make sense of what was being reported. They could not. Casey, knowing that something he had started had gone terribly wrong, moved to protect the agency. He asked President Reagan to rescind his finding that authorized antiterrorist teams, and he shut down the operation.[45]

The Saudis also moved quickly to cover their involvement. They spread a story that Israel was responsible for the bombing, and they leaked information to the Hezbollah that identified some of those involved in the bombing.

Because the threat of terrorist attacks still existed, Prince Bandar communicated an offer of $2 million to Sheikh Fadlallah in return for warnings of impending attacks on Saudi and American facilities. Fadlallah accepted the offer with the provision that payment be made in the form of food, medicine, and social services to his supporters. Fadlallah was good to his word. According to Bob Woodward's account, Prince Bandar offered the analysis that "[i]t was easier to bribe him [Fadlallah] than to kill him." William Casey was amazed by the simplicity of Bandar's solution to the problem of Hezbollah attacks against the United States.[42] Casey's biographer, Joseph Persico, reported that Bandar denied having anything to do with the bombing in Beirut.[46]

A reply to the bombing in Beirut was delivered five weeks later, on April 12, 1985, in Spain. Three hundred people were having breakfast at the El Descanso restaurant located about nine miles from central Madrid on the road to the Barajas Airport when an explosion tore through the ground-floor restaurant and brought down the three-story building that housed it. Seventeen people were killed in the blast, and eighty-two more were injured. Two of the dead and twelve of the injured were believed to be Americans from the U.S. Air Force base at Torrejon de Ardoz, near the restaurant.

After the explosion, local radio stations and newspapers received phone calls from people claiming to represent the separatist terrorist group Basque Fatherland and Liberty (Euzkadi Ta Askatasuna, ETA) claiming responsibility for the attack.[47] The Popular Front for the Liberation of Palestine-Special Command (PFLP-SC), a splinter group of the PFLP that operated out of southern Lebanon, also took credit for the bombing.[48]

Shared responsibility of both groups is possible because members of the ETA are known to have received training at camps in Lebanon where the PFLP-SC has its base.[49]

Terrorists again remembered the bombing in Beirut when they hijacked an airliner on June 14, 1985. TWA flight 847 had flown from Cairo to Athens and was to continue on to Rome. In Athens, two men smuggled pistols and hand grenades on board. Soon after the plane took off for Rome, the men commandeered it and ordered the pilot to fly to Beirut. While the airliner was refueled in Beirut, the hijackers, who were identified as members of Islamic Jihad, a.k.a. Hezbollah, demanded the release of 766 Lebanese Shiite Muslims who were being held by Israel. The plane flew to Algiers, where a small number of passengers were released, and then it returned to Beirut. Just after landing, the hijackers beat and shot a passenger, and they dumped his body from the plane onto the tarmac. The dead man was a U.S. Navy diver.[50]

When someone in the airport control tower condemned the murder over the radio, one of the hijackers shot back, "We have not forgotten the Massacre at Bir al-Abed" (the suburb of Beirut where hired assassins had attempted to kill Sheikh Fadlallah with a truck bomb).[51]

The hijacked airliner made one more trip to Algiers and returned to Beirut, continuing to leave small groups of passengers at each stop. When it made its final stop in Beirut on June 17, the Shiite Amal militia took charge of the remaining forty hostages, who were all men and all Americans. The Amal leader said that his group had adopted the hijackers' demands and that the hostages would not be released until Israel released its prisoners.[50]

Seventeen days after the beginning of the hijacking ordeal, the parties involved brought it to an end through an exchange of prisoners that was mediated by Syria. The Amal released the American hostages first, and Israel eventually released 735 Lebanese prisoners in several groups over the next five months. Israel said that it had not made a deal with anybody to release the men they held.[52]

ARMS FOR HOSTAGES

From the very beginning of his administration, President Reagan's foreign policy was unambiguous about its opposition to international terrorism. A week and a day after the forty Americans held hostage in Beirut were released, President Reagan said in a speech to the American Bar Association that terrorism was not the "erratic work of a small group of fanatics" but an organized program of "a confederation of terrorist states." These states were Iran, Libya, North Korea, Cuba, and Nicaragua. Notably absent from the list was Syria, which had won goodwill in Washington by negotiating the release of hostages from

Lebanon a week earlier. Reagan made a point of noting "the Soviet Union's close relationship with almost all of the terrorist states."[53]

Reagan's list of "terrorist states" set in place America's way of thinking about terrorism. It would be followed by the Department of State's somewhat different listing of "state sponsors of terrorism" (see appendix 4)[54] and by President George W. Bush's "axis of evil," which included Iran, Iraq, and North Korea.[55]

Within weeks of identifying the "terrorist states," Reagan and his administration stumbled into its greatest scandal by ignoring the presence of Iran at the top of the list. The sordid foreign policy mess that followed would become known as the Iran-Contra affair. It began with two distinct problems the Reagan administration faced. First, early in 1984, about the time the last U.S. Marines were leaving Lebanon, agents of Hezbollah began kidnapping Americans. By mid-1985, seven had been taken, including CIA station chief William Buckley, who was believed to be dead.[56] President Reagan wanted their release, and he was willing to be flexible on how this would be accomplished. Second, the Central American nation Nicaragua was under the control of that country's elected communist regime. Reagan and his administration wanted to support the right-wing Contra rebels who opposed the government, but Congress had prohibited aid to them by passing the Boland Amendment.[57]

The door to opportunity and disaster opened in June, as the Lebanon airliner hostage crisis was unfolding. An unofficial contact from Iran told an old friend of CIA director William Casey that Iran was willing to use its influence to gain the release of the hostages taken by Hezbollah in Beirut. In exchange, it wanted the United States to sell it TOW antitank missiles to be use in its war with Iraq. When Iran helped in getting the release of the forty airliner hostages, Casey and the Reagan administration took Iran's offer seriously. To get around an embargo on selling arms to Iran, they arranged for Israel to act as middleman in the sale.[58] The first shipment of weapons arrived in Iran on August 20, 1985. In December of that year, President Reagan got around to signing a retroactive finding authorizing arms shipments via Israel. The following month, he signed another finding that approved direct sales of weapons to the "terrorist state." In all, the United States sold Iran 2,004 TOW antitank missiles, 18 HAWK antiaircraft missiles, and "spare parts" for the HAWKs.[59]

Only the twisted logic of politics could rationalize what Reagan and his administration were doing. Half a decade earlier, Iran had held hundreds of Americans hostage in its own embassy. Iran had supported Hezbollah, the terrorist group that had destroyed the American embassy in Beirut, the embassy annex, and the marine barracks, killing hundreds of Americans and Lebanese. Iran was still backing Hezbollah, which had hijacked an airliner, murdered a sailor, and taken forty hostages just two months ear-lier. Only weeks before, President Reagan had branded Iran a "terrorist state." Nevertheless, Reagan and his advisors decided to reward Iran by selling it weapons in the hope that its client, Hezbollah, would release seven men it had kidnapped. Reagan and his men ran the operation out of the National Security Council to keep its illegality and stupidity a secret from Congress and the American people.

Iran paid top dollar for its antitank missiles, which made a tidy profit. The National Security Council added these funds to contributions from foreign countries and donations from wealthy Americans, which it then spent on President Reagan's other pet project, funding the Contra rebels in Nicaragua, in violation of the Boland Amendment.

The Iran-Contra operation began to fall apart on October 5, 1986, when an American-owned cargo plane carrying weapons to the Contras was shot down over Nicaragua. The one survivor, an American, said that he had been hired for the mission by the CIA. A month later, a Lebanese pub-lication reported that the United States had secretly sold weapons to Iran. On November 25, Attorney General Edwin Meese confirmed these two allegations and linked them by announcing that officials in his depart-ment had learned that profits from the arms sales had been used to fund the Contras.

The investigations, hearings, and trials stemming from the Iran-Con-tra affair would go on for almost eight years. Fourteen men were indicted on criminal charges that included crimes relating to the oper-ation and also crimes connected to a cover-up. The highest ranking of those charged were Secretary of Defense Caspar W. Weinberger and national security advisers Robert C. McFarlane and John M. Poindexter. Eleven of the defendants, including McFarlane and Poindexter, were convicted. Poindexter's convictions were reversed on appeal, as were those of Lieutenant Colonel Oliver North, who was responsible for managing the operation. In December 1992, President George Bush par-doned Weinberger, before trial, and McFarlane, after his conviction, along with four others, three of whom had been convicted.[57] Indepen-dent counsel Lawrence Walsh, who was leading the prosecution of the defendants, said sardonically of George Bush's mass pardons, "The Iran-Contra cover-up, which has continued for six years, has now been completed."[60]

When the arms-for-hostages deal had begun to foul the air, President Reagan claimed that only a small amount of weapons were sold to Iran for the purpose of supporting moderates in its government and improving relations. There was no quid pro quo in the arms for hostages deal, he said; as it eventually turned out, on that point he was telling the truth. Iran did arrange for the release of three hostages, but before long seven more

Chapter 7

Muammar Qaddafi

TARGET: MUAMMAR QADDAFI

Muammar Qaddafi, leader of Libya, continued to be a constant problem for numerous African states, European countries, and the United States because of his support of insurgents and terrorist organizations.[1] The United States began to take action against him and his country when American citizens abroad became targets of, in the judgment of the CIA, Libyan-trained and supported terrorists.

On December 27, 1985, terrorists attacked Christmas travelers at the Rome and Vienna airports, killing a total of nineteen people. Five of these were Americans, one of whom was an eleven-year-old girl. The CIA suspected that Libya had been involved, but there was no hard evidence to connect it to the attacks.[2] Nevertheless, the United States chose to make a statement to Qaddafi with the operation it designated "Prairie Fire."

On Sunday, March 23, 1986, the United States stationed a flotilla of forty-five ships off the coast of Libya, as it had done in August 1981, in a show of force challenging Qaddafi's power. Three of the ships, with more than a hundred planes as protective air cover, crossed over the "line of death"—as Qaddafi called it—south of the thirty-second parallel and into the Gulf of Sidra. Within two hours, Libya fired two antiaircraft missiles from land-based sites at two American planes, and it launched four more missiles in the hours that followed. No planes were hit. The United States responded by destroying Libya's radar installations with air-launched missiles. Libya then sent its patrol boats out after the overwhelming American armada, which sunk at least two of them during the battle.

Four days after it began Operation Prairie Fire, the United States ended the exercise and counted casualties. The American force suffered none, but Libya lost an estimated seventy-two men. It seemed that the United States had disciplined Libya and Muammar Qaddafi at a minimum expense to itself.[3]

Five days after the U.S. Navy ended Operation Prairie Fire, on April 2, a bomb hidden on board a TWA jet on a flight from Rome to Athens exploded. The blast of the bomb, which was apparently hidden under a seat, tore a three-foot-by-nine-foot hole in the fuselage, and four passengers were sucked out through the hole to their deaths. An unknown Arab terrorist group claimed responsibility for the attack as an act of retaliation for the navy's pummeling of Libyan missile sites and gunboats in the Gulf of Sidra a week earlier. Muammar Qaddafi denied any responsibility for the bombing of the airliner. Spokesmen for President Reagan were reluctant to pin responsibility on Qaddafi but declined to rule out his involvement. Reagan called the attack "a wanton action of international terrorism," and he promised retribution for those responsible.[4]

Authorities in Rome suspected that the bomb had been planted by a Lebanese woman who had occupied the seat on the flight's first leg from Cairo. She had changed planes in Rome to a flight for Lebanon. When she was questioned, she denied planting the bomb but admitted having taken part in actions against Israeli and Christian militia targets during Lebanon's civil war.[5]

On March 25, 1986, as the United States was sinking Libyan gunboats, its intelligence agencies intercepted a message sent from Tripoli to eight of Libya's "People's Bureaus"—its term for its embassies—which read in part, "Prepare to carry out the plan." The message gave no hint as to what the plan was. Ten days later, on April 4, the intelligence agencies picked up a message from the People's Bureau in East Berlin to its headquarters that read, "Tripoli will be happy when you see the headlines tomorrow." Then, in the early morning of April 5, the People's Bureau sent another message to Tripoli that read, "An event occurred. You will be pleased by the result."

Minutes after the U.S. intelligence agencies intercepted the last message, a bomb exploded in the La Belle disco in West Berlin, a hangout for off-duty American servicemen. The blast killed one American soldier and a Turkish woman; 230 people were injured, among them 50 GIs. The Reagan administration believed that the intercepted messages implicated Libya and Muammar Qaddafi in an act of terrorism.[6,7] West Germany was not convinced. A senior official of the West German domestic intelligence unit said in a television interview five days after the bombing that although they could not exonerate Libya from responsibility, they did not have any hard evidence to prove its guilt either.[8]

The National Security Council began planning an air strike against Libya as a response for the bombing of the Berlin disco. The rationale had been laid out in a report of the Task Force on Combating Terrorism, a group headed by former CIA director and then Vice President George Bush two months earlier. It concluded: "Use of our well trained and capable military forces offers an excellent chance of success if a military option can be implemented. Successful employment, however, depends on timely and refined intelligence and prompt positioning of forces." The report cautioned, however, that "[c]ounter terrorism missions are high-risk/high-gain operations which can have a severe negative impact on U.S. prestige if they fail."[8]

The National Security Council's antiterrorism expert, Oliver North, headed a small subcommittee that coordinated the planning and identified targets for a raid on Libya. The formally identified targets were the command and control center in Tripoli and key administrative and military facilities. The unstated objective of the raid, although nobody in the Reagan administration would ever admit it, was to kill Muammar Qaddafi. In case the question came up, one report said, Department of State lawyers were busily writing a position paper arguing that "in the context of military action, what normally would be considered murder is not."[8]

According to the CIA, Qaddafi was hated by many of his own countrymen. In late 1981, while riding in a jeep with a man he had just promoted to general, the man drew his revolver and pulled the trigger at point-blank range. Surprisingly, the would-be assassin missed, and he was shot and killed by Qaddafi's security guard. In 1984, the French counterpart to the CIA supported two operations by Libyan exiles to assassinate or overthrow Qaddafi. The exile teams were supplied with weapons, trained in the Sudan, and then infiltrated into Libya. Although one of the groups eventually engaged in a gun fight with Qaddafi loyalists near his headquarters at the Bab al Aziziya Barracks in Tripoli, fifteen of its members were killed.[8] By one account, in the two years preceding the spring of 1986, various groups had attempted coups against Qaddafi nineteen times, and he was the target of at least three assassination attempts.[9] Ronald Reagan and his advisors believed that some segment of the Libyan opposition would step in if they had some help in disposing of Qaddafi. They were prepared, even anxious, to give that assistance.[8]

The CIA had little access to information on potential targets within Libya, and William Casey approached Israel and its foreign intelligence service, the Mossad, for help. The Mossad fed back the requested information, with the key fact that Qaddafi and his family lived in Tripoli, in a two-story stucco house at the Bab al Aziziya military compound.[6] According to New York Times writer Seymour Hersh, who interviewed over seventy government employees who had firsthand knowledge of the raid, its target was not just Qaddafi but also his wife and children. The concept of attacking Qaddafi's family allegedly came from CIA officers who believed that Qaddafi would lose support of the Bedouin people if he could not protect his home and family.[8]

North's subcommittee, the National Security Council, and the Reagan administration built plausible denial into the planning of the raid on Libya. A former National Security Council official quoted North as saying, "'There was no executive order to kill and no administrative directive to go after Qaddafi.'" The official commented, "They've covered their tracks beautifully."[8]

In his autobiography, Oliver North brushed off Seymour Hersh's claims that Qaddafi was the primary target of the attack on Libya, without giving any information about how the attack was planned. North wrote, "In the old days, the United States would have found a way to assassinate Qaddafi. But despite what Seymour Hersh and other journalists have claimed, killing him was never part of our plan.... But if Qaddafi happened to be in the vicinity of the Bab al Aziziya Barracks in downtown Tripoli when the bombs started to fall, nobody would have shed any tears."[10]

Air force officers involved in the raid understood that the target was Qaddafi. An air force intelligence officer recalled, "There's no question they were looking for Qaddafi. It was briefed that way. They were going to kill him." An air force pilot remembered that "the assassination was the big thing." One air force intelligence officer said that pilots and weapons systems officers who flew on the raid were given reconnaissance photographs that separately identified the locations where Qaddafi could be found and where his family was in residence.[8]

Operation El Dorado Canyon began at 12:13 P.M. eastern standard time on April 14, 1986, when twenty-eight aerial refueling tankers took off from bases in England. They were followed by twenty-four F-111 attack bombers and five EF-111s carrying electronic jamming equipment. Their course would take them southwest, around Spain, through the Strait of Gibraltar, then east over the Mediterranean Sea. Their indirect course was mandated by France's and Spain's refusal to let them cross their territories on their way to bomb Libya.[11]

In late afternoon in Washington, about the time the F-111s from England were finishing their second refueling and were approaching the Strait of Gibraltar, congressional leaders arrived at the White House to be "consulted" on the operation-in-progress. Some of them grumbled that they were being notified, not consulted.[12]

As the air armada from England finished the last of four outbound refuelings and approached Tripoli, on the coast of western Libya, U.S. Navy aircraft carriers *Coral Sea* and *America*, cruising in the Mediterranean off Libya, launched about one hundred aircraft. The first of these planes to go into action approached Benghazi at 6:54 P.M. eastern standard time, 1:54 A.M. in Libya. They flew in at under 500 feet to avoid radar detection, and they used jamming equipment and missiles to take out Libyan radar sites. They were followed at exactly 2:00 A.M. Libyan time by a squadron of A-6s that bombed the airfield, destroying four MiG-23 fighters, two helicopters, and two propeller-driven aircraft. A second group of twelve A-6s attacked the military barracks and other targets in Benghazi.

Simultaneously, 400 miles to the west, the bomber flight from England struck Tripoli. Radar-jamming planes swooped in, and when the first wave of attackers had taken out the radar sites, the F-111s came in. Five of the bombers hit the military side of Tripoli's airport and destroyed five of Libya's nine Il-76 transport planes, which, it was believed, Libya had used to supply terrorists. A second group of F-111s attacked the Sidi Bilal naval base, doing only slight damage.[11]

Six F-111s were assigned to strike the twenty-acre Bab al Aziziya compound. Two of the six aircraft could not satisfactorily find their targets and did not release their bombs. The remaining four dropped a total of sixteen Paveway II laser-guided 2,000-pound bombs.[13] When the dust settled, the compound was riddled with craters. The windows of buildings were blown out, and a few walls had fallen; but not a single building was destroyed. The tent Qaddafi used for greeting visitors was still standing, although it had been struck by a falling utility pole.[11] Precision bombing, even with laser-guided munitions, was not yet an exact science.

Two bombs had hit about 150 yards from the home of Qaddafi and his family, shattering every window and demolishing the interior. Dr. Mohamed Muafa, who identified himself to reporters as Qaddafi's family physician, told of how he found Qaddafi's three youngest children in the rubble an hour after the bombing and rushed them to a hospital.[11] Qaddafi's three-year-old son, Camis, was semiconscious and bleeding when he arrived at the hospital. His four-year-old son, Sef al Arab, was unconscious and had deep cuts on his face. His fifteen-month-old adopted daughter, Hana, died of multiple skull fractures and internal injuries. Qaddafi's wife was, understandably, in shock. Muammar Qaddafi was reported to be either in his tent[14] or in a subterranean bunker[12] at the time of the attack, and he survived.

One of the F-111s dropped its bomb load over a residential area of Tripoli in error. The explosions damaged the French embassy and the residence of the Swiss ambassador and caused numerous civilian casualties.

Eleven minutes after the attack began, it was over. The A-6s were on their way back to their carriers; and the F-111s were back over the Mediterranean, starting their long return flight to England. Not all of them made it. Three pilots reported seeing an aircraft burst into a fireball and be swallowed by the sea about ten miles off shore. A search turned up no trace of the missing F-111 or of its two-man crew, who were presumed dead.[2, 11]

Libyan sources initially reported that thirty-seven people had been killed and ninety-three more were injured.[13] Estimates of the dead would rise to more than 100.[15]

Soon after the attack had been completed and U.S. warplanes were on their way back to their aircraft carriers and bases in England, President Reagan addressed the American people on television and radio, claiming victory:

My fellow Americans, at 7 o'clock this evening Eastern time, air and naval forces of the United States launched a series of strikes against the headquarters, terrorist facilities and military assets that support [Col.] Muammer [el-] Qaddafi's subversive activities.

The attacks were concentrated and carefully targeted to minimize casualties among the Libyan people, with whom we have no quarrel. From initial reports, our forces have succeeded in their mission....

Col. Qaddafi has engaged in acts of international terror, acts that put him outside the company of civilized men....

Self-defense is not only our right, it is our duty. It is the purpose behind the mission taken tonight....

We believe that this pre-emptive action against his terrorist installations will not only diminish Qaddafi's capacity to export terror, it will provide him with incentives and reasons to alter his criminal behavior.[16]

According to one National Security Council official, President Reagan's address contained a few paragraphs that were never made public. They were to be read if U.S. sources could confirm that Qaddafi had been killed in the raid. The text, following an analysis prepared by a Department of State legal adviser, claimed that the United States had the right to retaliate for the bombing in Berlin to preempt future terrorist attacks; and killing Muammar Qaddafi was neither retaliation nor a crime.[8]

With thirty-two tons of bombs dropped on Qaddafi's headquarters, over half of the sixty-ton total, Reagan administration officials began giving not very plausible denials when asked if the purpose of the raid was to kill Qaddafi.

Secretary of State George Schultz stated: "We did not have a strategy saying we wanted to go after Qaddafi personally. We have a general stance that opposes direct efforts of that kind."[17] Schultz also declared, "He was not a direct target."[12]

While denying that the administration intended to kill Qaddafi, an unidentified member of Reagan's circle admitted that the Bab al Aziziya compound had been targeted with "a reasonable expectation that he might be there." An unidentified Reagan strategist added, "The more of his places we hit at once, the better the odds." When asked the odds of what, he answered, "You can guess. That's all I have to say."[9]

Newsweek credited an unnamed "top official" with the candid statement that "the demise of Kaddafi [Qaddafi] is an end in itself."[9]

Another member of Reagan's administration said, "If Gaddafi [Qaddafi] had been killed, I don't think it would have been considered 'collateral damage,' " using the euphemism the military applies to civilian casualties.[11]

William Casey, director of the CIA, said to a reporter, "There was no decision to kill Qaddafi. But if it happened, I was ready to take all the heat you guys could dish out."[15]

In his memoirs, Ronald Reagan repeated the analysis of his advisors:

The attack was not intended to kill Qaddafi; that would have violated our prohibition against assassination. The objective was to let him know that we weren't going to accept his terrorism anymore, and that if he did it again he could expect to hear from us again. It was impossible, however, to know exactly where he would be at the time of the attack. We realized that it was possible, perhaps probable, that he might be at or near the intelligence center when our planes struck.[18]

Reagan also noted that he "deeply regretted" that "one of our missiles went off track during the attack and caused fatalities in a civilian neighborhood." Reagan did not mention the death of Qaddafi's adopted daughter or the injuries to the Libyan leader's other children.[19]

Although the raid on Libya failed to achieve its unstated but obvious aim—the elimination of Muammar Qaddafi—it set a precedent that would be convenient for administrations in decades to come. Reagan's advisors had gone through the tortuous reasoning of establishing that it was acceptable to kill a foreign leader provided his death was, or could be, rationalized as the unintended consequences of a morally justified military action. Furthermore, such a preemptive strike could be made to prevent an undefined military or terrorist activity against the United States or its interests at some unknown time in the future. This reasoning had its critics, but nobody of any political stature stood up after the raid to call it an assassination attempt.

The strategy for the future was clear. Demonize the enemy leader—the target—with public statements and the release of supportive information to the media. Attack his stronghold. If his body is pulled from the rubble, be prepared to characterize his death as collateral damage of a morally and legally justified military action. President Reagan's Executive Order 12333 and all laws prohibiting assassination became irrelevant.[20]

The day after the raid, Washington received intelligence reports claiming that there had been an attempted coup by the Libyan military and that Qaddafi had been wounded in the left shoulder. When he appeared on Libyan television two days after the raid, much to the disappointment of those in Washington, he showed no obvious physical injuries. Besides demonstrating that he was still in command, he took the opportunity to condemn Reagan and British prime minister Margaret Thatcher as "child murderers." "We will not kill your children," he said, reminding everyone of his dead adopted daughter. "We are not like you." He said nothing about reprisals.[12]

By the end of the week, Radio Tripoli was demanding revenge, and terrorists were striking back. In Lebanon, gunmen dumped the bodies of three men, an American University librarian and two British teachers, who had been kidnapped three weeks earlier. A note near the bodies read that the men had been killed in retaliation for the bombing of Libya. The note was signed by the "Arab Revolutionary Cells," a group believed to be aligned with terrorist leader Abu Nidal, who resided in Libya at the time. In Sudan, a communications officer at the U.S. embassy was shot in the head as he drove home; the injury left him partially paralyzed. Mobs of protesters marched on the embassy in Sudan, and Washington ordered that over two hundred embassy employees and members of their families leave for their safety. In London, security guards at Heathrow Airport found a bomb in the luggage of a woman boarding an El Al flight destined for Tel Aviv. British police believed the woman had been unknowingly used by her Arab lover to carry the bomb.[12]

THE USS *VINCENNES* AND IRAN AIR FLIGHT 655

The United States did not take sides in the Iran-Iraq war, which raged through the 1980s, but it did have an interest in how it progressed. The United States and its people remembered the humiliation of the 1979 to 1981 hostage crisis and Iran's support of Hezbollah, the Lebanese group responsible for destroying the U.S. embassy, the embassy annex, and the Marine Corps barracks, and—the arms-for-hostages deal that was part of the Iran-Contra affair notwithstanding—it leaned in the direction of Iraq. Furthermore, about half of the oil in the world that was exported came from Iraq's then-ally Kuwait. Iran's Revolutionary Guard operated a fleet of small gunboats that harassed tankers going to and coming from Kuwait. A good part of the oil these ships carried went to the United States. To safeguard its continued supply of oil, the United States kept a navy presence in the Persian Gulf that protected tankers registered under the American flag.[21]

Iraq almost lost the good will of the United States in May 1987 when one of its fighters fired a French-made Exocet missile at the frigate USS *Stark*, which was cruising in the Persian Gulf. The attack killed thirty-seven sailors. Saddam Hussein quickly offered an apology for the "accident" and paid $27 million in restitution to the families of the victims.[22]

On July 3, 1988, the U.S. Navy committed a blunder of its own in a way that looked to the Arab world like an act of terrorism.[21] It will help first to look at the account that was told by the navy and reported in the American press immediately after the incident.

Iranian military activity against the United States in the Persian Gulf was rising in mid-1988. In April, a marine helicopter with two men on board was lost; it was believed that an Iranian missile brought it down. Iran was placing Silkworm missiles in underground bunkers near the Strait of Hormuz, and the cruiser USS *Vincennes* was deployed to the area because of its antimissile capabilities to counter the new threat. On July 2, the USS *Elmer Montgomery* fired a warning shot at an Iranian gunboat that had attacked a Danish tanker.

Then at 10:10 A.M. on July 3, the tragic incident began, according to the navy, when Iranian speedboats fired on a reconnaissance helicopter from the USS *Vincennes.* The helicopter was not hit. Half an hour later, the *Vincennes* closed on the Iranian boats, fired its five-inch guns, and claimed to have sunk or damaged three of them.

Five minutes after dealing with the gunboats, radar aboard the *Vincennes* detected an aircraft taking off from an airport at Bandar Abbas, Iran, on a course that would take it toward the cruiser. Two minutes later, the *Vincennes* radioed a warning telling the aircraft to change its course. The aircraft continued on a course toward the *Vincennes* at an altitude estimated to be 7,000 to 9,000 feet. Four minutes after they began tracking the aircraft, the crew of the *Vincennes* concluded that the aircraft was an F-14 fighter approaching the ship with hostile intent. At 10:54, seven minutes after first detecting the aircraft, Captain Will C. Rogers, commanding officer of the *Vincennes,* ordered that two Standard surface-to-air missiles be fired at the approaching aircraft. The aircraft was about six miles away from the *Vincennes* and hidden by haze when at least one of the missiles struck it, and debris and bodies began raining down over the waters of the Strait of Hormuz. Only later did the captain and crew of the *Vincennes* learn that the aircraft they had downed was Iran Air flight 655, flying from Bandar Abbas to Dubai in the United Arab Emirates. All 290 passengers and crew aboard the Airbus A300 were killed.

President Reagan said about the destruction of the commercial passenger plane, "This is a terrible human tragedy. Our sympathy and condolences go out to the passengers, crew, and their families....We deeply regret any loss of life." Then he shifted the blame to Iran by saying that the *Vincennes* had "followed standard orders and widely publicized procedures, firing to protect itself against possible attack."

The people of Iran knew without a doubt that the United States had deliberately shot down the Iran Air plane, killing 290 innocent civilians. Iranian officials spoke of a "barbaric massacre," and it threatened, "We will not leave the crimes of America unanswered." The Ayatollah Khomeini demanded a "real war" against "America and its lackeys."[23] Despite the call for retaliation, Iran was preoccupied by its war with Iraq, and Khomeini's "real war" never materialized.

With as many witnesses and guilty consciences as were on American ships in the Strait of Hormuz, it was inevitable that the facts of the Iran Air incident would emerge. Four years after the incident, *Newsweek* published the findings of its investigation. The new, key revelations were as follows: Captain Will Rogers of the USS *Vincennes* had disobeyed an order by having his ship in the area at that time; the *Vincennes* was within Iranian territorial waters, in clear violation of international law, when it attacked the Iranian gunboats and shot down the Iran Air airliner; the airline had been within the commercial air corridor, contrary to the claim of the U.S. Navy; and contrary to another navy claim, the *Vincennes* was not rushing to the aid of a commercial ship under attack—there was no merchantman in the area at that time.

The American explanation of the fate of the Iran Air flight was, according to *Newsweek*, a cover-up that had been approved by Admiral William Crowe, who was at the time chairman of the joint chiefs of staff.

In the bureaucratic tradition of punishing the innocent and rewarding the guilty, the navy awarded all crew members aboard the USS *Vincennes* combat action ribbons. The ship's tactical commander for air-warfare received a commendation medal for "heroic achievement." Captain Will Rogers retired from the navy three years later without having been held accountable for his actions at the Strait of Hormuz.[21]

PAN AM FLIGHT 103

President Reagan's claim of success in controlling Libyan terrorism and Muammar Qaddafi's claim that he and his allies "will not kill your children" were challenged on December 21, 1988, when Pan Am flight 103 exploded over Lockerbie, Scotland, killing all 259 on board and 11 on the ground. Almost three years later, the United States and Great Britain presented a link between the air disaster and Libya. In November 1991, at simultaneous press conferences in Washington and Edinburgh, Scotland, the United States and Great Britain accused two Libyan intelligence agents, Abdel Basset al-Megrahi and Lamen Khalifa Fhimah, of planting the bomb. Libya refused to surrender the suspects; and in April 1992, the United Nations succumbed to intense American and British lobbying by imposing an embargo on Libya until it surrendered the accused men. Libya finally turned the suspects over for a trial before Scottish judges to be held in the Netherlands.[24]

On February 12, 2001, al-Megrahi was convicted of murdering 270 people and given a life sentence; his codefendant was aquitted.[25]

Chapter 8

Saddam Hussein

Iraq was both a sponsor and a practitioner of terrorism. Its principal victims have been its own people and those of neighboring states. The primary beneficiary of its terror has been Iraq's autocratic ruler, Saddam Hussein, who—as long as his regime lasted—held in his grip the power and diminishing wealth of a nation in isolation and under siege.

As a youth, Saddam Hussein was a malcontent with little education and few prospects, but with great ambitions. He had joined Iraq's Baath political party, a radical nationalist group with about three hundred members that had ambitions that matched Saddam's. It planned to seize power in Iraq after assassinating General Abdul Kareem el-Kassem, who himself had come to power after the murder of King Faisal II. In 1959, when he was twenty-two, Saddam joined a Baath assassination team that attacked General Kassem's car. They killed Kassem's driver, seriously wounded one of Kassem's aides, and inflicted injuries on Kassem that kept him in the hospital for a month. Saddam is reported to have received a leg wound as a result of fire returned by Kassem's guards.

Saddam spent the next four years in Cairo, where he finished high school and began studying law. He returned to Baghdad in February 1963, after army officers belonging to the Baath Party assassinated Kassem and seized control of the government. Nine months later, another army group kicked out the Baaths, and Saddam found himself in prison. He escaped in 1966 but managed to be on hand in 1968 when the Baaths again seized power. Saddam became deputy chairman of the Revolutionary Council with responsibility for internal security. For the next eleven years, he dealt ruthlessly with the enemies of the Baath Party and built his power base in Iraq.[1]

In July 1979, when the president of Iraq resigned—or was coerced into resigning—for reasons of health, Saddam moved up to the presidency and to the position of secretary general of the Baath Party. Saddam's will and Iraqi policy became one. His first significant action was to purge his possible opposition in the party and the government; he is reported to have ordered the execution of 500 people.[2]

Under Saddam Hussein, Iraq became a refuge for Arab terrorists and terrorist groups. Among these was Abu Nidal, whose organization has targeted the United Kingdom, France, Israel, moderate Arabs, the PLO, and the United States. Other terrorists who found safe haven in Iraq were Abu Abbas, who organized the hijacking of the cruise ship Achille Lauro, and groups on the radical fringe of the PLO.[3]

In September 1980, Iraq attacked Iran for the purpose of taking land and access to waterways along their mutual border. Saddam, who had no military experience, directed the battle himself and expected victory in two or three weeks. As the war dragged on, Iraq found support in its enemy's enemy, the United States. The Reagan administration's rationale was explained by Geoffrey Kemp, head of the National Security Council's Middle East section: "The memory of the hostages [taken from the U.S. embassy in Tehran, Iran] was quite fresh; the Ayatollah [Khomeini] was still calling us the Great Satan. . . . It wasn't that we wanted Iraq to win the war, we did not want Iraq to lose. . . . We knew he [Saddam Hussein] was an S.O.B., but he was our S.O.B."[4]

The United States began its support for Iraq in March 1982, ironically, by removing it from the list of countries that supported terrorism. Removal from the list made Iraq eligible to receive financial aid in the form of guaranteed credits for the purchase of rice and wheat from the United States. In 1984, the United States reestablished full diplomatic relations with Iraq, and the CIA began feeding Saddam's government satellite photos of Iranian positions on the battlefield.[3]

The cordial relationship between the United States and Iraq began to sour when, in November 1986, it was revealed that the United States had sold arms to Iraq's enemy as part of the Iran-Contra affair. The following year, an Iraqi plane fired an Exocet missile that hit a U.S. ship, killing thirty-seven sailors (see chapter 7). Saddam apologized for the error, but he was once again his own S.O.B.[5]

Iraq fought its war against Iran without regard for human rights or mercy. It used poison gas against enemy troops and the Iranian people. Thousands of Iranians taken as prisoners of war were executed as a matter of Saddam's and Iraq's policy.[6]

Saddam was equally brutal when dealing with those in Iraq who opposed him. Iraq's Kurds, wanting their own homeland, traditionally opposed the Iraqi leader. Saddam took his vengeance on them on March 16, 1988, sending his aircraft to attack the Kurd city of Halabja with poison gas. The agents included mustard gas, the nerve gases sarin and tabun, and VX, and they may have also included cyanide and biological agents. The attack lasted for three days. When it was over, the city with a population of 80,000 had an estimated 5,000 dead and another 10,000 injured.[7]

Iraq's war with Iran ended with the signing of a United Nations–mediated cease-fire in July 1988. Iraq had lost 120,000 men, with another 300,000 wounded. It had run up a debt of $70 billion. Saddam Hussein and Iraq claimed victory.[8]

THE PERSIAN GULF WAR

Saddam Hussein's agenda for aggression then turned to Kuwait, the tiny, oil-rich sheikhdom to its southeast. In a lightning strike, his Iraqi Army occupied Kuwait on August 2, 1990.[9] The United Nations (UN) Security Council condemned Iraq's invasion of Kuwait (Resolution 660, August 2, 1990).[10] President George Bush called Saddam Hussein a threat to "our way of life" and compared Saddam to Hitler. And of course, there was the need to keep the oil of the Middle East flowing freely to the West and to the United States.[11]

The United States assembled in the Persian Gulf region a ground force numbering about one hundred thousand soldiers and marines and an air fleet of about one thousand air force, navy, and marine aircraft flying from thirty bases and three aircraft carriers. There were so many aircraft that even if the United States and its allies wanted to bring in more, they could not; the facilities could not support them.

In mid-September, air force chief of staff General Michael J. Dugan briefed reporters on U.S. strategy—or at least his view of what it should be. According to Dugan, the United States planned to "decapitate" Iraq's leadership.[12] In the military jargon of the Cold War, "decapitation" meant removing the center of power and authority by, for example, dropping a nuclear warhead on Moscow or, alternatively, Washington. In Iraq, the same result might be achieved with conventional weapons. As Dugan explained it, "Saddam is a one-man show....If for any reason [he] went away, it is my judgment that those troops [in Kuwait] would...be back in Iraq in a matter of hours, in disarray."[13] As Dugan explained the war plan, the air force would personalize the impending war by attacking as targets President Saddam Hussein, his family, his senior commanders, his palace guard, and his mistress.[12]

When Secretary of Defense Richard B. Cheney read Dugan's remarks in the *Washington Post* and the *Los Angeles Times,* he went ballistic. As Cheney saw it, Dugan had emphasized the importance of the air force at the expense of the other services, made the political blunder of discussing contributions from Israel, and revealed classified operation plans. Cheney also noted that "decapitation," as described by Dugan, bore an uncomfortable resemblance to assassination, which was prohibited by executive order. He immediately fired General Dugan.[14]

On January 11, 1991, just days before military action against Iraq was scheduled to begin if it did not withdraw from Kuwait, the subject of a personal attack against Saddam Hussein came up again. The *Minneapolis Star-Tribune* reported, "U.S. Forces will attempt to kill Iraqi President Saddam Hussein during the initial phase of the war with Iraq.... According to Defense officials, Bush ordered Colin Powell, Chairman of the joint Chiefs of Staff, to target Saddam for attack shortly after Iraq's August 2 invasion of Kuwait."[15] The events that followed a few days after this newspaper report give reason to believe that it contained at least a kernel of truth.

The forces allied against Iraq began Operation Desert Storm, their war against Iraq, in the closing hours of January 16, 1991. U.S. Air Force crews flying F-117A stealth attack fighters took the battle to Baghdad. They carried 2,000-pound GBU-27 laser-guided bombs. At exactly 3:00 A.M., January 17, Baghdad time, one F-117A dropped its 2,000-pound bomb on the twelve-story International Telephone and Telegraph building. The explosion cleared the antennas that studded the concrete roof and punched a hole in its center. Two more F-117As, approaching from different directions, dropped two more 2,000-pound laser-guided bombs through the hole. The explosions turned the top two stories of the building to powder.

During the first full night of the air war, U.S. Air Force F-117As used the same tactic on key facilities in Iraq: punch a hole in the target with the first bomb, then drop a second bomb through the hole to pulverize the target's contents. In Baghdad, they also bombed the Tower for Wire and Wireless Communications, the Iraqi Ministry of Defense building, and the Air Force headquarters. They bombed five command centers, both in- and outside Baghdad, that monitored early-warning radar and controlled interceptor aircraft and several hardened bunkers believed to be sites of air defense centers.[16]

The first wave of attacks was carried out in the middle of the night with the pin-point accuracy of laser-guided bombs to minimize "collateral damage" and civilian casualties,[17] but one target site was clearly personal: the presidential palace.[16] Many other targets that first night of the air war were also personal, but less obviously so. The F-117As hit every known Iraqi command bunker with the hope and expectation that Saddam Hussein would be present in one of them. According to the air commander of Desert Storm, Air Force Lieutenant General Charles Horner, "he should have been present for duty." But he was not.[18]

Two days later, on January 19, the air force ordered a crash program to build two 5,000-pound laser-guided bombs, to be given the designation GBU-28—GBU being the Air Force acronym for Glide Bomb Unit. The

GBU-28s were built at the Watervliet Arsenal in upstate New York. They were fashioned from eight-inch hardened-steel howitzer tubes that were fitted with tapered nose cones. The purpose of the bombs was easily guessed by those building them. A worker at the Watervliet Arsenal inscribed on one bomb "The Saddamizer." A senior officer of the Central Command commented to a reporter on the selection of the bombs target. "I would be lying to you," he said, "if I told you they weren't meant for Saddam." When completed, the bombs would be shipped to Saudi Arabia, and then on to their target in Iraq.[18]

While the bombs were being built, the air force kept hammering sites in Iraq it thought were command sites. One of these was a bunker in the Amariyah section of Baghdad. On February 13, F-117As dropped two 2,000-pound bombs on the bunker. The first opened a hole in the bunker's concrete roof, and the second bomb fell through the hole and exploded inside the structure. Washington and the world were soon shocked to learn that the bunker was being used as a civilian air raid shelter. More than four hundred people, many of them women and children, were killed. The Bush administration regretted the civilian deaths but continued the war.[19]

By late February, President Bush was under intense pressure from Saudi Arabia and Egypt to stop the fighting. Saudi Arabia especially wanted an end with the Iraqi civil structure intact so that it would not be faced with a radical Shiite Muslim faction trying to form its own state at its northern border. The United States had but a few hours in which to take its last shot at Saddam Hussein.[20]

The GBU-28 5,000-pound bombs arrived aboard a U.S. Air Force C-141 transport plane at an air base in the Saudi Arabian desert at 7:19 P.M. on February 27. As the pilots and weapons officers of two F-111F bombers were being briefed on their mission, the bombs were being loaded onto the aircraft. One GBU-28 was mounted to the bomb rack under a wing of an F-111F, and a more conventional 2,000-pound unguided bomb was mounted under the opposite wing to help balance the weight.

The target of the two aircraft was a hardened bunker at the al-Tajir airfield about fifteen miles northwest of Baghdad. On three occasions, the air force had hit the base with 2,000-pound bombs with little effect. Intelligence analysts estimated that the bunker was approximately two hundred feet square, several stories deep, and protected from above by as much as twenty feet of concrete and dirt. Because it appeared to be the hardest surviving bunker, U.S. strategists reasoned that Saddam would use it as a refuge in what appeared to be the final night of the Persian Gulf War.

The laser-guided GBU-28s hit the al-Tajir bunker in sequence following the air force's bunker-busting technique: one bomb to open the roof, the second to fall through the hole and destroy the interior. Several seconds after the explosions, smoke began to billow from the bunker's six entrances. Intelligence sources reported that several high-ranking Iraqi commanders had been killed, but Saddam was not in the bunker and survived.[18]

President Bush ordered a cease-fire to begin at 8:00 A.M. on February 28, just hours after the last attempt during the Persian Gulf War to kill Saddam Hussein.[21]

When the dust of Desert Storm had settled and the senior American players wrote their memoirs, they told a somewhat different, yet revealing, story about the attitude of U.S. officials toward Saddam Hussein.

Colin Powell, former chairman of the joint chiefs of staff, the man who was allegedly ordered by President George Bush to target Saddam for an attack,[15] wrote:

President Bush had taken to demonizing Saddam in public.... "We are dealing with Hitler revisited," he said on one occasion, and described Saddam as "a tyrant unmoved by human decency." ...I preferred to talk about the "Iraqi regime" or the "Hussein regime." Our plan contemplated only ejecting Iraq from Kuwait. It did not include toppling Saddam's dictatorship. Within these limits, we could not bring George Bush Saddam Hussein's scalp. And I thought it unwise to elevate public expectations by making the man out to be the devil incarnate and then leaving him in place.[22]

General H. Norman Schwarzkopf, who commanded Operation Desert Storm, took a more pragmatic approach to the dirty work of war, and he reported on it more candidly:

After the shooting started we repeatedly asserted that the United States was not trying to kill Saddam Hussein—President Bush said so himself—and that was true, to a point. But at the very top of our target list were the bunkers where we knew he and his senior commanders were likely to be working. Because of Iraq's highly centralized system of command and control, Saddam was what military theorists call an enemy center of gravity—an aspect of the opposing force that, if destroyed, will cause the enemy to lose its will to fight. (Clausewitz, the great Prussian philosopher of war, defined the concept of a center of gravity in his 1832 book, Vom Kriege.) For our purposes, it was sufficient to silence Saddam—to destroy his ability to command the forces arrayed against us. If he'd been killed in the process, I wouldn't have shed any tears.[23]

In his memoir A World Transformed, written with Brent Scowcroft, his national security advisor, George Bush confirmed that he and his administration had targeted Saddam Hussein. He candidly wrote about his attitude toward Saddam in the days before Operation Desert Storm and the Persian Gulf War:

We discussed again whether to go after him [Saddam Hussein]. None of us minded if he was killed in the course of an air attack. Yet it was extremely difficult to target Saddam, who was known to move frequently and under tight security. We had problems locating Noriega in Panama, a place we knew well. Saddam was far more elusive and better protected. The best we could do was strike command and control points where he may have been. There were several, and they were on our target list anyway. We later learned Saddam had been caught in one military convoy attacked by coalition aircraft but escaped unharmed.[24]

Bush wrote in his diary on January 31, 1991:

I just keep thinking the Iraqi people ought to take care of [him] with the Iraqi military. Seeing their troops [and] equipment getting destroyed—they've got to do something about it. I wish like hell *we* [Bush's emphasis] could.... This is a war and if he gets hit with a bomb in his headquarters, too bad.[24]

Bush wanted Saddam dead, and his intention rolled down through the executive and military organization all the way to the 2,000- and 5,000-pound bombs that U.S. aircraft dropped on his refuges.

Seven years after Operation Desert Storm, George Bush wrote in a letter to Bob Woodward, "I see respected columnists constantly criticize me for not 'getting' Saddam Hussein, going in, finding him, killing him." The criticism offended Bush, but he did not say whether he was more upset by the criticism or by not "getting" Saddam.[25]

TARGET: GEORGE BUSH

George Bush was defeated by Bill Clinton in the 1992 U.S. presidential election. Nevertheless, Bush was still a hero in Kuwait, and he agreed to visit that country to receive its thanks. His trip to Kuwait began badly. The emir of Kuwait had sent a refurbished jet to pick him up in Houston. After Bush, his wife, and their group boarded the aircraft and it took off, it returned to make an emergency landing because a piece of a wing had fallen off. The airplane was repaired, and Bush and his entourage embarked on their journey the following day.[26]

Bush's three days in Kuwait were days of triumph and celebration. On April 14, 1993, the emir of Kuwait, Sheikh Jabir al-Ahmed Al Sabah, presented Bush with the tiny nation's highest civilian award in thanks for rallying the international coalition that expelled the Iraqi Army. The following day, Bush addressed the Kuwaiti parliament and received an honorary doctorate degree from Kuwait University. On April 16, the final day of the ex-president's visit, he met some of the 1,500 U.S. troops still stationed in Kuwait.

On April 27, eleven days after Bush had left for home, the Kuwaiti defense minister announced that days before the ex-president made his triumphant visit, his government had broken a plot orchestrated from Iraq to assassinate Bush.[27] U.S. officials wanted to examine the evidence and interview witnesses before committing the country to a response, and the FBI and CIA sent a joint team to Kuwait to investigate the alleged plot. By late June, the team reported back to Washington what it believed to be the facts based on the evidence.

The plot to assassinate ex-President George Bush was initiated by the Iraqi Intelligence Service on April 9, 1993, in the Iraqi city of Basra, when it gave its orders to the leader of the group, Wali al-Ghazali. Along with his orders, the Iraqi Intelligence Service gave al-Ghazali a white Toyota Land Cruiser with 80 kilograms (about 175 pounds) of explosives hidden inside. On the night of April 12, al-Ghazali and his team smuggled the deadly vehicle across the border into Kuwait and hid it in a warehouse.

The assassins had three basic scenarios that they would use, in sequence, in attempting to kill Bush. In their primary attempt, they would park the Land Cruiser on a street near Kuwait University. As Bush arrived by motorcade to receive his honorary degree, and his car passed near the parked vehicle, the assassins would detonate the bomb by remote control. If for some reason the bomb was not or could not be detonated, the Land Cruiser would be moved to Bush Street, where the assassins would again wait for Bush's car to pass nearby. If these two scenarios should fail, Wali al-Ghazali, the leader of the assassination ring, would strap a bomb to his waist and get as close as possible to Bush, then detonate the bomb, killing both Bush and himself.

The plot came apart the day after the assassination team smuggled the Land Cruiser into Kuwait. When three members of the assassination team went to the warehouse where the bomb-laden Land Cruiser had been parked, they found it surrounded by Kuwaiti police. Fourteen conspirators—eleven Iraqis and three Kuwaitis—were in police custody before Bush and his entourage arrived safely in Kuwait.

Based on the testimony of the conspirators and on the construction of the bomb itself, the FBI-CIA team concluded that the plot was real and orchestrated by the Iraqi Intelligence Service. The men in custody named as their controllers minor bureaucrats in the Iraqi Intelligence Service, names known to the CIA. The bomb itself was identical to one found in Turkey in 1991, during the Persian Gulf War, in the possession of an Iraqi agent.[28]

The United States and President Clinton had little choice but to respond to the evidence of an Iraqi-planned assassination plot against ex-President Bush; they had to demonstrate that terrorists could not target its citizens for attacks on its own soil or elsewhere in the world without incurring consequences. The response began on Saturday June 26, 1993, at 4:22 P.M. eastern standard time (12:22 A.M. in Baghdad) when the U.S. destroyer *Peterson,* sailing in the Red Sea, and the cruiser *Chancellorsville* in the Persian Gulf began launching Tomahawk cruise missiles at Baghdad. Within twelve minutes, they had fired a total of twenty-three missiles. They were aimed at the headquarters of the Iraqi Intelligence Service in downtown Baghdad, a compound that contained a large main intelligence headquarters building and several dozen smaller buildings used for support services. The attack was planned to take place in the early hours of Sunday morning when few if any people would be in the complex. President Clinton and his advisors had no problem with killing the top intelligence personnel, but they had no interest in harming secretaries and maintenance personnel.

The missiles reached Baghdad about an hour and a half later, between 6:00 and 6:05 P.M. eastern standard time (2:00 and 2:05 A.M. Baghdad time). Sixteen Tomahawks hammered the intelligence headquarters building, and four others hit elsewhere in the compound. Three missiles struck a residential area near the intelligence compound. Iraq claimed that it had shot down one of the missiles.[29]

An hour after the Tomahawk missiles blasted Baghdad, President Clinton addressed the nation to tell of the attack and to explain the reasoning behind it. After describing the plot to assassinate ex-President Bush, he said, "It is clear that this was no random act. It was an elaborate plan devised by the Iraqi Government and directed against a former President of the United States because of actions he took as President. As such, the Iraqi attack against President Bush was an attack against our country and against all Americans." Clinton stretched the facts by calling a dedicated but unexecuted plot an attack. Then he announced, "We could not, and have not, let such action against our nation go unanswered....Therefore...I ordered our forces to launch a cruise missile attack on the Iraqi Intelligence Service's command and control facility in Baghdad." The source of the assassination plot was the target of the missile attack.[30]

The day after the attack, foreign reporters were allowed to photograph damage in the residential areas of Baghdad, but they were kept away from the primary target, Iraqi Intelligence Service headquarters. The Iraqi News Agency reported that eight people had been killed in the attack and more than a dozen seriously injured. The casualties were remarkably light considering that each of the twenty-three Tomahawks carried a 984-pound warhead.[29] It is noteworthy that in the operation, U.S. personnel did not cross into Iraq and were never at risk.

SADDAM HUSSEIN REVISITED

Since the 1991 Gulf War, a presidential finding signed by George Bush authorized covert actions against Iraq. Although the finding did not alter the prohibition against involvement in assassinations, it did sanction the use of methods by the CIA that might lead to deaths.

The United States made no secret of its support, both moral and financial, to groups within Iraq that opposed Saddam Hussein and his regime.

One of these groups, the Iraqi National Congress (INC), counted among its members Kurds and other dissidents in northern Iraq. The Clinton administration and the CIA had no expectation that the INC could bring down Saddam Hussein and did not completely trust the group, but it gave limited support to the INC because it was a nuisance to Saddam Hussein. Some senators, however, pressed the administration for more support because staff members of the Senate Select Committee on Intelligence were favorably impressed by the INC after a visit to northern Iraq.

With the backing of the United States, the INC planned a military offensive against the Iraqi government for March 1995. CIA agents on the scene in northern Iraq learned that the INC intended to kill Saddam Hussein as part of the campaign, in a scenario that had become all too familiar. The leader of the assassination plot was Wafiq Samarrai, a former chief of Iraqi military intelligence who had defected. The assassination, as Samarrai described the operation, would take place as Saddam traveled through his hometown of Samarra, about seventy miles northwest of Baghdad on a tributary of the Tigris River. He and about twenty members of his large family would take up positions at both ends of the Samarra bridge. As Saddam's convoy crossed the bridge, they would attack the first and last cars of the caravan, trapping Saddam in the middle of the span. Then they would methodically kill everybody in the caravan.

The CIA agents who heard Samarrai's plan told CIA headquarters about it. Headquarters, foreseeing indiscriminate carnage and sensing the potential for both tactical and political disaster, turned down the plan and ordered its agents in the field not to discuss it again.

But the INC continued to discuss the plot, specifically with Iranian intelligence officers. As the U.S. National Security Agency (NSA) monitored Iranian communications, it learned of the plot and alleged CIA involvement and informed the White House. CIA agents in Iraq were subsequently instructed to tell the INC that their plot had been compromised. If they went through with it anyway, they would lose all support from the United States. The FBI investigated this plot to assassinate Saddam and found no evidence that the agents in the field and the CIA were involved in illegal acts.[31]

STATE SPONSORS OF TERRORISM

In 1993, the U.S. Department of State finally organized its thoughts and formally identified seven states it believed supported terrorism: Cuba, Iran, Iraq, Libya, North Korea, Sudan, and Syria.[32] The states named on the list have not changed in subsequent years.[33] The Department of State has been vague in defining its criteria for placing a state on or taking it off the list. Consequently, presence on the list may reflect political biases accumulated over time in addition to solid evidence of current support of terrorist groups.

When the Department of State published its annual report on terrorism for the year 2000, the document made passing reference to Afghanistan, which during the late 1990s and most of 2001 was controlled by the Taliban. The report read, "The Taliban...continues to harbor terrorist groups, including al-Qaida, the Egyptian Islamic Jihad, al-Gama'a al-Islamiyya, and the Islamic Movement of Usbekistan."[34] Presumably, the Department of State did not put Afghanistan on its list of state sponsors of terrorism because the United States, like most countries, refused to accept that Afghanistan had a legitimate government that could sponsor terrorism. Somalia was also omitted from the list for a similar reason: the East African country has not had a stable government since 1991. Since then, it has been a battleground for warring clans and a playground for terrorist groups, most notably Al Qaeda.[35]

Appendix 4 gives a summary of the cases presented by the Department of State in May 2002 against the seven states it identified as sponsors of terrorism.[36] It noted that "Sudan and Libya seem closest to understanding what they must do to get out of the terrorism business," and it gave Iran, North Korea, and Syria credit for their limited cooperation in international antiterrorist activities. However, the Department of State did not appear close to removing any of the seven from its list of state sponsors of terrorism.[33]

Chapter 9

The Blind Sheikh and the Mastermind of Terror

THE WORLD TRADE CENTER

Terrorism from the Middle East made its American beachhead in 1990 when Sheikh Omar Abdel-Rahman entered the United States on a tourist visa, despite his presence on a government watch list of suspected terrorists. Few Americans will remember his name, but many will remember him by the name the press called him: "the blind cleric."

Abdel-Rahman developed diabetes as a child and became blind as a result of that disease. Nevertheless, he studied Islamic law at al-Azhar University in Cairo. He adopted a fundamentalist view of Islam and became critical of Egypt's secular government and institutions. His dissent allegedly took a criminal turn in 1981 when that country's president, Anwar Sadat, was assassinated. Abdel-Rahman was arrested as an accessory. He had issued a *fatwa*, a decree that sanctioned the assassination of those perceived as enemies of Islam. He was acquitted because the prosecutors could not prove a relationship between Abdel-Rahman and Sadat's assassins.

For the balance of the decade, Abdel-Rahman preached to Muslims in Afghanistan, Britain, Pakistan, Saudi Arabia, Sudan, Switzerland, and the United States, urging them to join the mujahideen in their battle against the Soviet Union in Afghanistan.[1]

Sheikh Abdel-Rahman was unambiguously identified as a terrorist when an Egyptian court convicted and sentenced him in absentia for the 1989 murder of a police officer and for conspiring to overthrow the Egyptian government. The conviction resulted in Abdel-Rahman's name being placed on the Department of State's "Automated Visa Lookout System," which was created to identify suspected terrorists before granting them permission to enter the United States.[2] In 1990, Abdel-Rahman applied for a visa to enter the United States at the American embassy in Sudan. The embassy worker who arranged for issuing the visa was a CIA officer working undercover in the consular section. Some have speculated that the CIA arranged for Abdel-Rahman to enter the United States as a way of buying his goodwill, which would be valuable if Muslim extremists managed to take over Egypt.[3]

When Sheikh Abdel-Rahman arrived in the United States, he was in his early fifties, he had a gray beard cut off square a few inches below his chin, and he wore large sunglasses to cover his blind eyes. He associated himself with the Masjid Al-Salaam, the Mosque of Peace, which occupied the space above a store in Jersey City, New Jersey.[4] The sheikh preached the militant message of radical Islam: "Hit hard and kill the enemies of God in every spot, to rid it of the descendents of apes and pigs fed at the table of Zionism, communism and imperialism."[2] Abdel-Rahman soon had a small group of like-minded followers who were not afraid of action.

Among the first of those who joined Sheikh Abdel-Rahman in prayer was a young Arab named El Sayyid Nosair, who would gain notoriety when he was tried for the murder of Rabbi Meir Kahane. Rabbi Kahane was a Zionist, a zealot who hated Arabs, and he was the founder of the Jewish Defense League. On November 5, 1990, according to the prosecutor, Nosair shot Kahane in front of some sixty people who had come to hear the rabbi speak at the Marriott Hotel at Forty-ninth Street and Lexington in Manhattan. The assailant, gun in hand, then ran from the hotel. When he could not find his getaway car, he kept running until he came face to face with a postal inspector. Nosair shot the man in the chest, but because the inspector was wearing a bulletproof vest, his injury was minor. The postal inspector returned fire, bringing down Nosair with a slug from his .357 magnum. When Nosair's case came to trial a year later, the jury inexplicably acquitted him of charges of murder and attempted murder but convicted him of assault and firearms violations. The judge, who called the verdicts "devoid of common sense and logic," sentenced Nosair to the maximum of seven and one-third to twenty-five years.[4]

The FBI developed an interest in the Al-Salaam Mosque and its congregation at the time of Nosair's trial. It planted an informant at the mosque, a man named Emad Salem, who was at that time also an Egyptian intelligence agent. Before long, Sheikh Abdel-Rahman proposed to Salem that he assassinate Egyptian president Hosni Mubarak. Salem reported the proposal to Egyptian authorities, but the plotting was not taken any further.

In June 1992, the radicals frequenting the mosque began developing plans to build a dozen pipe bombs. The idea originated with El Sayyid Nosair, who was in residence at Attica Penitentiary, and his cousin Ibrahim

El Gabrowny, who was Nosair's link to the mosque. The bombs, once made, would be used to kill Judge Alvin Schlessinger, who had sentenced Nosair to prison, and New York assemblyman Dov Hykind, who had loudly denounced Nosair in court. The rest of the bombs were to be used against Jewish targets in New York. The FBI supported Salem in gathering information but drew the line at letting him build bombs, which was a criminal offense. It stopped using him as an informant in July because of doubts about his credibility. Salem ended his contacts with the conspirators, and the pipe-bomb plot withered away.[5] The FBI decision to drop Salem as an informant was unfortunate because those he had associated with at the mosque were about to make the transition from talk to action.

On September 1, 1992, a man arrived in New York from Pakistan with an Iraqi passport issued to a man named Ramzi Ahmed Yousef. He was twenty-four or twenty-five years old, six feet tall, and 180 pounds. His face was lean with an olive complexion, and he sometimes wore a beard. His appearance said he was from somewhere in the Middle East. Although he is now commonly identified by the name Ramzi Yousef, he had used so many aliases and left such a convoluted trail of false identities behind him that his true identity is a matter for debate.[6]

Immediately after stepping off the airplane at Kennedy Airport, Yousef gave his passport to a U.S. immigration officer and asked for political and religious asylum, which he received. Yousef had flown to America with a Palestinian man named Ahmad Ajaj. Ajaj presented a different immigration officer an obviously doctored Swedish passport. He was questioned about it in detail, and an agent searched his luggage. She found a collection of passports from different nations with different names. She also found a small library of books, documents, maps, aerial photographs, and videotapes. Some of the books concerned explosives; one booklet was titled *Rapid Destruction and Demolition.* One of the videotapes dealt with the suicide bombing of a U.S. embassy; another gave a chemistry lesson on the manufacture of explosives. Ajaj was taken to jail as his traveling companion Yousef entered the United States.[7]

Yousef took up residence in the "Little Cairo" section of Jersey City, where he associated with a group of young Arab men who were in the ideological orbit of Sheikh Omar Abdel-Rahman. Within about a month, under Yousef's guidance and leadership, the nebulous pipe-bomb plans had been transformed into a plot to bring down the World Trade Center with a truck bomb.

During a period of about four-and-a-half months, Yousef organized his terrorist team, designed the bomb, converted raw chemicals into an explosive, built the bomb, and delivered it to the World Trade Center. Yousef's team included at least six men in addition to himself. His primary apprentice was Muhammad Salameh, a Palestinian, who shared an apartment with Yousef, contributed capital, and ran errands. Nidal Ayyad, another

Palestinian, had a degree in biochemical engineering and a job with a chemical company; he contributed money and ordered chemicals for the bomb. The other conspirators ran errands, mixed chemicals, and paid bills. Although Nidal Ayyad had training in chemistry and engineering, it is generally accepted that Yousef brought the bomb-building knowledge with him to the United States, was the mastermind of the plot, and probably had the idea of destroying the World Trade Center in his mind before stepping on the airplane that brought him to New York.[8]

Beginning in early January 1993, Yousef and Salameh mixed chemicals in their apartment in Jersey City to make the explosive urea nitrate. They did this by mixing crystalline urea with concentrated nitric acid. The explosive they produced was a relatively stable solid, but the fumes from the nitric acid corroded every metal surface in the apartment and ate away at their lungs. They stockpiled the materials that they made in the apartment, and by the end of February, they were ready to assemble the bomb.[9]

Salameh rented a Ford Econoline van from Ryder Rentals. Ayyad drove it to a storage space the conspirators had rented, and they put three tanks of hydrogen gas into the van. Their next stop was Yousef and Salameh's apartment, where the bomb components were stored. Yousef and his gang loaded the van with plastic garbage bags containing urea nitrate. Because urea nitrate is hard to detonate, they added cushioned containers of nitroglycerine as triggers. They connected blasting caps to the nitroglycerine and twenty-foot-long fuses to the caps—four fuses in all. To give the bomb an added kick, they put the three tanks of compressed hydrogen gas next to the urea nitrate.[10]

Evidence uncovered later indicated that Yousef and his group may have included sodium cyanide in the construction of the bomb. If the blast would have blown the sodium cyanide into a vapor that was sucked into the World Trade Center's ventilation system, it could have poisoned anyone who inhaled it. If it had indeed been part of the bomb, it was most likely burned into less-harmful compounds.[11]

Investigators believed that Yousef had hoped to build a "radiological bomb," one in which a conventional chemical explosion is used to scatter dangerous radioactive isotopes into the atmosphere and cause a deadly fallout. Yousef, working through a conspirator in Pakistan, tried to get a supply of strontium-90 or cesium-137. Fortunately, Yousef's contact in Pakistan failed to deliver.[12]

At about 4:00 A.M. on February 26, 1993, the yellow Ryder van holding a 1,200-pound bomb pulled out of the driveway of Yousef and Salameh's apartment building in Jersey City with Yousef behind the wheel and Salameh in the seat beside him. A red Chevrolet and a dark blue Lincoln occupied by their coconspirators followed them. They stopped at a gas station to fill up the van, and then they drove on to Manhattan. Yousef and his group stopped in midtown Manhattan to pick up another man, a Jordanian named Eyad Ismail, who was comfortable driving New York streets; Ismail drove the rest of the way to the World Trade Center. They arrived about noon, eight hours after they had begun their short trip across the Hudson River. Why they had taken so long to make the trip remains a mystery.[13]

The rented yellow van, followed by the red Chevrolet, entered the underground garage. Yousef picked the place to park the van, under the corner of the North Tower that was closest to the South Tower. He lighted the twenty-foot-long fuses and then joined the rest of the conspirators in the red Chevy. They had twelve minutes to get as far from the World Trade Center as possible.

The bomb exploded at 12:17 P.M. It shook the twin towers, and many people in lower Manhattan thought that the ground was being rocked by an earthquake. Dense acrid smoke poured up through ventilation shafts and stairwells. Some people panicked. It took five hours to evacuate the building complex. When the casualties were counted, only six people were dead, but more than a thousand had sustained injuries.

Down below, in the parking garage, the explosion had hollowed out a cavity 200 feet across that penetrated six floors of the structure under the World Trade Center. It tore out support columns and utility feed lines, and it weakened the retaining wall that held back the water of the Hudson River.[14, 15]

FBI investigators who studied the damage concluded that the terror-ists had parked the van carrying the bomb next to a support column of the North Tower with the purpose of causing that tower to topple into the South Tower, destroying it also. Ramzi Yousef said, after he came into the custody of U.S. officers, that he had hoped the explosion and collapse of the buildings would kill as many as 250,000 people.

But the World Trade Center stood. The complex of buildings had redun-dant structural supports. The two massive towers had been engineered to survive hurricane-strength winds and the impact of a 707 jetliner crashing into it.[15] American engineering had triumphed. The terrorists had taken their best shot at the living symbol of American capitalism and failed. Construction crews went to work rebuilding the underground supports and the parking garage; utility workers repaired the damage to the build-ings' infrastructures; housekeeping crews swept up the dust and aired out the offices; and everybody went back to work.

One of the first investigators to examine the destruction under the World Trade Center was Joseph Hanlin, a senior officer from the explosive technology branch of the Bureau of Alcohol, Tobacco, and Firearms (ATF). Hanlin and his team explored the crater and the piles of rubble illumi-nated by improvised lighting and flashlights they carried. Besides pulver-ized concrete, they found crushed automobiles and flattened exterior parts and body panels that had been torn from vehicles by the blast. As they explored the edge of the crater on the B-2 level, the same level on which the bombers had left the Ryder truck, Hanlin noticed interior parts, fragments from within a vehicle that could have been blown out of a vehicle by an explosion that began in the same vehicle. He found a gear assembly, a cover for a gear assembly, and then a differential housing, all of which had formed a single unit, which he thought must have been directly below the bomb. Hanlin wiped the housing and found a series of numbers: a vehicle identification number (VIN). It was a case of luck and fate favoring the prepared mind.

Hanlin turned the VIN over to the FBI; after a few phone calls, its agents knew that the housing was from a truck owned by Ryder and that it had been rented by a Ryder agent in Jersey City to a man who identified himself as Mohammad Salameh. Salameh had told the rental agency that the truck had been stolen. The FBI staked out the rental office, and on the sixth day after the bombing, Salameh walked in to claim the deposit he had left on the truck. The FBI arrested him, and they found in his pockets identification papers, addresses, and other bits and pieces of information that led to other suspects.[16]

Within a few weeks, investigators had in custody four accused bombers: Mohammad Salameh, Nidal Ayyad, Ahmed Ajaj, and a man named Mahmud Abu Halima, who had been picked up in Egypt. The FBI had interviewed another man named Abdul Yasin and found him to be open and helpful. The day after talking to the FBI, Yasin flew to Jordan and then moved on to Baghdad.[17]

By the time investigators learned that a man going by the name Ramzi Yousef was involved in the bombing of the World Trade Center, he was long gone. Three days before delivering the bomb, he had purchased a one-way ticket for a Pakistan International Airlines flight from Kennedy airport to Karachi under the name of Abdul Basit. Yousef/Basit left America on February 26, the day of the bombing.[18] Another suspect, Eyad Ismail, who drove the bomb-laden truck into the World Trade Center garage, is believed to have left the United States for Jordan at the same time Yousef left for Pakistan.[19]

Four men were defendants in the first World Trade Center bombing trial: Mohammad Salameh, Nidal Ayyad, Ahmed Ajaj, and Mahmud Abu Halima. In early 1994, they were all convicted in a federal court on terrorism charges, and all four were sentenced to 240 years in a federal penitentiary.[20]

THE NEW YORK AND UNITED NATIONS BOMBING CONSPIRACY

After the FBI discovered that several of the men accused of bombing the World Trade Center had been followers of Sheikh Omar Abdel-Rahman, it patched up its differences with its mole, Emad Salem, and sent him back to the sheikh's mosque in New Jersey. Before long, Salem was bringing back stories of planned terrorist activities in the New York area led by a Sudanese man named Siddig Ibrahim Siddig Ali. Bombing targets included the Holland and Lincoln Tunnels, which connect Manhattan and New Jersey, the George Washington Bridge, which crosses the Hudson River from upper Manhattan to New Jersey, the United Nations Building, and the Federal Building in Manhattan. Siddig Ali and his group also discussed bombing the Statue of Liberty and midtown Manhattan's Diamond District, which employed a large number of Hassidic Jews.

Wishful thinking turned to conspiracy, and talk became action when Siddig Ali asked Emad Salem, the FBI's mole, to find a place where they could build bombs. Salem rented a warehouse in Queens, where Siddig Ali's group set up shop, and the FBI planted bugs and video cameras. A little over a month later, in the early hours of June 23, 1993, an FBI team assaulted the bomb factory. They caught five men in the act of mixing fertilizer—most likely ammonium nitrate—and diesel fuel. Three other men were arrested at their homes, and several more accused conspirators were arrested later. Sheikh Omar Abdel-Rahman was arrested about a week after the bomb factory raid.[21, 22]

The case came to trial in federal court in New York in mid-1995 with ten defendants sharing fifty charges, the key charge being that they had engaged in seditious conspiracy against the United States.[23] The seditious conspiracy law, which has been invoked infrequently since it was written soon after the Civil War, requires only proof of discussion and planning of action against the government for a conviction. Because it does not require evidence that any action has been taken, it has been criticized as coming perilously close to restricting freedom of speech.[24]

During the trial, the prosecution singled out Sheikh Abdel-Rahman as the leader of the conspiracy and relegated Siddig Ibrahim Siddig Ali, who led the terrorist group, to the role of one of many coconspirators. On October 1, the jury found the defendants guilty of forty-eight of the fifty charges against them. Two were acquitted of the charge of taking direct part in the bombing plot. In addition to being convicted of directing the bombing conspiracy, Sheikh Abdel-Rahman was convicted of plotting to assassinate President Hosni Mubarak of Egypt.[23]

One inconvenient fact that was largely overlooked at the trial was that two members of the Sudanese mission to the United Nations were involved in the conspiracy to bomb that institution. Siddig Ibrahim Siddig Ali, who was from Sudan, had arranged to get from the two Sudanese diplomats diplomatic license plates that would let the plotters bring a truck full of explosives into the parking garage under the UN buildings. The two Sudanese had diplomatic immunity and could not be tried with the other conspirators. Incredibly, the United States did not expel them from the country until April 1996, almost three years after the conspiracy was exposed. The U.S. government apparently did not confront the Sudanese government with evidence that two of its diplomats were coconspirators in a plot to commit acts of terror and war against it. The Clinton administration had its prosecutors deal with the terrorists, but it failed to identify and deal with the sponsors of terrorism. It was easier not to know.[25]

RAMZI YOUSEF AND GLOBAL TERROR

After the 1993 bombing of the World Trade Center, Ramzi Yousef found his way back to Pakistan, and he is believed to have lived a good part of the following three years at the Bayat Ashuhada (House of Martyrs) guesthouse in Peshawar, which was financed by Osama bin Laden.[26] After his success in damaging—if not, as he had hoped, destroying—the World Trade Center, he appears to have been in demand as a terrorist for hire. In July 1993, he accepted a contract to assassinate Benazir Bhutto, a secular candidate for prime minister of Pakistan. Yousef and two associates intended to place a bomb outside of Bhutto's residence. The bomb went off prematurely, injuring Yousef severely enough to take him out of action for a few weeks. He later planned to shoot Bhutto with a sniper's rifle, but he was unable to get an appropriate weapon for the job.[27]

In March 1994, Yousef and several others attempted to attack the Israeli embassy in Bangkok, Thailand. Building on an earlier success, they rented a truck, loaded it with a ton of plastic explosives, ammonium nitrate, and fuel oil. The bombers got into a traffic accident on their way to the target and abandoned the vehicle. Thai police later found Yousef's fingerprints on the bomb.

It is believed that in June 1994, Ramzi Yousef also led the bombing of the Shrine of Reza, which Iranian Shiite Muslims hold as their holiest site. He was hired for the job by the Mujahedin-e Khalq Organization (MKO), a terrorist group opposed to the government of Iran. Few details of the operation are known, but the results were spectacular. The blast knocked down an entire wall and the dome above the prayer hall. It killed at least twenty-six pilgrims and injured more than two hundred others.[28]

Although it is not clear how and when and with whom he began his planning, Yousef left Pakistan in August 1994 for the Philippines, where he began preparing for more terrorist attacks on the United States.[29] Yousef had visited the Philippines before he orchestrated the World Trade Center bombing, and some believe that Osama bin Laden or his agents asked him to return there to train members of the Abu Sayyaf terrorist group in the use of explosives. Yousef had been in the Philippines about three months when emissaries from bin Laden, then residing in Sudan, asked him to kill President Bill Clinton when he visited Manila in mid-November 1994 on his way to the Asian Pacific Economic Conference.[30]

Yousef considered using a ground-to-air missile to take down Air Force One as it was either landing or taking off. A second approach was to use a bomb to stop the president's motorcade as it drove through the streets of Manila. Once the vehicles were stopped, Yousef would attack them with a cloud of phosgene gas, a chemical weapon used with deadly effect during World War I. Investigators later found among Yousef's possessions chemical manuals describing how to produce phosgene. Fortunately for President Clinton and those around him, Yousef could not surmount the difficulties of obtaining a ground-to-air missile or of manufacturing phosgene, and he went back to building bombs.[29, 31]

During his months in the Philippines, Yousef had developed a small nitroglycerine bomb that was equipped with a timer adapted from a Casio digital watch. To test his bomb, he gave one of the devices to a confederate named Wali Khan Amin Shah, who took it to the Greenbelt Theater in Manila, where he left it under a seat. The bomb exploded on schedule at 10:30 P.M., causing the expected amount of damage. Fortunately, no one was sitting in the seat above the bomb, and it caused only minor injuries to several people in the theater.[31]

Yousef conducted the next bomb test himself on December 11, 1994, when he carried one of his bombs through the security gate and onto a Philippines Airline Boeing 747 bound from Manila to Tokyo via Cebu, in the Philippines. After the plane was airborne, he asked the stewardess if he could move to seat 26K because, he told her, the view was better from there.[32] It is more likely he chose the seat because he knew from studying 747 blueprints that it was above a point of vulnerability.[33] Yousef set the timer, placed the bomb in the life vest under his seat, and disembarked at Cebu. Two hours later, as the airliner was flying over one of Japan's southernmost islands, the bomb exploded, shredding the bottom half of the body of the man who had taken seat 26K. The blast seriously injured six other passengers. The explosion also tore a hole in the floor and cut the control cables leading to the ailerons.[32]

Ailerons are control surfaces on the main wings of an airplane that control its ability to bank and make turns. Without them, an airplane is seriously crippled. The pilot used only the rudder to guide his plane through wide turns and a safe landing at an airport in Okinawa. Back in Manila, Ramzi Yousef called the Associated Press news agency to give credit for the airliner bombing to the Abu Sayyaf terrorist group.[32]

Yousef, now knowing that he had a reliable design, began making more bombs. To make more, he needed more explosive chemicals, which he cooked up in the apartment he shared with an old friend named Abdul Hakim Murad on one of the higher floors of a six-story building overlooking President Quirino Boulevard, a major Manila thoroughfare.[31] Late in the evening on January 6, 1995, Yousef's cooking pot seems to have gone out of control. Clouds of thick, acrid smoke poured from whatever he was cooking and billowed out of the apartment. Yousef and his room-mate Murad apparently got the cause of the smoke under control in the kitchen sink. Hearing fire engines approaching, they calmly left the building and let the firefighters air out the apartment.

Some time after the fire brigade had left the apartment, Yousef persuaded Murad to return to the room to retrieve Yousef's possessions, which included his papers, books, and laptop computer. As Murad was scooping up all of this, he was confronted by a squad of police officers with a search warrant. They arrested Murad and began collecting evidence, which included technical manuals, chemicals, timing devices, four small pipe bombs, and Yousef's computer. Yousef did not return to the apartment but found his way back to Pakistan.[34]

A computer expert working for the Philippines National Police cracked the encryption Yousef had used to protect his computer files, and these files described in detail Yousef's many terrorist plots.[35] The files revealed that because Yousef could not find a way to get at President Clinton, he had decided instead to assassinate Pope John Paul II when the pope visited Manila in mid-January 1995. Yousef's apartment had been ideally situated as a command center for such an attack; it was about five hundred feet from the residence of the Vatican's ambassador to the Philippines, where the pope was to stay, and on a road the pope would use frequently as he commuted to events. Yousef's plots included a suicide attack and an airplane bombing run on the "Popemobile," but because of their inherent difficulties, these plans did not progress far beyond the planning stage.

Another of Yousef's plans was to have his friend and collaborator Murad, who was a pilot, fly a light aircraft loaded with poison gas into CIA headquarters in Langley, Virginia; and should Murad not want to become a martyr to the cause, Yousef also considered spraying poison gas from an airplane flying over the area.[36]

The most terrifying of the plans on Yousef's computer was in the file named "Bojinka," the Serbo-Croat word for explosion.[31] The plan described how five terrorists working simultaneously would plant bombs on eleven American airliners flying from Asia to the United States. The goal was to destroy the aircraft over the Pacific Ocean, killing all of the several thousand people on board. Yousef gave each of the five terrorists a code name and an assignment:

• **"Mirqas"** was to take a United Airlines flight from Manila to Seoul, Korea. He would plant a bomb and get off the plane in Seoul. The plane would continue on toward San Francisco and be destroyed by the bomb over the Pacific Ocean. Mirqas would take a Delta Airlines flight from Seoul to Taipei and plant a second bomb. He would change planes in Taipei for a flight that would eventually take him to Karachi, Pakistan. The plane with the second bomb would continue on to Bangkok but never reach its destination.

•"**Maroka**" would board a Northwest Airlines flight from Manila to Tokyo, planting his first bomb. He would leave that plane before it left for Chicago and its
doom. Before that happened, Maroka would board a Northwest Airlines flight
from Tokyo to Hong Kong. He was to plant his second bomb, get off in Hong
Kong, and continue on to Pakistan. The Northwest flight would continue on
toward New York and be destroyed over the Pacific.

•"**Obaida**" was to plant his first bomb on a United Airlines flight from Singapore
to Hong Kong. After he left the plane, the bomb would explode on the next leg of
the airplane's trip to Los Angeles. Obaida would leave his second bomb on a
United flight from Hong Kong to Singapore. He would get off in Singapore and
fly directly to Pakistan. Meanwhile, the airplane with the second bomb would go
down on its return trip to Hong Kong.

•"**Majbos**" was to leave his first bomb on a United airliner going from Taipei to
Tokyo. As it left for Los Angeles and disaster, he would fly United Airlines from
Tokyo to Hong Kong and plant his second bomb before that aircraft continued on
to New York and destruction.

•"**Zyed**" was probably the code name for Yousef, and he was assigned to place
three bombs. The first was to be left on a Northwest Airlines flight from Manila
to Seoul that continued on to Los Angeles; the second bomb would be planted on
a United Airlines flight from Seoul to Taipei, continuing on to Honolulu; the third
bomb was intended for a United flight from Taipei to Bangkok, with its destruction on the next leg over the Pacific to San Francisco. By the time that happened,
Zyed would be on his way from Bangkok to Karachi, Pakistan.[35]

The "Bojinka" file on Yousef's laptop computer could not be dismissed
as a fanciful plan. After Yousef had been taken into custody in Pakistan by
FBI agents, he told them that had his plan not been cut short by the apartment fire, he and the other terrorists would have bombed the airliners
"within a week or two."[37] Yousef had already tested a prototype bomb
with lethal consequences in December 1994 on the Philippines Airways
flight to Tokyo.[32] Also, FBI and Filipino investigators believe they know
the identities of the five bombers. They were to be Yousef, his friends and
fellow terrorists Abdul Hakim Murad and Wali Khan Amin Shah, one of
Yousef's brothers, and Khalid Shaikh Mohammad, who was believed to
be Yousef's uncle.[35]

Ramzi Yousef had a history of letting his fellow terrorists take the risks
whenever there was a chance that he might be caught by a law enforcement officer. After the 1993 attack on the World Trade Center, he fled to
Pakistan, leaving behind several of his coconspirators to deal with the FBI.
In Manila, he bullied Murad into taking the risk of retrieving his documents and his computer, an act that led to Murad's arrest. After Yousef
fled from the Philippines to Pakistan, he began using a friend named Ish-
tiaque Parker to run dangerous errands and to prepare for terrorist
attacks. Yousef may have threatened to harm Parker's wife and child if he

did not comply. When Yousef told Parker to deliver a package to a Shiite mosque in Islamabad, Parker called the U.S. embassy in Islamabad and asked to talk to someone about a terrorist. He told an agent of the Department of State's Diplomatic Security Service that he knew the whereabouts of Ramzi Yousef, the man wanted for the bombing of the World Trade Center; and, by the way, he also knew about the $2 million reward the United States had offered for Yousef.[38]

Although the United States did not have an extradition agreement with Pakistan, taking Yousef into American custody turned out to be much easier than one might expect. Benazir Bhutto had become prime minister of Pakistan. She believed that the Islamic terrorist movement to which Yousef belonged was a danger to her country, and this belief was probably solidified by her knowledge that she had once been Yousef's target for assassination. Prime Minister Bhutto offered her government's help to capture the terrorist fugitive and even let U.S. agents assist in his capture.

FBI agents sent to Pakistan following Parker's tip tracked Yousef to the Su Casa guest house in Islamabad, which was owned by a member of Osama bin Laden's family.[39] On February 7, 1995, the FBI team sent Parker into the guesthouse to confirm that Yousef was actually there. When Parker emerged and gave the prearranged signal that Yousef was still there, the FBI agents accompanied by Pakistani officers burst into Yousef's room. Once satisfied that they had their man, they bound his hands and feet, blindfolded him, and sped him away in a waiting car; Pakistan then surrendered custody of Yousef to the United States.[40]

In September 1996, Ramzi Yousef, Abdul Hakim Murad, and Wali Khan Amin Shah were convicted in the federal district court in Manhattan on charges of conspiracy to destroy American airliners and kill Americans traveling outside the United States.[41]

In November 1997, Yousef was found guilty in federal court for his participation in the 1993 attempt to destroy the World Trade Center.[42] Eyad Ismail, who drove the bomb-carrying truck to the World Trade Center, was arrested in Jordan and returned to the United States for trial. In 1997, he was convicted of federal terrorism charges and like the others, given a 240-year sentence.[43]

The convictions of six men in the 1993 plot to destroy the World Trade Center and three men in the 1995 "Bojinka" plot to destroy eleven airliners over the Pacific gives the impression of closure, but this may be an illusion. In mid-2002, FBI sources revealed their belief that yet another man, Khalid Shaikh Mohammed, was involved.[44] Mohammed had been born in Kuwait and was believed to be a relative of Ramzi Yousef.[45] Mohammed was already known to have been involved in the 1995 "Bojinka" plot. After his name was linked to the World Trade Center bombing, the chief police investigator of the Philippines gave more details of his involvement in the 1995 plot. Not only was Mohammed to plant some of the bombs; he was a conduit for financing the schemes, appearing at luxury hotels in Manila posing as a wealthy Saudi sheikh.[46] Mohammed's name would turn up again in investigations of other terrorist plots, and he would show up on the FBI's Most Wanted Terrorist list (see appendix 2).

Although imprisoned, Ramzi Yousef is still an enigma. The commonly told biography of the man now in a federal penitentiary for leading the 1993 bombing of the World Trade Center and for the Bojinka plot says that he was born Abdul Basit Mahmoud Abdul Karim in 1968 in Kuwait of a Pakistani father and a mother of Palestinian descent. Abdul Basit, later known as Ramzi Yousef, lived his early life in Kuwait; in 1986, he entered the Swansea Institute in Wales, where he began studying engineering. The school had a large enrollment of Muslim and Middle Eastern students, and from encountering them he developed an enthusiasm for revolutionary causes and Islam. During summer break in 1988, Basit went to Pakistan to be near the war against the Soviets in Afghanistan. Although he did not fight in Afghanistan, the FBI believes that he spent several months at a training camp that was financed by Osama bin Laden. When the summer ended, Basit returned to Wales to complete his education, earning a Higher National Diploma (an academic level a rung lower than a degree). Basit is believed to have been back in Kuwait in August 1990, when the Iraqi Army invaded that oil-rich country. He has been accused of having been a collaborator, although there is scant evidence to support the accusation.[47] Basit's whereabouts immediately after the Gulf War are unknown, but he is believed to have arrived in the Philippines in December 1991, where he gave specialized training to Abu Sayyaf guerrillas.[39] He appeared next on September 1, 1992, at an Immigration and Naturalization Service desk at Kennedy Airport, where he identified himself as Ramzi Ahmed Yousef.[48]

Sorting out his activities over the years is complicated by the fact that the man who is now known as Ramzi Yousef used some forty aliases.[47] Judge Kevin Duffy, who sentenced Yousef to 240 years in prison, believed he was sentencing the man responsible for the World Trade Center bombing, but he doubted he knew the man's name or personal history. After sentencing Yousef, Duffy said, "While normally a prisoner in administrative detention might have some visitors from his family, in your case I would expect the prison to require proof positive that one is in fact a member of your family. We don't even know what your real name is. You have used a dozen aliases. Having abandoned your family name, I must assume that you have abandoned your family also."[49]

Laurie Mylroie, a scholar of Iraq and biographer of Saddam Hussein, has made a disturbing proposal about the identity of Ramzi Yousef. The young electronics engineer, Abdul Basit, got caught up in the Iraqi invasion of Kuwait in 1990, and he emerged after the Gulf War as an ambitious terrorist. Mylroie suggests that the real Abdul Basit was a casualty of the war and that the man who took his identity was an agent of Iraq who would become a terrorist with as his primary target, Iraq's most hated enemy, the United States.[50] Why didn't the United States pursue the possibility that Ramzi Yousef was an agent of Iraq? Because if the possibility was found to be fact, the United States would have to do something about it. Nobody wanted to deal with the consequences of discovering state sponsorship of Yousef's terrorist attacks against the United States, and nobody wanted to restart the Gulf War.

OKLAHOMA CITY

At 9:00 A.M. on April 19, 1995, a twenty-foot-long truck painted yellow with the black trim colors of the Ryder Rental Company pulled up in front of the Alfred P. Murrah Federal Building in Oklahoma City. A man got out—the driver—and walked away. A minute or two later, a bomb in the truck believed to be made of 2,000 pounds of ammonium nitrate, a common fertilizer, and a similar weight of fuel oil exploded. The explosion destroyed the front half of the nine-story building, which faced the truck, and excavated a crater thirty feet deep. The final tally of casualties told that the explosion killed 168 people, 19 of them children in a day care center in the building, and injured 503 others. The blast damaged 530 other structures in the area near the federal building. The estimated cost of recovery from the destruction was $651 million.[51] On the basis of the numbers of dead and injured, the Oklahoma City bombing was the worst case of terrorism experienced by the United States until then.

An hour and a half after the explosion, an Oklahoma highway patrolman arrested Timothy McVeigh eighty miles north of Oklahoma City on misdemeanor charges of driving a car that was not displaying a license plate, having no insurance verification, and carrying a concealed weapon. Before McVeigh could be released on bail, federal agents had concluded that he had rented the Ryder van that carried the bomb, and they took him into custody.[52] A few weeks later, Terry Nichols, a friend of McVeigh since they had served together in the army, was first held as a material witness and then charged as McVeigh's accomplice.[53] Largely on the basis of circumstantial evidence, McVeigh was convicted of several charges relating to the Oklahoma City bombing and sentenced to death.[54] Nichols was convicted of conspiracy but not of participation in the bombing itself.[55]

McVeigh's lawyer, Stephen Jones, has argued that not only did the federal government fail to give his client a fair trial in its zeal to get a conviction, but it also failed to explore the possibility of a wider conspiracy involving international terrorists. Jones has developed a scenario in which his client was the designated fall guy, and Terry Nichols was the organizer who received help in planning, training, and possibly financial support from terrorists in the Philippines, most notably Ramzi Yousef.

The story of Nichols's connection to the Philippines begins in 1990, not long after he left the army with a hardship discharge and divorced his first wife. He soon found a second wife through a mail-order bride service in the Philippines. Nichols traveled to Cebu City on Cebu Island, the country's second-largest city, where, at the age of thirty-five, he married sixteen-year-old Marife Torres. While his new wife waited for a visa, Nichols went to Michigan, where he had family. Sometime in 1991, Marife joined him there. She brought along her infant son, who was fathered by another man. The boy died in an accident, and Nichols and Marife subsequently had a daughter.

Over the next four years, Nichols, who had trouble finding and keeping a job, made numerous trips back to the Philippines in search of "business opportunities." He took his last trip there in November 1994; his wife and their daughter had left for Cebu in September. Before he left the United States, Nichols gave his ex-wife a package with ominous instructions to open it only in the event of his death or if he did not return in sixty days. She did not wait and opened the package. Inside were instructions that led her to Nichols's hidden treasure, which, she said, included $20,000 in cash, gold bars, and precious stones. The package also contained a farewell letter to be delivered to Timothy McVeigh that read in part, "Go for it, you're on your own."[56]

Nichols returned to America in mid-January 1995, four months before the Oklahoma City bombing. Little is known about what he did in the Philippines for two months, but McVeigh's lawyer claims to have learned of his most significant activity. McVeigh's lawyer had his agent in the Philippines look for contacts Nichols might have had with terrorists. He found a man in police custody who said he had met Terry Nichols. The man, whose name was Edwin Angeles, was formally being held in "protective custody" while he talked about terrorists in the Philippines; he probably knew a lot because the Philippine police had documentary evidence that he had been a cofounder of the Abu Sayyaf terrorist group and was its second in command.

Angeles said that sometime in the early 1990s, he met a man who called himself "the Farmer" at a meeting at Davao, on the island of Mindanao.[57] Nichols had grown up in a rural area of Michigan, and before going to the Philippines in November 1994, he worked as a farmhand in Kansas.[57] Angeles produced a pencil sketch of "the Farmer" that McVeigh's lawyer described as "a dead ringer for Terry Lynn Nichols." Angeles identified others at the meeting as a man calling himself Abdul Basit, a.k.a. Ramzi Yousef, Abdul Hakim Murad, and Wali Khan Amin Shah.[58] If Nichols was "the Farmer" who met Yousef, the meeting must have taken place in November or December 1994, when both men were in the Philippines.[58]

Angeles said in a videotape recording and repeated in a written statement that three topics were discussed at the meeting: "bombing activities, providing firearms and ammunition, and training in making and handling bombs."[59]

Soon after their alleged meeting, Nichols returned to the United States, Yousef fled to Pakistan, and Murad and Shah were arrested for plotting to bomb eleven airliners owned by American carriers. Murad learned of the Oklahoma City bombing while he was in a New York jail awaiting trial. He told a guard and later repeated in a written statement his belief that the destruction of the Murrah Federal Building was the work of Ramzi Yousef's "Liberation Army."[60]

The story put together by Timothy McVeigh's lawyer linking Ramzi Yousef to the bombing of the Murrah Federal Building in Oklahoma City is built on circumstantial evidence, suspect testimony, and an incomplete investigation, but then the same could be said of the scenario used by the prosecution to convict McVeigh and Nichols. The most promising leads that could have shown a link between Yousef and the Oklahoma City bombing were the videotaped and written statements of Edwin Angeles. Unfortunately, he is no longer available to give additional information. He was murdered in January 1999.[61]

Timothy McVeigh was executed by lethal injection at the Federal Penitentiary in Terre Haute, Indiana, on June 11, 2001.[62] Although he paid the supreme penalty for his crime, the World Trade Center bombers did not. They received sentences of up to 240 years in prison because the death penalty for federal terrorist cases did not come into being until 1994, the year after the World Trade Center attack and the year before McVeigh bombed the Oklahoma City federal building.[49]

Chapter 10

America in Retreat

SOMALIA

In 1992, Bill Clinton was elected to the presidency to a large extent on the voters' acceptance of his unofficial campaign motto, "It's the economy, stupid." The Soviet Union was dead; the United States became, by default, the world's only superpower; and America had turned inward because of concerns about its pocketbook. Foreign affairs, though still important, took second place to the major domestic issue, the economy. Nevertheless, the United States still had foreign commitments and a military presence around the world. One of these was in the East African country of Somalia, where it would face the challenges of anarchy and international terrorism.

Like many African countries, Somalia did not emerge from colonialism with a stable government or a clear national identity. In 1991, the Somali government collapsed, and rival warlords fought for control of the country. Within a year, a large part of its population was starving because the fighting groups hoarded the limited food supplies for their own people. A UN task force entered Somalia on the humanitarian missions of bringing peace and ending starvation. The United States sent a contingent as part of the group in Operation Restore Hope.[1]

On their way to Somalia, some American troops stayed at a hotel in Yemen, at the southern end of the Arabian Peninsula across the Gulf of Aden from Somalia. On December 29, 1992, after the Americans had moved on, a bomb exploded at the hotel, killing two Austrian tourists. At the same time, several terrorists were arrested near Aden Airport as they were about to fire rockets at American aircraft. American investigators learned later that Al Qaeda operatives had placed the bomb in the hotel and that the rocket-wielding terrorists had been trained by Al Qaeda. Both operations were apparently under the control of Muhammed Atef, who would later achieve notoriety as Al Qaeda's chief of military operations and the third-ranking member of that group. Atef, accompanied by several Al Qaeda members who had been in Yemen at the time, boarded an airplane for Somalia immediately after the bombing. In Somalia, they gave military training and assistance to recruits of Somali warlords.[2]

When the U.S. Army got on the ground in Somalia, it soon learned that its—and the United Nations'—efforts were being opposed by the supporters of General Mohammed Farah Aidid, who controlled the capital city, Mogadishu. The UN peacekeepers moved to neutralize Aidid by arresting his top aides. On October 3, 1993, a U.S. Army task force, while on a mission to arrest two of Aidid's lieutenants in Mogadishu, found themselves in a life-or-death battle. This encounter is remembered principally because it became the subject of the best-selling book by Mark Bowden, *Black Hawk Down*, and a successful movie of the same name.[3]

The battle of Mogadishu lasted fifteen hours. When it was over, General Aidid's two lieutenants were in UN custody, as intended; but the casualties were staggering. Eighteen U.S. soldiers had been killed, and dozens more were seriously wounded. One army helicopter pilot had been captured, but his Somali captors returned him eleven days later. By one conservative estimate, 500 Somalis were killed and at least another 500 wounded.[1]

Several years after the battle of Mogadishu, U.S. intelligence sources would confirm that Al Qaeda had been on the scene. One of its senior terrorists, Mohammed Saddiq Odeh, had trained Somali fighters who participated in the battle. Odeh would show up again in 1998 in Nairobi, where he would play a role in planning the bombing of American embassies.[4]

The American losses in Somalia might have been accepted by the American people had not someone with a video camera been at the scene after the battle. Television stations around the world and in the United States were soon broadcasting images of Somali mobs abusing and dragging the bodies of two dead soldiers through the dusty streets of Mogadishu. The people of the United States were outraged.[1]

Somali warlord General Aidid claimed victory, and the United States retreated in defeat. President Clinton had been under bipartisan pressure from Congress to withdraw American troops from Somalia.[5] Clinton gave in under the pressure just three days after the battle. He announced a series of actions to prop up Operation Restore Hope that included a short-term increase in troops, but, he said, "All American troops will be out of Somalia by March 31," less than six months in the future.[6]

The Somalia experience reversed America's willingness to take on battles in foreign lands. America's success in the Gulf War, that of driving

Iraq forces out of Kuwait while sustaining incredibly low casualties, had restored its faith in its military abilities, which had sunk to a low during the Vietnam War. The sight of the corpses of American sons being dragged through the streets of Mogadishu, however, was repellent and terrifying. After Somalia, America would fight its battles at a safe distance, with smart bombs and cruise missiles rather than with boots on the ground.

BACK IN THE UNITED STATES

Frank Corder went to the Hartford County Airpark in Maryland on September 11, 1994, where he intended to steal an airplane. According to his friends, Corder was despondent. During the previous year, he had been treated for alcoholism and arrested on a drug charge, his trucking business failed, his father died, and he broke up with his third wife. One of Corder's friends said that he had threatened "to get a plane and kill himself" by flying into the White House.[7]

Sometime in the first hour of September 12, Corder, who had a pilot's license but limited flying experience, took off in a Cessna 150, a two-seat, propeller-driven aircraft of a type often used as a trainer. He flew toward Washington, D.C., about sixty miles to the southwest. Corder's flight path approached the center of the city from the north, flying low over Seventeenth Street. When he began to cross over the Mall, he banked to the left, just west of the Washington Monument, and turned his course due north on a flight path that led directly to the White House.

Seconds later, Corder, in his stolen Cessna, crossed over E Street and the south fence of the White House grounds. Secret Service agents on the scene had just enough time to run for cover before the tiny aircraft hit the south lawn, bounced into a magnolia tree, and crashed into the lower wall of the White House, two floors below the president's bedroom. Corder, the pilot, was killed on impact. The crash of the airplane caused some damage to the landscaping, but damage to the building was not significant.

President Clinton and his family were not in the White House at the time. They had been living in Blair House, across Pennsylvania Avenue, while a maintenance crew was making repairs to the ventilation system.[8]

The misguided pilot probably achieved his aim, killing himself, but his exploit pointed out serious security deficiencies in the nation's capital. Downtown Washington was—and is—surrounded by an envelope of restricted air space that includes the White House, the Capitol, the Mall, and major monuments.[8] It was—and is—defined by imaginary boundaries that provide no physical protection. The flight path to Washington National Airport (now Reagan National Airport) was a twenty-second flight away, which gave security officers minimal time to react to an incursion. There was speculation that the Secret Service had stinger missiles that could bring down any aircraft that approached and threatened the

White House, but their use in downtown Washington would have probably caused unacceptable collateral damage.[9] As a senior White House official pointed out, "If you missed, E Street becomes pretty ugly, pal."[8]

If Frank Corder had stolen a larger aircraft and intended to do more than kill himself, he could have caused significant damage. He demonstrated that the White House and the president were easy targets for aerial terrorists and assassins. It is likely that some improvements have been made since his flight, but the terrain around the White House and the Capitol has not changed. The White House has probably remained an achievable target. The factors that defined the vulnerability of the White House also applied to the Pentagon and to the World Trade Center on September 11, 2001.

ATTACKS IN SAUDI ARABIA

The United States developed a friendly military relationship with Saudi Arabia in the mid-1960s, and it began sending its personnel to that Middle Eastern country in the mid-1970s. Their primary mission was to train the 80,000 members of the Saudi National Guard in the maintenance and operation of military equipment it had purchased from the United States. Their secondary mission was to keep as low a profile as possible in this most conservative of Islamic states, which has resisted all foreign influences. Americans came in mass during the 1991 Gulf War, and many stayed afterward.[10]

The first warnings of danger to American military personnel came as faxes to the U.S. embassy in Saudi Arabia and to *al-Quds al-Arabia,* a newspaper based in London that was owned by Palestinians and sympathetic to Iraq. The faxes, which arrived in April and early July 1995, demanded that American and British forces leave Saudi Arabia by June 28 or become "legitimate targets" of attacks. The latter of the two messages stated, "The movement will use all available means to move 'the crusader forces' off the peninsula of Islam." The sender of the faxes identified itself as the Islamic Change Movement.

In the late morning of November 13, 1995, a van parked near a military training and communications center of the Saudi National Guard in central Riyadh, the capital of Saudi Arabia. Two men got out of the van, and moments later, the 250-pound bomb inside the van exploded, tearing into the three-story building. The blast killed seven people; five of them were Americans. Sixty others, many of them Americans, were injured. Three groups claimed credit for the Riyadh bombing: the Islamic Change Movement and two others that were previously unknown.[10, 11]

President Clinton made the pro forma response to terrorist attacks. He promised to "increase our efforts to deter terrorism, [and] to make sure that those responsible for this hideous act are brought to justice."[10]

The following April, Saudi authorities reported that they had arrested four men who had committed the Riyadh bombing. In confessions broadcast on Saudi television, the men said that they had also planned to commit kidnappings and assassinations. They claimed that they were inspired by a Saudi dissident based in London who advocated overthrowing the Saudi royal family and replacing it with a more conservative Islamic government. No mention was made of the Islamic Change Movement, which threatened attacks on foreigners, or other groups that might have sponsored the attack.[12]

American authorities wanted to question the four men who had made the public confessions, and they had a lot of questions about the men's motivations and sponsorship. The Saudis did not permit it.[13] Thirty-one days after the public confessions, they executed the accused men by public beheading.[10]

Seven months after the Riyadh bombing, terrorists struck again in Saudi Arabia. After the Gulf War, members of the U.S. Air Force were stationed at the Abdul Aziz Air Base near Dhahran, where they supported Operation Southern Watch, the operation that enforced the prohibition on Iraqi military activity in the no-fly, no-drive zone south of the thirty-second parallel. The air force personnel lived at the Khobar Towers, a complex of high-rise buildings near the base.

Just before 10:00 P.M. on June 25, 1996, a tanker truck drove into the housing complex and parked at a security barrier about thirty-five meters from a building occupied by Americans. An air force security officer who saw the truck park alerted both Saudi and American security personnel; he then began evacuating the building. When a Saudi officer approached the truck, two men jumped from it, got into a car that was apparently driven by an accomplice, and sped away. Less than four minutes later, the truck exploded.

The blast tore the face off the eight-story apartment building and caused its partial collapse. It gouged a crater eighty-five feet long and thirty-five feet deep. The explosion killed nineteen and injured hundreds. Eighty of the injured were hospitalized.[14] The number and seriousness of the casualties would have been greater had not residents, who were evacuating the building, been in interior stairwells when the bomb went off.

The type of explosive used and its quantity was not immediately determined. According to initial estimates by the defense department, the truck bomb contained the equivalent of 3,000 to 8,000 pounds of TNT. The Defense Special Weapons Agency reported later that a more accurate figure was about 20,000 pounds of TNT.[15]

President Clinton said about the terrorist attack, "We will pursue this. America takes care of our own. Those who did it must not go unpunished."[15]

But who should be punished? Saddam Hussein was an obvious suspect because air force fighters from Saudi Arabia were making a daily commute to patrol the skies over Iraq, but U.S. investigators apparently did not give much credence to that possibility. For a while, Osama bin Laden was a suspect, but the available information did not reveal any direct connections, and bin Laden declined to take credit. When he was interviewed by CNN reporters Peter Bergen and Peter Arnett in May 1997, he told them, "I have great respect for the people who did this. What they did is a big honor that I missed participating in."[16]

Just a few days short of the five-year anniversary of the bombing of the Khobar Towers and the expiration of the statute of limitations, the United States indicted thirteen Saudis and one Lebanese for crimes related to the attack. The charges against the fourteen men included murder, attempted murder, conspiracy to kill U.S. nationals, conspiracy to kill U.S. employees, and use of weapons of mass destruction against U.S. nationals. According to FBI director Louis Freeh, an unspecified number of those accused were in the custody of a government or governments friendly to the United States. Attorney General John Ashcroft said that "the Iranian government supported and supervised members of Saudi Hezbollah," the group the accused men belonged to. He said that planning for the bombing began in 1993 with "extensive surveillance [by the accused] to find American targets in Saudi Arabia." Ashcroft also said that "the charged defendants reported their surveillance activities to Iranian officials and were supported and directed in those activities by Iranian officials." However, the United States did not indict any Iranian officials or take any action against Iran. It was easier to let the blame for the Khobar Towers bombing fall on fourteen men who were apparently beyond the jurisdiction of the government.[17]

SADDAM HUSSEIN AND WEAPONS OF MASS DESTRUCTION

As a condition of the cease-fire to end the Persian Gulf War, Saddam Hussein had agreed to open Iraq to UN inspectors who would verify that his country would not produce and would destroy its "weapons of mass destruction," (WMD) a broad category that included chemical, biological, and nuclear weapons. Hussein's compliance with this agreement was poor to nonexistent for nearly seven years, and toward the end of 1998, the United Nations' Iraq inspection team left in disgust. The United States and Britain took action on behalf of the United Nations, although without its consultation or approval. On December 16, they began a campaign of air strikes, which were intended, according to President Clinton, to "degrade Iraq's ability to develop and deliver weapons of mass destruction and its ability to threaten its neighbors."[18]

The brief air action, named "Operation Desert Fox," entailed attacking about a hundred sites in Iraq with some 415 Tomahawk cruise missiles and 650 sorties flown by U.S. and British aircraft. The bombing campaign lasted seventy hours and was over almost before anyone at the United Nations, in the Arab world, or in the United States or Britain could voice a significant objection. There were no casualties or aircraft lost on the side of the United States and Britain.[19]

The point of the exercise, other than being a punitive action, was less obvious than President Clinton claimed. The title of *Time* magazine's article covering it asked, "What Good Did It Do?"[20] The subheading of *Newsweek's* article read, "Bombs rained down on Baghdad for days, but with no guarantee that they would remove Saddam from power. So what was the purpose of Desert Fox?"[21] After this attack on Iraq, the United Nations' Iraq inspection team was not likely to return to do its job. The answer might be found in some of the targets hit. The major targets were the Directorate of Military Intelligence, military command centers, weapons-production facilities, Republican Guard barracks, and other sites associated with the Republican Guards.[20] The U.S. Department of Defense had unconfirmed reports that casualties in the Republican Guard ranged from 600 to 2,000.[22]

Other sites that were hit suggested that some Tomahawk missiles and laser-guided bombs were targeted at specific people, including Saddam Hussein. In a press briefing a few weeks after the assault on Iraq, General Anthony Zinni, who commanded Operation Desert Fox, said, "We are looking at reports that...there were senior leadership members in there who were part of the casualty lists, especially in the special security organizations and in the Republican Guard."[22] Among the sites bombed, where Saddam Hussein might have hoped to find refuge, were the Secretariat Presidential, the working office building of the leadership of Hussein's regime,[23] his daughter's palace in Tikrit,[21] and his sister's residence.[22] Most fascinating, of course, was an unconfirmed report that one target destroyed during Operation Desert Fox was the house where Saddam Hussein rendezvoused with his mistress.[24] Saddam Hussein apparently survived Operation Desert Fox physically intact; but according to General Zinni, "he was shaken and the regime was shaken."[22]

So why would the United States try to kill Saddam Hussein if, as it claimed, its purpose in the air attack was to reduce Iraq's abilities to use weapons of mass destruction and lessen its ability to threaten its neighbors? A possible reason was given by Saftor, Inc., a private intelligence-analysis firm. After reviewing thousands of pieces of publicly available information, Saftor claimed that the raids on Iraq were timed to coincide with a coup backed by the United States. The scenario of an assassination attempt accompanying a coup was reminiscent of the CIA's plan to assassinate Castro at about the time of the Bay of Pigs invasion.[25] As would be expected, American officials denied that there was any truth to the reported coup attempt against Saddam Hussein.[26]

Corporal Steve W. Kirtley, a marine security guard at the U.S. embassy in Tehran, Iran, was one of fifty-three Americans held hostage for 444 days. (Photograph courtesy of U.S. Marine Corps, photo no. 20015249525.)

President and Mrs. Reagan review the caskets holding the remains of the Americans killed on April 18, 1983, when a suicide truck bomb destroyed the U.S. embassy in Beirut, Lebanon. The bomb killed sixty-three people and injured 120. (Photograph courtesy of the Ronald Reagan Library, photo no. NLS-WHPO-A-C14159[28A].)

The explosion of a truck bomb at the marine barracks in Beirut, Lebanon, on October 23, 1983, created a cloud of smoke that was visible from miles away. The blast destroyed the barracks building, killed 241 marines, and injured hundreds more. (Photograph courtesy of U.S. Marine Corps, photo no. 2001101810128.)

After the destruction of the marine barracks building in Beirut, Lebanon, the survivors searched through tons of rubble for their missing comrades. (Photograph courtesy of U.S. Marine Corps, photo no. 20011018101413.)

A U.S. Navy F-14A Tomcat releases a 500-pound laser-guided bomb during an ordnance testing exercise. Similar laser-guided bombs were used in attacks on Muammar Qaddafi's headquarters in Libya on April 15, 1986, and on sites in Iraq frequented by Saddam Hussein during the 1991 Persian Gulf War. (Photograph courtesy of U.S. Department of Defense, photograph no. 960510-N-0000P-001.)

The World Trade Center in New York was the target of a terrorist bombing on February 26, 1993, which killed six people and injured a thousand. (Photograph courtesy of the National Archives, photo no. NWDNS-412-DA-5204.)

After the Iraqi invasion of Kuwait, President George Bush watches a performance of Saddam Hussein on television. (George Bush Library, National Archives, photo no. P 39220-2.)

On April 19, 1995, the explosion of a truck bomb built by domestic terrorists tore through the Alfred P. Murrah Federal Building in Oklahoma City, killing 168 people and injuring hundreds more. (Photograph courtesy of the Federal Emergency Management Agency [FEMA].)

The explosion of a fuel truck next to the Khobar Towers, the residence of U.S. military personnel stationed at the King Abdul Aziz Air Base near Dharan, Saudi Arabia, on June 25, 1996, killed 19 Americans and sent 64 to the hospital; 200 others were treated for their injuries and released. (Photograph courtesy of U.S. Department of Defense, photo no. 960626-N-00000-002.)

An army honor guard carries the remains of a victim of the bombing of the U.S. embassy in Nairobi, Kenya, at a ceremony at Andrews Air Force Base, Maryland. (Photograph courtesy of U.S. Department of Defense, photo no. 980813-F-7466S-003.)

A Tomahawk cruise missile is launched from a navy destroyer. Missiles of this type were used in U.S. attacks on Al Qaeda camps in Afghanistan on August 20, 1998, and on "presidential" sites in Iraq during the December 16–20, 1998, assault. (Photograph courtesy of U.S. Department of Defense, photo no. 960903-N-8202E-003.)

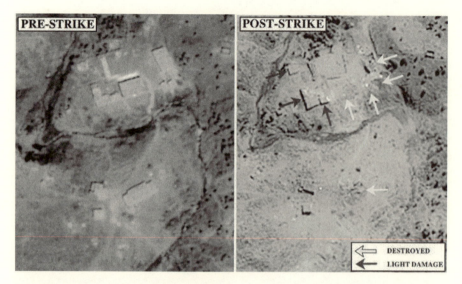

Satellite photographs of Osama bin Laden's main Al Qaeda camp at Khowst, Afghanistan, taken before and after the cruise-missile attack on August 20, 1998. Seven buildings were either severely damaged or destroyed. (Photograph courtesy of U.S. Department of Defense, photo no. 990113-O-0000X-001.)

The U.S. Navy recovered the cockpit data recorder from Egypt Air flight 990, which was, according to the National Transportation Safety Board, intentionally crashed by its copilot on October 31, 1999. (Photograph courtesy of U.S. Department of Defense, photo no. 991113-N-9407M-506.)

The guided missile destroyer USS *Cole* (DDG 67) had a hole blown in its hull when a small boat loaded with explosives and piloted by a suicide bomber crashed into the ship and exploded during a refueling operation in the port of Aden, Yemen, on October 12, 2000. The blast killed seventeen sailors. (Photograph courtesy of U.S. Department of Defense, photo no. 001012-N-0000N-002.)

A smoke plume rises over lower Manhattan from the collapsed twin towers of the World Trade Center, September 11, 2001, as seen in this photograph taken from the International Space Station. (Photograph courtesy of NASA, photo no. ISS003-ESC-5588.)

The Pentagon burns in the night after hijackers crashed an airliner into it on September 11, 2001. The point of impact is seen in the wall to the left of center of this photo. The illuminated dome of the U.S. Capitol is visible in the distance. (Photograph courtesy of U.S. Navy, photo no. 010911-N-1350W-077.)

Firefighters and urban search-and-rescue teams work amid the rubble of the collapsed World Trade Center, September 11, 2001. (Photograph courtesy of the Federal Emergency Management Agency [FEMA].)

U.S. Navy SEALS found this propaganda poster in an Al Qaeda classroom in the Zhawar Kili area of eastern Pakistan, January 2002. An illustration of an airliner crashing into a tower of the World Trade Center can be seen to the left of Osama bin Laden. (Photograph courtesy of the U.S. Navy, photo no. 020114-N-8242C-005.)

Chapter 11

Osama bin Laden

Osama bin Laden's background emerges from a fog of vague and often-contradictory tales, and the details should be taken with a small helping of skepticism. The following, however, is a commonly accepted and reasonable approximation of the man's background—until a better story comes along. He was born into uncertainty, if not conflict, sometime in the mid-1950s in Saudi Arabia. His father, Mohammed bin Laden, had in his lifetime put together Saudi Arabia's biggest construction company, making him and his family prodigiously wealthy. Osama bin Laden was born to one of the last of Mohammed bin Laden's many wives, and he had about fifty siblings. His father died in 1967, leaving Osama independently wealthy.

There are stories that in his late teens, Osama bin Laden lived the life of a playboy in London or Beirut. A more credible story has him attending King Abdul Aziz University, in Jedda, Saudi Arabia, where his belief in Islam became focused into commitment to a radical interpretation of jihad, holy war against the infidels, that would bring the world under the rule of ancient Islamic principles.

The Soviet Union gave Osama bin Laden his chance to be a part of the movement by invading Afghanistan in December 1979. Bin Laden joined the Afghan rebels, and at first he used his expertise in the construction industry and his organizational skills to help refugees who had escaped to Pakistan. By 1986, he had made the personal transition from logistical support to combat. According to various reports, he and the Arab unit he led were remarkably brave in the face of the better-equipped enemy.[1]

As the war in Afghanistan against the Soviet invaders was nearing its end, bin Laden began to think globally. In 1988, he formed a new organization called Al Qaeda, "the military base," which counted among its members the leaders of terrorist organizations and had as its purpose the worldwide expansion of radical Islamic groups.[2] The war against the Soviet Union in Afghanistan ended in 1989 when the Soviet Union withdrew its forces, but warfare continued as rival Afghan forces fought for control of what was left of the country.

In 1990, back in Saudi Arabia, bin Laden thought he had another righteous cause: the defense of his country against Iraq, which had invaded its neighbor Kuwait. He apparently acquired his hatred for the United States when the Saudi government chose it rather than him to defend its country. He was horrified to learn that the Americans—the infidels, the friend of Israel and the Jews—would base troops on the sacred soil that was the site of Islam's holy shrines at Mecca and Medina.

Bin Laden left his home in Saudi Arabia in April 1991, and after a short stay in Pakistan, he arrived in Sudan. With the approval of the Sudanese government, he pursued his two main interests. He invested in banks, agriculture, and construction; and under the umbrella of Al Qaeda, he set up training camps for Islamic warriors. Bin Laden's revolutionary efforts stretched across East Africa. His agents set up the blundering attack in Yemen against American troops on their way to join the UN task force in Somalia, and they trained the Somalis who were involved in the notorious "Black Hawk Down" incident that killed eighteen American soldiers (see chapter 10).[3] In 1993, they also began planning for an attack on the U.S. embassy in Nairobi, Kenya.[4] The following year, Saudi Arabia, tiring of bin Laden's militant escapades, revoked his citizenship.[1]

By 1996, Osama bin Laden's support of terrorist activities became a concern to the United States and to Egypt, and both countries pressured Sudan to expel him, thereby cutting him off from his business enterprises and his terrorist infrastructure—or so they thought. Bin Laden returned to Afghanistan in May of that year, where he was accepted as a guest by the Taliban, who were consolidating their control of the country that had been torn apart by tribal warfare. Far from being neutralized by his expulsion from Sudan, bin Laden took the offensive against the country he saw as the enemy of Islam and God. On August 23, he issued "The Declaration of Jihad on the Americans Occupying the Country of the Two Sacred Places [Mecca and Medina in Saudi Arabia]."[5] A little more than a month later, the Taliban drove the remnants of the Afghan government out of Kabul and declared themselves the legitimate government of that country.[6]

Al Qaeda and the Taliban were an odd couple whose relationship was based primarily on its fundamentalist religious philosophy. Taliban is the plural of *Talib*, a word that means "religious student." They were young Afghans who had attended religious schools in Afghanistan and Pakistan, and they were led by an Islamic cleric by the name of Mullah Mohammed

Omar.[7] Al Qaeda members and its leader were mostly Arabs, usually better educated and with a far more sophisticated understanding of the world beyond Afghanistan. Their respective leaders, Mullah Omar and bin Laden, developed a close personal relationship. They are reported to have spent long hours discussing the principles of Islam. Bin Laden declared Mullah Omar caliph, the leader of the faithful, and he swore an Islamic oath of fealty to the Taliban leader. Al Qaeda gave financial support to its Taliban hosts. In return, bin Laden and Al Qaeda received the hospitality of Afghanistan and influence over its government. Bin Laden had—he thought—a secure base from which to launch his war against the infidels.[8]

The foundation, of course, had been laid in the war against the Soviet Union that began a decade and a half earlier and paid for, in part, by the enemy through the CIA. During Afghanistan's war with the Soviet Union, the CIA had laundered the money it spent to support the mujahideen, the Islamic forces fighting the Soviets, by funneling it through Pakistan's Inter Services Intelligence agency (ISI). The ISI spent the money—$3 billion in all—according to its own conservative priorities, and a good chunk of it went to build training camps and other infrastructure controlled by Islamic zealots.[9] After the Taliban took control of Afghanistan, some of these camps, most notably the camp at Khowst, eventually fell under the control of bin Laden. By early 1997, bin Laden was establishing additional training camps that catered to Arab recruits.[10]

Documents collected by American forces after the assaults on the Taliban and Al Qaeda in late 2001 and early 2002 indicate that the camps had organized and sophisticated curricula. The camps had two tiers of instruction. The general program was designed to produce irregular ground troops, guerrillas, whom American military instructors described as "a competent grunt." They learned the basics of firearms, land mines, and stinger missiles. Their training manuals, which the students laboriously copied by hand, were based on Soviet and American military training manuals.

Those students who showed superior abilities were directed into advanced courses that taught terrorist techniques. Subjects included instruction on how to make explosives from common, innocuous materials and enough electrical engineering to allow students to construct timing and detonation devices.[11]

How many guerrillas the Al Qaeda camps in Afghanistan graduated during their five years of operation is a matter of speculation. French intelligence officials estimate that the camps trained as many as ten thousand people, who then dispersed to cells in more than fifty countries.[12] American officials estimated that the camps trained twenty thousand men.[11] The trained terrorists who graduated from the camps are a fraction of that total, but obviously a number that could be in the thousands. In view of the destruction caused by only nineteen terrorists on September 11, 2001, the unknown number of terrorists bin Laden's camps trained is cause for grave concern.

In February 1998, Osama bin Laden appeared as the leader of a new federation of terrorist organizations calling itself the International Islamic Front for Jihad Against the Jews and Crusaders. One of its first actions was to issue a *fatwa*, or decree, signed by leaders of five militant Islamic groups, with Osama bin Laden's name at the top of the list. The following excerpt gives the flavor of the document and illustrates why bin Laden was seen as a serious threat by U.S. security agencies:

No one argues today about three facts that are known to everyone....

First, for over seven years the United States has been occupying the lands of Islam in the holiest of places, the Arabian Peninsula [specifically, at military bases in Saudi Arabia], plundering its riches, dictating to its rulers, humiliating its people, terrorizing its neighbors, and turning its bases in the Peninsula into a spearhead through which to fight the neighboring Muslim peoples [especially Iraq]....

Second, despite the great devastation inflicted on the Iraqi people by the crusader-Zionist alliance, and despite the huge number of those killed, which has exceeded 1 million,...despite all this, the Americans are once again trying to repeat the horrific massacres, as though they are not content with the protracted blockade imposed after the ferocious war or the fragmentation and devastation....

Third, if the Americans' aims behind these wars are religious and economic, the aim is also to serve the Jews' petty state [Israel] and divert attention from its occupation of Jerusalem and murder of Muslims there....

On this basis, and in compliance with God's order, we issue the following *fatwa* to all Muslims: The ruling to kill the Americans and their allies—civilians and military—is an individual duty for every Muslim who can do it in any country in which it is possible to do it.[13]

In this *fatwa*, bin Laden escalated his 1996 declaration of war against America by calling for attacks on civilians, as well as military targets, anywhere in the world. Bin Laden's call for radical Muslims to murder Americans was not reported at that time by the American news media.

As Osama bin Laden escalated his language and his terrorist activities, he was largely unknown by the people of his primary enemy, the United States. There were, however, a few intelligence officers within the government who understood him as a threat. Possibly the first time anyone noticed bin Laden was during the investigation of the 1993 bombing of the World Trade Center. His name was included on a list of donors to a charity that had contributed to financing that attack, and one of the defendants had been overheard mentioning a "Sheikh Osama." Richard A. Clarke, who was the White House's national coordinator for counterterrorism, said that the CIA was also generating reports that mentioned "financier Osama bin Laden." Gradually, a few changed their perception of bin Laden from "financier" to "leader."[14]

The files on Osama bin Laden grew thicker, and in 1996 the State Department circulated a dossier outlining his operations and antipathy for the United States. It linked him to the 1992 bombing of the hotel used by American troops in Aden, Yemen, and it stated that bin Laden's followers had trained the Somali irregulars who killed eighteen American soldiers in the 1993 battle in Mogadishu. Also in 1996, the CIA created a group that it code-named "Alex" to monitor bin Laden's global activities. Regrettably, it appears that this was the totality of intelligence gathering on Osama bin Laden. It was limited to newspaper clippings and electronic intelligence. The United States, as we learned later, was woefully deficient in "human intelligence" collected by informants and spies.[15]

America's television stations were ahead of the government in putting its agents in the field in Afghanistan to dig out the story of the self-proclaimed leader of the holy war against the infidels. The first Western journalists to make the trek to Afghanistan to interview Osama bin Laden were Peter Arnett and Peter Bergen of CNN. Bin Laden lectured the two journalists for over an hour on the theme of the evils visited on the Islamic world by the United States in collaboration with the Jews; and he repeated his intention to attack American military forces stationed in Saudi Arabia. CNN broadcast its profile on Osama bin Laden on May 12, 1997, to more than a hundred countries; but in the United States, according to Bergen, "the story had little impact."[16]

A year later, a crew from ABC News interviewed bin Laden and got a similar story. The terrorist leader repeated his threats against Americans, including the warning he made in the *fatwa* of February 1998, that he made no distinction between military personnel and civilians. ABC broadcast its interview with bin Laden on Wednesday, June 10, 1998, as part of its *Nightline* program, which aired after most Americans had gone to bed.[16, 17]

The subliminal, though not necessarily intended, message of the interviews with bin Laden was that he was not much of a threat. Here was a man who wore robes, who needed a shave and probably a bath, and who lived in a cave high in the mountains of Afghanistan. He and his men were armed with Kalashnikov rifles, Russian PK submachine guns, and rocket-propelled grenades; but in Afghanistan, who wasn't? He talked big, but how could someone whose base of operations was so remote and so primitive that it did not even have indoor plumbing be a significant threat to the world's only superpower? Those who dismissed bin Laden forgot that the mujahideen had defeated the Soviet Union in the same mountains with the same weapons and that nearly four decades earlier, a far smaller band of mountain-dwelling rebels led by Fidel Castro had taken over Cuba and then made their revolution felt on the international scene.

Osama bin Laden had declared war on America, and America ignored him.

Chapter 12

Al Qaeda's War

THE EMBASSY BOMBINGS

At 10:30 A.M. on August 7, 1998, in a residential section of Dar es Salaam, Tanzania, the U.S. embassy's water truck pulled through the perimeter fence into the embassy compound and stopped to be inspected by security guards. Moments later, a massive explosion destroyed the water truck, instantly killing five security guards and four others. A crater behind where the truck had been indicated where the bomb had detonated and where, according to witnesses, a light truck had followed the water truck.[1] The explosion destroyed the entrance to the embassy and tore a side off the three-story white-stone embassy building.[2]

Four minutes later, in Nairobi, Kenya, 450 miles north of Dar es Salaam, a similar scene played out. The U.S. embassy in Nairobi, unlike the one in Dar es Salaam, was in the downtown area, on the corner of a busy intersection, across the street from a railway headquarters and adjacent to office buildings. The streets were filled with traffic and shoppers.

A 3.5-ton truck pulled into the access road that led to the parking lots of the embassy in Nairobi. As it sped toward the lots, a security guard lowered a barrier to stop the truck. A man jumped from the passenger side and demanded that the guard open the barrier. When the guard did not comply, the man threw a hand grenade. The guard ducked; the grenade fell behind him. The guard ran behind the building shouting into a walkie-talkie that the embassy was under a terrorist attack. Then the truck exploded. The five-story embassy building took a hard hit to its side, with damage extending inside, but it remained standing. A seven-story building adjacent to the embassy building and next to the truck was leveled. A twenty-one-story building across the access road from the embassy also sustained major damage. People were killed in all three buildings, in the area of the embassy access road, and on the streets of Nairobi. Hundreds were dead and thousands injured.

It took days to treat the wounded and to find and count the dead. The sum of those killed in the bombings at Dar es Salaam and at Nairobi was 257; the sum of the wounded by both bombings was estimated at over 5,000. Of those killed, only twelve were Americans. The rest were mostly Africans.

FBI agents and explosives experts from ATF converged on the two embassy sites to sift through the rubble for physical evidence; but even before they arrived, a suspect was in custody. On the day of the bombing, August 7, 1998, Pakistani authorities detained a man who was attempting to enter the country at Karachi International Airport with a Kenyan passport that appeared to be counterfeit. The man was thirty-two-year-old Mohammed Saddiq Odeh (also written Mohammed Saddiq Howaida). When questioned, he is reported to have admitted being involved in planning the bombings. Pakistan turned him over to the FBI.[1]

FBI agents in Nairobi who examined local hospitals for patients who checked in on the day of the bombing found Mohammed Rashed Daoud al'Owhali, who was identified as having been a passenger in the truck that carried the explosives.

Within two weeks of the embassy bombings, Odeh and al'Owhali were in New York facing prosecution in federal court. According to government sources, after they were taken into custody, the accused bombers said that they were part of Al Qaeda and that they had both taken training at its camps in Afghanistan. The trail, according to the government, led directly to Osama bin Laden.[3] Within about a week, bin Laden, who had been virtually unknown in the United States, became the most recognized—if not the most feared—leader of international terrorism.

TARGET: OSAMA BIN LADEN

President Clinton had charged his national security team headed by national security advisor Samuel (Sandy) Berger to explore military options as retaliation for the embassy bombings. They recommended a cruise missile attack against Osama bin Laden's camps in Afghanistan. Later, a Sudanese pharmaceutical factory that the administration claimed was a potential manufacturer of nerve gas was added as a target. Thursday, August 20, 1998, was selected as the date of the attack because intelligence reports indicated that top officials of bin Laden's terrorist network would meet at the camp in Afghanistan on that date. President Clinton is reported to have stipulated that if bin Laden and his group postponed or canceled their meeting, the United States should attack other, more important targets in Afghanistan. Clearly, the target was top-ranking personnel.[4, 5]

The assault began when a flotilla of U.S. Navy ships cruising in the Arabian Sea fired a barrage of sixty Tomahawk cruise missiles at Osama bin Laden's camps in Afghanistan. Some of the missiles carried the standard 1,000-pound high-explosive warhead. Others carried clusters of 166 bombs the size of hand grenades intended to destroy small targets such as vehicles and to kill people.[4, 5]

The missiles arrived at 10:00 P.M. local time at the Zhawar Kili Al Badr base camp, training camp, and support complex, about ten miles south of Khowst. Spy satellite photographs taken after the attack revealed that a significant number of buildings at the camps were destroyed or severely damaged. The Taliban government reported that at least twenty-one people were killed.[4] Osama bin Laden escaped death, but a government source insisted that he had been in the complex of camps at the time of the missile assault.[5]

In an almost-simultaneous attack, two U.S. ships in the Red Sea fired twenty Tomahawk cruise missiles at Sudan. They arrived at the Shifa Pharmaceutical manufacturing complex in northeast Khartoum at 7:30 P.M. local time.[6] The twenty Tomahawks obliterated the pharmaceutical factory and an adjacent candy factory. One person was killed and about ten others injured. A Sudanese searching the rubble found a metal label that had apparently been part of one of the missiles. It bore the inscription, "MADE IN THE U.S.A., WITH PRIDE."[5]

At 1:55 P.M. on August 20, while he and his family were vacationing at Martha's Vineyard, Massachusetts, President Clinton made a brief statement to the press at a local elementary school. He got right to the point:

Today I ordered our Armed Forces to strike at terrorist-related facilities in Afghanistan and Sudan because of the threat they present to our national security. . . . We saw its [terrorism's] twisted mentality at work last week in the embassy bombings in Nairobi and Dar es Salem, which took the lives of innocent Americans and Africans and injured thousands more. Today we have struck back. . . .

Our target was the terrorists' base of operation and infrastructure. Our objective was to damage their capacity to strike at Americans and other innocent people.[7]

The Clinton administration had justified the attack on the pharmaceutical factory on the basis of a soil sample taken sixty feet from the Shifa property that was contaminated with a trace of a chemical used to manufacture VX nerve gas. Subsequent testing did not confirm the original finding, and the administration failed to produce any information linking Osama bin Laden to the factory. Lacking evidence to the contrary, the Shifa factory appears to have been nothing more than what Sudan claimed it to be, a pharmaceutical manufacturing plant, and its destruction an unjustified attack on an innocent target.[8]

Even before the Tomahawks took off for their targets in Afghanistan, the U.S. government had put together its justification of the attacks as both moral and legal. The decision makers in Washington claimed to have "credible evidence" that Islamic terrorists had plans to attack embassies in Albania, Eritrea, Malaysia, Uganda, and/or Yemen. Therefore, an attack on the terrorists' base would, as President Clinton asserted, "damage their capacity to strike at Americans and other innocent people."[7]

More problematic was the government's claim that the attack on bin Laden's base in Afghanistan was aimed at facilities rather than people. Should the claim lose the little credibility it had, the administration was prepared to argue that an attack intended to kill Osama bin Laden and his lieutenants could not be construed as an assassination attempt. Their camps in Afghanistan were legitimate military targets.[5] For legal support of this view, the administration pulled out and dusted off a memo prepared by the office of the army judge advocate general nine years earlier.[9] It stated in part, "The clandestine, low visibility, or overt use of force against legitimate [human] targets in the time of war, or against similar targets in time of peace, where such individuals or groups pose an immediate threat...does not constitute assassination."[10]

While members of the administration denied that the cruise missile attack on the camps in Afghanistan were an attempt to kill bin Laden, Defense Secretary William S. Cohen told a different story when visiting American troops stationed at Eskan Village, thousands of miles from home in the desert of Saudi Arabia. Cohen stated explicitly that Osama bin Laden, along with Islamic militant colleagues, had been a target of the attack. He said, "When we saw Osama bin Laden carry out that bombing attack [in Africa], we sent a very strong message by going after his colleagues, and himself, hopefully, in Afghanistan. We weren't quite successful...to hit as many [terrorists] as we wanted, but we sent a message."[10]

The rule of law took notice of Osama bin Laden on November 4, 1998, when a federal grand jury in the Southern District of New York publicly issued a 238-count indictment against bin Laden and a similar indictment against Muhammad Atef, whom the indictment described as bin Laden's chief military commander. Bin Laden was charged with murder of U.S. nationals outside the United States, conspiracy to murder U.S. nationals outside the United States, and attacks on a federal facility resulting in death, the bombing of the U.S. embassies in Dar es Salaam, Tanzania, and Nairobi, Kenya.[11] The government immediately posted rewards of $5 million each for information leading to the arrest and conviction of bin Laden and Atef.

On November 4, federal prosecutors also revealed that bin Laden had been indicted earlier—in June 1998, more than a month before the embassy bombings—by the federal district court in Manhattan on charges of leading a terrorist conspiracy to attack American installations. Prosecutors also charged in the June 1998 indictment that members of Al Qaeda, who included Muhammed Atef and two men charged in the embassy bombings, Mohammed Saddiq Odeh and Haroun Fazil, had also been in Somalia in spring 1993 to train the Somalis who fought U.S. Army forces in the Mogadishu battle of October 3 and 4, 1993. The indictment was sealed, presumably to prevent tipping off bin Laden that American agents wanted to arrest him.[11] Ironically, the U.S. government got around to announcing that it wanted to give Osama bin Laden a fair trial three-and-a-half months after it tried to execute him by a cruise missile attack.

One more alleged conspirator in the bombing of the embassies in Kenya and Tanzania came to light in June 2002, as a result of investigations into the September 11, 2001, attacks. An unnamed senior intelligence official told reporters—without divulging details—that Khalid Shaikh Mohammed had been tied to embassy bombings. He had earlier been identified as one of Ramzi Yousef's accomplices in the 1995 plot to simultaneously destroy eleven American-operated airliners over the Pacific Ocean and the 1993 bombing of the World Trade Center. The government source said that Mohammed was also suspected of being the "mastermind" behind the September 11, 2001, terrorist attacks. A senior official in the Bush administration quipped, "He is the Forrest Gump [the fictional character in the book and movie of the same name who appeared at key events in American history] of Al Qaeda. He has more presence in some of their plots than we had previously known."[12]

Osama bin Laden stayed out of sight after the United States' cruise missile attack and while his enemy went through the motions of indicting him and offering a reward for his arrest. He moved into public view again late in 1998 when he offered interviews to *Time* and *Newsweek* magazines.[13, 14] The fact that the U.S. government had tried to kill him four months earlier gave bin Laden much more prestige than he possessed when he was just another Arab terrorist, and the magazines were apparently delighted to send reporters to his camp in Afghanistan. Although he repeated his anti-American diatribe, he had nothing new to say in his interviews; but the American people could be justified in thinking that he was a very scary man.

Then in February 1999, bin Laden disappeared into the hills of Afghanistan. The Taliban reported to the world, "Our guest has gone missing. We did not order him to leave; we do not know where he has gone."[15]

The Tomahawk cruise-missile attacks against bin Laden's camp in Afghanistan and on the pharmaceutical plant in Sudan turned out to be public relations disasters for the Clinton administration, both domestically and globally. Although the navy kept submarines loaded with cruise missiles within range of Afghanistan just in case an opportunity to strike at bin Laden presented itself, the government turned to other approaches to combat terrorism. The United States increased its efforts with friendly governments to arrest members of terrorist cells, and at the time, this appeared to be a productive approach.[16]

The United States also began covert operations to either capture or kill Osama bin Laden. Soon after the terrorist attacks of September 11, 2001, former president Bill Clinton admitted at a news conference, "I authorized the arrest, and, if necessary, the killing of Osama bin Laden, and we actually made contact with a group in Afghanistan to do it and they were unsuccessful." Clinton also noted that special forces had been trained for an operation against bin Laden in Afghanistan, but they did not go into action because they lacked the necessary intelligence about bin Laden's whereabouts.[17]

Although Clinton mentioned "special forces," it now appears that the CIA led the secret effort against bin Laden. It sent officers to northern Afghanistan to enlist the support of Ahmed Shah Massoud, military leader of the Northern Alliance, which opposed the Taliban, bin Laden's ally. The CIA offered Massoud large sums of money if his group could help eliminate bin Laden. How much effort Massoud and the Northern Alliance put into finding the terrorist leader is not known. Although the Northern Alliance did not launch an attack against bin Laden, another Afghan group did. That group reported to the CIA that it had attacked a convoy in which it believed bin Laden was traveling, but it did not find him. The CIA said it had neither approved nor planned that assault.[18]

The Clinton administration also solicited the aid of Pakistani prime minister Nawaz Sharif. It offered to lift sanctions on Pakistan and give the country economic aid if it would cross the Pakistan-Afghanistan border in pursuit of bin Laden. Sharif accepted the offer, and the CIA equipped and began training sixty commandos of the Pakistani intelligence agency for the mission. The operation was cut short when, in October 1999, Prime Minister Sharif was overthrown in a military coup.[19]

It has also been reported that the U.S. military was developing a relationship with the military of Uzbekistan to give arms and training in exchange for a unit to hunt bin Laden. That unit never began its mission.[16]

The core feature of the United States' covert program to defuse or destroy the threat of terrorism by Al Qaeda was to eliminate its leader. It would not pursue bin Laden with its own agents or special forces, but it offered the contract to Afghanistan's Northern Alliance, Pakistan, and Uzbekistan. Perhaps no one should be surprised that it failed to achieve that goal.

EGYPT AIR FLIGHT 990

Egypt Air flight 990 started in Los Angeles with a stop in New York to refuel, board passengers, and take on a new crew. The Boeing 767 lifted off from the runway at Kennedy Airport at 1:20 A.M. on October 31, 1999, carrying 217 passengers and crew. Twenty-four minutes later, it leveled off at an altitude of 30,000 feet, flying east toward Cairo, the destination it should have reached in about eleven hours. The flight lasted thirty-one minutes, and much of what is known about what happened aboard the aircraft was learned from the cockpit voice recorder and the flight data recorder.[20]

On long commercial flights, a second flight crew is required to be on board to relieve those at the control a few hours into flight. The relief copilot on flight 990 was a friendly, heavy-set man named Gamil al-Batouti. Batouti was said to be a family man, a practicing Muslim, but not a fanatic. He was known to be a moderate drinker. He was also just three months shy of sixty and mandatory retirement.

Barely twenty minutes after takeoff, Batouti entered the cockpit and talked the copilot into giving up his seat. Twenty-eight minutes into the flight, the pilot left the cockpit to use the toilet. He left Batouti to fly the airplane, which, at that stage of the flight, consisted of letting the autopilot do all the work.

Twenty-eight-and-a-half minutes into the flight, Batouti was heard to say softly on the cockpit voice recording, "Tawakkalt ala Allah," which translates into English as "I rely on God."

The autopilot was disengaged. Four seconds later, Batouti was again heard to say, "I rely on God." The flight data recorder showed that the aircraft's two jet engines were moved back to medium idle, and the airplane's elevators were shifted to a down position. The airplane went into a steep dive. Batouti, in a calm voice, repeated, "I rely on God," seven times.

Sixteen seconds after the airliner began its dive, the captain returned to the cabin and demanded to know what was happening. Batouti answered, "I rely on God."

The captain apparently began struggling with the controls at the pilot's seat and against the input Batouti gave to them from the copilot's seat. Thirty seconds into the dive, the aircraft had plunged from 33,000 feet to 20,000 feet, and it reached the speed of sound.

Batouti shut off the flow of fuel to the engines. As the engines died, the aircraft lost electrical power. The voice and data recorders stopped acquiring data when the plane reached 16,416 feet. The airliner with all on board was falling in the dark.

Investigators reconstructed the rest of the flight from radar data. At about 16,000 feet, flight 990 began to climb steeply. It reached an altitude of 24,000 feet, banked to the southeast, and began breaking up. Two-and-a-half minutes after beginning its dive, Egypt Air flight 990 crashed into the Atlantic Ocean about sixty miles south of Nantucket Island, killing all on board. Of the 217 people who died, 100 were Americans, 89 were Egyptians, 22 were Canadians, and the remainder were other nationalities.[20]

The Egyptian government asked the United States to conduct the salvage operation and do the necessary investigation. As with investigations of all aircraft accidents conducted by the United States, the job was the responsibility of the National Transportation Safety Board (NTSB). The NTSB investigation found no evidence that the crash of EgyptAir flight 990 was caused by bad weather, mechanical failure, or a bomb. That left the evidence of the flight recorders. In May 2001, the NTSB completed a draft report on its investigation, which concluded that Gamil al-Batouti, the relief copilot, gave the airplane "control inputs" that caused it to crash. The NTSB avoided language that implied that Batoui had committed suicide or mass murder. Nevertheless, Egyptian authorities, who apparently hoped for a less socially and politically inflammatory conclusion, demanded that the American investigators continue to look for a mechanical problem that caused the crash.[21]

Within weeks of the disaster, long before the NTSB produced its draft report that suggested that Batouti was responsible for the crash of flight 990, the FBI had reached that conclusion and asked the question, why? The two most likely explanations were that Batouti was suicidal and committed an act of self-destruction or that he was committing an act of terrorism.[22]

There are few precedents for a pilot intentionally crashing a commercial airliner. In the twenty years preceding the crash of flight 990, there were only three cases, all involving foreign carriers, in which suicide was considered the cause of a crash.[22] Examples of terrorists hijacking an aircraft with the intention of crashing it are about as rare. Three known examples ended in failure. In February 1974, a man attempted to hijack an airliner with the intention of crashing it into the White House. He was shot by a policeman and committed suicide (see chapter 1).[23] In April 1994, a disgruntled flight engineer aboard a Federal Express transport attacked the three-man crew with hammers and a spear gun. He intended to crash the aircraft into the company's Memphis hub. Fortunately for all involved, the injured crew members managed to subdue their assailant and land the aircraft.[24] On Christmas Eve 1994, four Islamic militants hijacked an Air France airliner with the intention of blowing it up over Paris. During a stop in Marseilles, French commandos stormed the plane and killed the hijackers.[25] Other reports of this incident say that the hijackers intended to crash the airliner into the Eiffel Tower.[26]

The FBI and to a lesser extent the NTSB considered the possibility that Batouti was depressed and suicidal, and they began collecting information on Batouti's state of mind. They found sources who claimed that Batouti was a sexual exhibitionist and an occasional stalker of women while in America. Another source claimed that before leaving New York, Batouti had had an argument about his behavior with the chief pilot of flight 990. Much of this evidence—if not all of it—appeared to be hearsay and speculation by sources less credible than those used by American tabloids. Batouti's family and colleagues stepped forward to attest to the man's character and give an opposing opinion.

The FBI considered the possibility that Batouti had committed an act of terrorism, but it found no evidence that he was associated with any terrorist group. The Egyptian government, which was more likely to have access to information linking one of its nationals to terrorists, gave no relevant information on the subject.[20]

A few days after the crash, a U.S. Defense Department spokesman told reporters that thirty-three Egyptian military officers, traveling in five separate groups, were on Egypt Air flight 990.[27] One source in Cairo reported that the dead included four Egyptian Air Force officers: two brigadier generals, a colonel, and a major. The source also said that the Egyptian Army lost nine senior officers: two major generals, one brigadier general, four colonels, and two lieutenant-colonels. Just days after the crash, the FBI discounted the possibilities of sabotage or terrorism, saying that they had no information suggesting that the Egyptian officers were targets of an attack.[28] Egypt has been silent about the significance of the loss of these men to its military forces.

The NTSB issued its final report on the crash of Egypt Air flight 990 in March 2002, more than two years after the disaster. It found that the aircraft crashed as a result of deliberate actions taken by copilot Gamil al-Batouti. It did not delve into why he might have wanted to crash the aircraft. Egyptian authorities, who had done little to support the investigation, held that the airplane crashed because of a mechanical malfunction of the control surfaces on the tail. The NTSB stated clearly that there was no evidence of a system malfunction.[29]

We may never know if Gamil al-Batouti was despondent about a personal problem or if he consciously committed an act of terrorism. But within weeks after his act, the news media had carried the story around the world that one man who was willing to die had destroyed an airliner and killed himself and 216 others, and that he had struck a significant blow—intended or not—at the Egyptian military. Most people were no doubt appalled, but some may have been inspired. This much is known. Less than a year after the crash of Egypt Air flight 990, Osama bin Laden's disciples were in the United States taking flight training and spending time in a Boeing 727 simulator.[30]

THE MILLENNIUM PLOTS

America was watching the calendar as if it was an odometer ready to tick over from 1999 to 2000. Its people were optimistic about what the new millennium had in store for them, but Osama bin Laden and his terrorist followers planned to deliver America a surprise.

Night had fallen on December 14, 1999, when the last ferry from Victoria, on Vancouver Island in Canada, slipped through the fog and docked at Port Angeles, on Washington's Olympic Peninsula. Thirty-five cars

drove off and were quickly processed through the customs and immigration checkpoint. The thirty-sixth car was a steel-blue Chrysler sedan with
only the driver inside. When he presented his identification to custom
inspector Diana Dean at the checkpoint, she noticed that the driver's
hands were shaking and he was sweating. She asked him to step out of the
car and open the trunk. The driver stepped out of the car and ran. Two
customs agents chased after him and caught him six blocks later.

When the customs officers opened the trunk of the car, they found ten
large bags containing a white powder and two jars of a syrupy liquid rest-
ing in a bed of sawdust. They thought the obvious: drugs. They were
wrong. The contraband turned out to be 130 pounds of explosives, enough
to make one and possibly more big bombs; that information helped
explain the four timing devices that they also found in the trunk.

The FBI took control of the case and quickly learned that the driver of
the explosives-laden car was Ahmed Ressam, a thirty-three-year-old Algerian who had lived in Montreal for five years, where he worked as a gro-
cer and supplemented his income with the proceeds of petty thefts. The
more important questions were unanswered: What was the intended target or targets of the explosives? And were more terrorists in other vehicles
loaded with explosives in transit to American targets?

By the morning after Ressam's arrest, the FBI knew that he had a reser-
vation at the Best Western Inn in Seattle, near the Space Needle. That dis-
covery and the suspicion that the Seattle landmark was a potential target
caused the city to cancel its millennium New Year's celebration.

The twentieth century passed and the new millennium arrived, and
everybody breathed easier with the knowledge that the United States had
not been attacked on its own soil by terrorists. Following a trail of evidence that Ressam had left behind, the FBI arrested several other men it
accused of being Ressam's accomplices. Ressam refused to talk as his case
approached trial.[31]

Federal investigators tied Ressam to the Al Qaeda organization. They
learned that in 1998 he had traveled to Pakistan and from there to an Al
Qaeda camp in Afghanistan where he learned the trade of terrorism.
Ressam returned to Montreal in February 1999 with a manual on how to
build bombs, a small supply of bomb-making chemical, and $12,000 from
Al Qaeda for expenses.

Ressam's attitude about sharing information with federal investigators
changed after he was convicted and facing 130 years in a federal penitentiary. He told investigators, among other things, that he had intended to
bomb the Los Angeles International Airport.[32]

A large part of the story of the millennium plots—if not all of the story—
eventually emerged. The bombing of the Los Angeles airport was to be
accompanied by other attacks against American targets. On January 3,
2000, the USS *The Sullivans* made a refueling stop in the port of Aden

Yemen. Terrorists had intended to pilot a boat loaded with explosives into *The Sullivans*, but they bungled the attack. U.S. investigators learned of this failed attack only after a similar attack on the USS *Cole.* According to a suspected conspirator in the *Cole* bombing who was in Yemeni custody, the boat full of explosives had been overloaded and sank within a few feet after casting off on its course to *The Sullivans.* One of the bombers left in disgust, never to return. While the others went for help, the outboard motor on the sunken boat was stolen. The conspirators took the next ten months to buy back their stolen motor, repair the water damage, and prepare for another attack, this time on the USS *Cole.*[33]

In Jordan, authorities arrested several suspects accused of plotting to attack two Christian pilgrimage sites and the Radisson SAS Hotel in Amman, all of which were frequented by American tourists. These attacks were also planned for January 3. And in the United States, Tuesday, January 3, was the first business day after the three-day holiday weekend. One would expect the Los Angeles airport to have been crowded with the last of the vacationers returning home and business travelers going back to work.

President Clinton's top terrorism advisor on the National Security Council, Richard A. Clarke, summed up the potential for disaster that had been averted. "What if January...had started with 1,000 Americans dead at six or seven locations around the world?" he asked. "We came very close to having that happen."[34]

THE USS *COLE*

The destroyer USS *Cole* had spent two months on its way to join the Fifth Fleet in patrolling the Persian Gulf. It had come from Norfolk, Virginia, cruised through the Suez Canal and down the Red Sea, and would stop at the port of Aden to top off its fuel tanks before going on to the Persian Gulf.[35]

The fueling stop in Yemen was as much political as operational. The United States had been courting the government of Yemen for the purpose of undercutting its occasional dealings with Iraq and inspiring the country to shut down terrorist groups that operated there. Visits of U.S. Navy ships to Yemen gave the United States visibility in that country and also gave Yemen a chance to earn American dollars.[36]

The air temperature approached the mid-nineties as the USS *Cole* cruised into the harbor of Aden in the morning of October 12, 2000. The ship would tie up to a fueling station in middle of the harbor for the few hours it would take to load fuel, then be on its way. As part of safety and security precautions, the Cole's commanding officer, Commander Kirk Leopold, had ordered all below-deck hatches "closed and dogged," and he placed armed personnel on deck.

Several small boats hovered nearby, their crews helping the *Cole* tie up to buoys. One boat with two men on board approached the *Cole*, and when it reached the ship, the boat exploded. The blast tore a hole forty feet by forty feet into the port (left) side of the hull. Water flooded in, and the ship began to list, but because below-deck hatches were closed, the *Cole* did not sink. The attack killed seventeen and injured thirty-three others. It took days to recover the bodies of all those who had died.[35]

President Clinton gave a variation of his now-familiar response to terrorist attacks. He said, "If, as it now appears, this was an act of terrorism, it was a despicable and cowardly act. We will find out who was responsible and hold them accountable."[37]

The government of Yemen initially dismissed the explosion that damaged the *Cole* as an accident, and it resisted getting involved in any investigation. Under U.S. pressure, it eventually agreed that the *Cole* had been attacked, and it began rounding up suspects. Within a few weeks, Yemen had six men in custody, but it did not turn them over to the United States because extradition was not allowed by its constitution.[38]

U.S. officials gave the press general descriptions of information it had that linked those accused of attacking the *Cole* to Osama bin Laden and his organization. Telephone records showed communication between the *Cole* suspects and bin Laden's agents in East Africa before the bombings of two American embassies in 1998, which the U.S. government had blamed on bin Laden and Al Qaeda. One suspect in Yemeni custody said that he had trained at a camp in Afghanistan operated by bin Laden and that he had fought with the contingent sent to Bosnia by bin Laden in 1994. Yemeni officials identified the alleged leader and financier of the attack on the *Cole* as a Saudi-born Yemeni named Mohammed Omar Al-Harazi, a.k.a. Abdul al-Nassir.[39] U.S. and Yemeni officials concluded that its primary suspects fled to Afghanistan after the attack on the *Cole*.[40]

Seven months after the attack of the *Cole*, a videotape circulating among Islamic militants surfaced that showed bin Laden's followers taking credit for the attack. In it, masked men at a training camp were seen and heard singing a song that had the lines, "We thank God for granting us victory the day we destroyed *Cole* in the sea." Bin Laden also appeared on the tape making an oblique reference to the American ship, but he did not take credit for the attack.[41]

After the September 11, 2001, terrorist attacks on the United States, a few more shards of information emerged that suggested a link of the attack on the *Cole* to Al Qaeda and bin Laden. Two of the September 11 hijackers, Khalid Al-Midhar and Salem Alhazami, had been on an immigration "watch list" because they were suspected of being associates of bin Laden. Furthermore, a source in U.S. intelligence claimed that Al-Midhar had been caught on videotape meeting in Kuala Lumpur, Malaysia, with an unnamed suspect in the attack on the *Cole*.[42] Also, in October 2001, Pakistan turned over to the American authorities a twenty-seven-year-old Arab man named Jamil Qasim Saeed Mohammed who was wanted in the bombing of the *Cole.* Neither the United States nor Pakistan described the case against him.[43]

The information that came out of the investigation of the attack on the *USS Cole* was at best circumstantial. It was as if the investigators were saying, we know Osama bin Laden was ultimately responsible, but we can't prove it. As time moved on after the bombing of the *Cole,* the United States did nothing. Those responsible no doubt thought that they could continue to attack the United States and that as long as they were not caught red-handed, they could get away with it.

COUNTERTERRORISM PROGRAMS

For those who are impressed by numbers, President Clinton did a lot to defend the country from terrorism. The FBI devoted less than 4 percent of its resources to fighting terrorism when Clinton came into office in 1993 but 10 percent by the time he was clearing his desk. The CIA does not give out similar information, but the best estimates are that its counterterrorism center nearly tripled its budget and personnel during the same time period. According to the Office of Management and Budget, the Clinton administration spent $5.7 billion to combat terrorism in fiscal 1996, $9.7 billion in 1999, and $11.1 billion in 2001. During the last twenty-nine months of Clinton's term in office, three-quarters of the counterterrorism budget was spent on increased security at both overseas and domestic sites. That left about $2.8 billion to track down terrorists and put them out of business, which, as subsequent events demonstrated, was not enough.[44]

When Clinton's time came to leave office, neither of his would-be-successors, Vice President Al Gore nor George W. Bush, raised terrorism as a campaign issue; and it did not become a top-priority item for President George W. Bush. His Counterterrorism Security Group did not begin to develop a comprehensive strategy for dealing with Al Qaeda until March 2001, and it did not have a draft plan until September. The key feature of the Counterterrorism Security Group's plan was a $200 million CIA program to support the enemies of bin Laden's ally in Afghanistan, the Taliban. This seems to be a large commitment until one realizes that it amounted to only about 7 percent of what the government was already spending on proactive programs against terrorism. A senior member of Bush's staff told reporters that the draft plan was to be presented to President Bush on September 10, but because he was traveling that day, the presentation was postponed. The following morning, of course, the basic assumptions had changed, and the plan was irrelevant.[45]

Chapter 13

The Past and the Future

Terrorism's war on America began over four decades ago with the first airliner hijackings, but with the exception of outrageous attacks that took place at widely spaced intervals in time, its people and leaders were inclined to view these incidents as aberrations. After the disintegration of the Soviet Union, the United States was the world's only superpower, and as such, it seemed invulnerable. Foreign nations could not mount a successful attack against it, and rag-tag terrorists were less likely to do so. September 11, 2001, showed America the dangers of self-delusion and hubris.

In the twenty-twenty hindsight of that traumatic national experience, and as more than a few observers have pointed out, every part of those attacks had a historical precedent. Terrorists had hijacked airliners, some had conducted suicide attacks, the World Trade Center had been bombed, and U.S. government buildings had come under attack. The surprises of September 11 were the audacity of the attacks and that they were destructive beyond the hopes and expectations of the terrorists.

MOTIVES

There has been much talk and analysis directed at determining what motivates terrorists. Finding the answer is simple—listen to what the terrorists have said:

- In the mid-1960s, Fidel Castro said that revolutionary movements were engaged in a "struggle against imperialism, colonialism, and neocolonialism, especially against Yankee imperialism."[1]

- Che Guevara echoed the sentiment that their revolution was "a battle cry against imperialism and a call for the unity of peoples against the great enemy of the human race: the United States of North America."[2]
- Palestinian skyjacker Leila Khaled justified her actions by saying that "Israel is a colony of America and the Americans are giving the Israelis Phantom planes."[3]
- The Ayatollah Khomeini of Iran condemned "criminal U.S. imperialism," "American imperialism," and "international Zionism."[4]
- Sheikh Abdel-Rahman, who inspired terrorist attacks against targets in the New York area in the 1990s, listed among the enemies of God, "Zionism, communism and imperialism."[5]
- Osama bin Laden, in one of his *fatwa*s declaring war on the United States, takes issue with America's military presence in Saudi Arabia, its leadership in the 1991 Gulf War against Iraq, and its support of Israel.[6]

Motives commonly cited by these terrorists were opposition to American neocolonialism, opposition to Zionism and America's support of Israel, and their own religious beliefs. They were unanimous in their opposition of what they perceived as America's imperialism and neocolonialism. In the post–World War II era, after the European powers lost or divested themselves of their colonies, the United States became the Western power with the greatest international presence—if not actual colonies—and it inherited the enmity accumulated over the preceding centuries by those powers. Despite the fact that America has for decades been a net importer of goods, its export of its music, movies, and popular culture has resulted in it being accused of "cultural imperialism." America is powerful and rich and has often been overbearing when pursuing its political and commercial interests around the world. Because of its success, it has become hated by those left behind by technology, commercial development, and prosperity. Nobody should be surprised that those not sharing the wealth are throwing rocks through the windows of the mansion.[7]

The grievance cited second in frequency, especially by those who originate in the Middle East, is America's consistent support of Israel at the expense of its Arab neighbors, principally the Palestinians. America, they believed, had taken the side of Israel in the bloody feud that spanned most of the twentieth century and had religious and cultural roots that reached millennia back in time.

Religion came in a distant third in the terrorists' list of grievances, even when voiced by those claiming to be religious leaders. The oft-touted Islamic jihad, or holy war, against the infidels may have its roots in a fundamentalist reading of the Koran, but it is fertilized by a complex group of political, economic, and cultural differences between Islamic and Western societies. In addition, a lust for power and greed have often marched side by side with religion as motives for war. Osama bin Laden planned to lay the groundwork for reestablishment of the caliphate, the authority that would govern the united Islamic nations, just as the Ottoman Empire had done until the early twentieth century. Some believed he wanted to be the new caliph.[8]

THE CHANGING FORMS OF TERRORISM

Both terrorists and counterterrorists have learned from the experiences of the past four decades. In the 1960s, terrorists learned that hijacking commercial airliners was an effective way to gain attention for their causes. In the following decade, countries engaged in air commerce learned that this form of terrorism could be countered by improved security measures. Over the decades, terrorists have learned that there is a direct relationship between the number of people they kill in an incident and the attention they get. They have devised increasingly lethal tactics, and the number of people they have killed in single incidents has increased from a handful of individuals in the 1960s to hundreds in the 1980s to thousands in 2001.

The viciousness of terrorist attacks and the numbers of casualties in each attack increased when religious fanatics joined those with nationalist and political ideologies. This trend is rooted in part in differing beliefs and values. Secular fanatics and terrorists are, to some extent, concerned about social approval. They want freedom, justice, or a better life—as they perceive it—for those they represent. They want political power and, if possible, approval for their cause. The degree of social approval they can achieve decreases as the number of casualties from their operations increases. Religious zealots, on the other hand, have only one constituency: their God. The more they do to bring their God's dominion to earth, the more they will earn their God's favor. The more destruction they cause, the more of the ungodly they kill, the greater will be their virtue in the eyes of their God. They will reap their reward in the afterlife, and innocents on earth will pay for it with their blood.[9]

We now take it for granted that terrorists are organized; they communicate and act through networks such as Al Qaeda. This understanding took a long time to develop. One of the first investigations into organized international terrorism was done by journalist Claire Sterling in her book *The Terror Network*.[10] Sterling presented her thesis that not only did separate terrorist groups communicate and cooperate but their activities were supported by and directed by the Soviet Union for the benefit of the Soviet Union.[11] When the book was published, Secretary of State Alexander Haig and CIA director William Casey embraced its conclusion of Soviet sponsorship as if it had been handed down on stone tablets. Unfortunately, the CIA had been spreading disinformation that may have led Sterling to believe that the Soviet Union sponsored much of the world's terrorism. Disclosure that her key conclusion may have been based on CIA disinformation undermined some of the credibility of Sterling's book.[12, 13]

If Sterling—and Haig and Casey—went wrong, it was not in pointing to the existence of networks but in accepting the premise that the Soviet Union had run a terrorist organization in a hierarchy it controlled from the top down. As much as the Soviet leadership might have wanted to benefit from nationalists and insurgents terrorists, they gave mostly token support to the uncontrollable terrorists.[14]

Two decades later, we are more comfortable with the concept of networks and their loose, ever-changing relationships of people and organizations. In retrospect, we can see networks in the relationships of the Palestinian and Libyan terrorist groups formed in the 1970s and 1980s, as well as in their support by the Arab and Islamic states of the Middle East. In a recent incarnation, we have seen terrorists operating without significant state support in the Al Qaeda network, which assimilated lesser terrorist groups and forged a fatal alliance with the Taliban. It should not be surprising if, in the aftermath of America's "War on Terrorism," the remnants of the Taliban and Al Qaeda seek out and form new alliances in the ever-changing network of terrorism.

PERCEPTIONS AND REACTIONS

After the attacks of September 11, 2001, many Americans were asking why no one saw that it could happen. The fact is that a small minority did see that massive terrorist attacks on the United States were possible, and they saw the threats not as a theoretical possibility but as a tangible atrocity, with dead bodies and devastation littering the American landscape. After the foiled millennium plot, a few intelligence officials began to fear that terrorist cells, especially ones with ties to Al Qaeda, were operating in the United States; but their concern apparently did not saturate the system or move up the government hierarchy.[15, 16]

John O'Neill, who had been chief of the FBI's counterterrorism unit for several years during the 1990s, faced a wall of bureaucratic apathy when he tried to alert it to the threat of terrorist sleeper cells in the United States and attacks sponsored by Al Qaeda. He gave up in frustration in mid-2001 to take the job as chief of security at the World Trade Center. After he began working there on August 23, he advised friends, "We're due." O'Neill's body was found in the rubble that had once been the World Trade Center.[15]

After the September 11 attacks, it became known that FBI field agents had made uncannily accurate warnings, which FBI headquarters discounted. In summer 2001, an FBI agent in Phoenix sent a memo to FBI headquarters urging the bureau to investigate Middle Eastern men who were taking flight training. He suggested that these men might be followers of Osama bin Laden and that they might be preparing for terrorist operations. Also in 2001, when Zacarias Moussaoui was arrested in Minnesota on immigration charges, it was learned that Moussaoui had enrolled in a flight school. An agent on the scene speculated in a report that Moussaoui might have planned to pilot an aircraft into the World Trade Center. After September 11, Moussaoui was perceived to be the twentieth hijacker and tried as a conspirator in the plots. The FBI took no action on either warning from its field agents.[17]

The House of Representatives and Senate intelligence committees formed a joint panel to investigate possible intelligence failures that preceded the September 11 attacks. The panel's preliminary report revealed that in the summer of 2001, the intelligence-gathering agencies had collected dozens of pieces of information that suggested a terrorist attack on the United States was imminent, but none of them contained useful specific details. Nevertheless, the CIA found the accumulated information sufficiently significant that in July 2001, it reported to senior government officials that "based on a review of all-source reporting over the last five months, we believe that UBL [bin Laden] will launch a significant terrorist attack against the U.S. and/or Israeli interests in the coming weeks. The attack will be spectacular and designed to inflict mass casualties against U.S. facilities or interests. Attack preparations have been made. Attack will occur with little or no warning." White House staff declined to tell the House-Senate intelligence panel if President Bush had been told of this CIA warning at his daily intelligence briefing.[18]

After four decades of terrorist attacks at home and on its interests abroad, America had become complacent. It dismissed the warnings of imminent attack and forgot the experience of decades of terror. It ignored the warning of nearly a decade of attacks by Osama bin Laden's Al Qaeda organization. In retrospect, the 1993 bombing of the World Trade Center, the Bojinka plot of 1995, and the millennium plot (see chapters 9 and 12) were clear indicators of their intentions. It should have been obvious that Al Qaeda would try again, sometime, somewhere, and, if it could, in the United States. America was unprepared and paid the price. It remains to be seen if intelligence gathering and analysis and the homeland security measures that followed the September 11 attacks will be more effective than those that preceded them.

Despite being the target of terrorist attacks for more than four decades, the people of the United States were largely ignorant of the nature of international terrorism and unconcerned about terrorism's threat to itself and world peace. Although its leaders occasionally spoke of the threat of international terrorism, they failed to implement effective programs to protect the United States. Several key points that are summarized from information in the preceding chapters illustrate a history of intelligence and strategic action blunders that spanned decades:

- President Reagan did not respond to the bombings of its embassies and the marine compound in Beirut, and President Clinton did not respond to attacks against American soldiers on a peacekeeping mission in Somalia and against the USS *Cole*. These failures to take action against those responsible—granted, their identities were suspected but not known with certainty—invited more attacks. (See chapters 6, 10, and 11.)

- When the United States did respond to terrorist attacks, it often did so with personal attacks against the leaders of those believed responsible. These attempts to kill Sheikh Fadlallah of Hezbollah, Muammur Qaddafi of Libya, Saddam Hussein of Iraq, and Osama bin Laden were uniformly failures and were often accompanied by the deaths of uninvolved civilians, which the government characterized as "collateral damage." (See chapters 6, 7, 8, and 11.)

- Government antiterrorist officials have claimed that they knew about Osama bin Laden and his terrorist activities as early as 1993; however, before the attacks on American embassies in Africa in 1998, Osama bin Laden was virtually unknown in the United States. (See chapters 11 and 12.)

- Despite the first attack on the World Trade Center in 1993, the highly organized plot against the United Nations and targets in New York, and the millennium plot, most Americans and leaders in the federal government believed that the homeland was invulnerable.

- Despite more than forty years of hijacking of airliners and numerous attempts to use them as weapons, and despite nearly two decades of suicide bombings against its facilities overseas, Americans and their leaders blissfully failed to understand that hijacked airliners could be used as weapons in suicide attacks, as they were on September 11, 2001.

During the past several decades, as the United States has been the target of terrorist attacks, it has also been accused by foreign countries and groups of being a terrorist government and a supporter of terrorists. The U.S. government has fueled this point of view by its actions and those of its agents. Several examples illustrate this point:

- CIA director William Casey's outside-the-system attempt to punish Hezbollah for its attacks on U.S. facilities and personnel in Beirut killed at least ninety-two people. Residents of Beirut draped a banner across a damaged Beirut apartment building that read "Made in U.S.A."[19] (See chapter 6.)

- The downing of Iran Air flight 655 in July 1992 by missiles fired from a U.S. cruiser was followed by condemnations by Iranian officials speaking of a "barbaric massacre" and "the crimes of America."[20] (See chapter 7.)

- After the United States bombed Libya in April 1986, killing more than a hundred people, mostly civilians, Libyans demonstrated in the streets, condemning the United States. A Libyan man in a devastated neighborhood of Tripoli told an American reporter, "Now you see who is the terrorist."[21] (See chapter 7.)

- After the bombing of its embassies in Tanzania and Kenya, the United States fired twenty Tomahawk cruise missiles at a factory in Sudan that it believed was used by Osama bin Laden's followers to manufacture VX nerve gas. The target, the Shifa Pharmaceutical manufacturing complex, was destroyed; one person was killed and ten others injured. The government's "evidence" that the plant was involved in manufacturing nerve gas turned out to be incorrect. (See chapter 12.) Nevertheless, the United States destroyed the core of Sudan's indigenous pharmaceutical industry. It has yet to apologize for the act, make restitution, or rebuild the plant.

The U.S. government has called these and other tragedies errors or collateral damage, or it has failed to acknowledge its mistakes. Others have called these acts of terrorism. The difference is more than semantic. The United States adopted tactics used by those it condemned as terrorists. The bombed-out resident of Tripoli had a right to ask, "Who is the terrorist?"

THE FUTURE OF TERROR

After the attacks of September 11, 2001, it has been commonly agreed that terrorists will continue to attack the United States and that the attacks are likely to become more vicious. Terrorists are now expected to acquire and use "weapons of mass destruction" (WMD). Specifically, these are chemical, biological, radiological, and nuclear devices. Their use requires a high degree of technical sophistication, but the payoff in destruction, death, confusion, and terror may be worth the extra effort for terrorist groups. The concern about WMD is exacerbated by the fear that terrorist groups may already have or will in the future acquire them from one of the Department of State's designated state sponsors of terrorism, especially Iraq, or from the stockpiles that were built by the defunct Soviet Union.[22]

Terrorist groups have already dabbled in the production and use of WMD, and although the destructive effects have been less than their hopes and expectations, these incidents suggest what the future may hold. The Centers for Disease Control published a survey of chemical and biological weapons incidents, both domestic and international, from 1960 to 1999.[23] About 80 percent of the 415 events cataloged in the survey turned out to be hoaxes, and many more were unsuccessful. The most successful use of chemical weapons by a terrorist group were those of the religious cult Aum Shinrikyo. In June 1994, that group staged an attack in the Japanese city of Matsumoto with the nerve gas sarin. The deadly cloud killed seven people and sent five hundred others to hospitals. Aum Shinrikyo struck again in March 1995, when it released sarin into the Tokyo subway. That attack killed twelve and injured nearly thirty-eight hundred others.[24] Deadly though they were, the experiments of the Japanese cult with chemical warfare appeared amateurish compared with Iraq's attack on the Kurds living in Halabja in 1988. That assault, using several chemical agents, killed an estimated five thousand people.[25] (Also see chapter 8.)

Biological weapons have been used less frequently than chemical weapons. The Aum Shinrikyo staged several attacks with biological weapons with botulinum toxin and anthrax between 1990 and 1995. There were no reported injuries.[24] The cult's anthrax attacks apparently failed because it used a strain of bacteria that was not capable of causing disease.[26]

The first known successful use of a biological weapon by terrorists was committed in the United States in 1984 by the Rajneeshee, an Indian religious cult. The group produced cultures of the bacterium *Salmonella typhimurium*, which it used to contaminate food at restaurant salad bars in the town of The Dalles, Oregon. Its objective was to incapacitate voters at the time of a local election so that it could seize political control of the county. The salmonella attack resulted in 751 cases of food poisoning, but fortunately, there were no deaths. The plot to intentionally release salmonella became known when disenchanted cult members became informants.[23]

This attack with salmonella is significant for several reasons. It was, until then, the first use of a biological weapon by terrorists that achieved its purpose of harming people. It was relatively low tech; the biological agent could be prepared with easily obtained, inexpensive materials and equipment found in most home kitchens by people who had taken a college microbiology laboratory course. The attack affected a large number of people, showing how great an effect a committed group of terrorists can have with limited resources.

The post–September 11 attack on the United States with anthrax killed five and sickened eighteen. Tens of thousands of others who might have been exposed received prophylactic antibiotics. Several government buildings through which anthrax-contaminated mail passed were shut down for decontamination, and the down time and decontamination cost several billion dollars.[26]

There are to date no known—or significant—instances in which terrorist groups have used radiological weapons (also called "dirty bombs"), those using conventional explosives to disperse radioactive materials.

There are only two known instances in which nuclear weapons have been used against people: the attacks on Hiroshima and Nagasaki in 1945. However, the thought of the use of nuclear weapons has been terrifying enough to influence the policies and actions of states. At the height of the Cold War, political pundits described the standoff between the East and West as the result of both possessing nuclear weapons, thereby creating a "balance of terror."[27]

The world may be the target of WMD attacks by terrorists in the future, but as we should have learned on September 11, 2001, the most dangerous and reliable WMD is a man—or woman—willing to give his life for his cause. The nineteen airliner hijackers who brought down the World Trade Center and severely damaged the Pentagon were not armed with WMD, but with carton cutters that can be bought at any stationery store for fifty-nine cents each.

For all of the destruction and death that terrorists have caused over the past several decades, their failure to achieve their political aims has been stunning. Nobody should be surprised. Once the moment of shock and fear has passed, the natural reaction of the targets is to resist intimidation and to retaliate. Powerful nations like the United States have always had the ability to strike back at poorly organized and ill-equipped terrorist groups. Their major problems have been to find the terrorists and to implement a coherent policy for dealing with them.

The United States has blundered along for four decades, responding to terrorist attacks with impotent verbal assaults, inaction, or ill-conceived acts of retaliation. The latter have, unfortunately, killed more innocents than have the terrorists. America's most significant act to thwart terrorism over the decades was the institution of airliner passenger screening, which began in 1973[28] and which failed catastrophically in September 2001.

International cooperation to counterterrorism has been, until recently, sporadic and manifestly inadequate. The civilized nations of the world, working together, should put terrorists out of business without adopting their tactics. The last part will be the hardest. Humankind's history has shown that violence breeds violence, and the more it escalates, the harder it is to tell which side represents anarchy and evil and which represents civilization and justice.

Epilogue

America finally got around to declaring war on terrorism on September 14, 2001, three days after the attacks on the World Trade Center and the Pentagon. Congress passed a resolution that authorized the President "to use all necessary and appropriate force against those nations, organizations, and persons he determines planned, authorized, committed, or aided the terrorist attacks that occurred on September 11, 2001."[1] The resolution gave the president unprecedented authority to act against unnamed enemies and discretion in how to wage the war.

Within weeks, Al Qaeda's bases in Afghanistan were rubble, its organization in disarray, and its leader, Osama bin Laden, nowhere to be found. The fundamentalist Taliban regime, which had been Al Qaeda's protector, was destroyed. An indigenous government cobbled together from the leadership of often feuding local factions replaced the Taliban. American troops stayed in Afghanistan to protect and stabilize the new Afghan government.

A year and a half later, American troops with the support of a much smaller contingent of British forces and the backing of a mostly symbolic coalition of other nations invaded Iraq for the purpose of—according to United States leaders—removing the threat of Iraq's weapons of mass destruction (WMD). Within a few weeks, the major fighting was over, and American troops controlled Iraq's major cities and roads. Saddam Hussein had disappeared in the fog of war.

Although Iraq had used poison gases during the 1980s and was developing biological and nuclear weapons in that decade (see chapter 8), as of this writing, no credible evidence of WMD have been found in Iraq. It appears unlikely that Iraq had significant numbers of such weapons or that they were operational and a threat to international security. In the absence of a stable indigenous government, the United States military is digging in for a protracted occupation of Iraq.

After the September 11 attacks, the United States government also moved to protect its home front. In late 2001, President Bush signed the executive order that would create the Department of Homeland Security.[2] Congress passed the USA Patriot Act, which those in government heralded as a bold step in protecting the security of America. Civil libertarians called it an attack on constitutional rights.[3]

These overwhelming exercises of military power and government control, according to popular thought, should have made America safer and more secure, but this may not be the outcome. The list of recent terrorist activities against Americans gives cause for a sense of insecurity:

- In the fall of 2001, the United States postal system was used to deliver five letters—possibly more—contaminated with anthrax. This biological attack killed five people and sickened 18 others. The person or persons responsible for this attack, whether foreign terrorists or home grown, are unknown.[4]

- On December 22, 2001, a little over two months after the synchronized airliner hijackings and the attacks on the World Trade Center and the Pentagon, a terrorist attempted another attack on America, but failed. Richard Reid, a British citizen who claimed to be a follower of Osama bin Laden, boarded an American Airline flight from Paris to Miami. When he attempted to light the fuse connected to explosives hidden in his shoes, alert flight attendants overpowered him. Had he been successful, Reid would have killed all 197 people on board the aircraft.[5]

- On October 12, 2002, members of Jemaah Islamiya detonated a truck bomb outside a nightclub on the Indonesian island of Bali. The explosion killed nearly 200 people and injured 300 more. One of the first suspects to be arrested, a man named Amrozi, is reported to have said, "They wanted to kill as many Americans as possible. They hate Americans. They tried to find where the Americans are gathering." The greatest numbers killed in the bombing, however, were Australians. Jemaah Islamiya, which has cells in countries across Southeast Asia, is believed to receive support from Al Qaeda.[6]

- As midnight approached on May 12, 2003, terrorists attacked three sites in Riyadh, Saudi Arabia, with truck bombs. The common denominator of the targets was association with the United States. The targets were housing complexes occupied by employees of joint U.S.–Saudi ventures or by Americans and other foreigners. The attack killed at least twenty-nine people, including seven Americans and nine suicide bombers. Al Qaeda was at the top of the list of suspects.[7]

- On the home front, on May 1, 2003, a man named Iyman Faris, a naturalized American who was born in Kashmir, pleaded guilty of charges that he conspired with and provided material support to terrorists. Court papers gave evidence that he had been in contact with the now notorious Khalid Sheik Mohammed in early 2002. (Mohammed, believed to be Al Qaeda's chief of operations, was taken into U.S. custody March 1, 2003.) Faris admitted plotting the destruction of the Brooklyn Bridge and a target in Washington during a simultaneous attack.[8]

In these attacks and plots since September 11, 2001, American casualties have been relatively low, but the ambitions of the terrorists have been high. American security efforts have probably prevented many acts of terrorism, but America may also have been lucky. The wars in Afghanistan and Iraq may have upset terrorists' plans and damaged their infrastructures, but the wars have also given support to the belief of many in the Arab world and in countries with large Muslim populations that the United States is the real terrorist. Al Qaeda and other groups have been exploiting the resulting hatred to recruit new members. Younger and more fanatical terrorists are joining terrorist groups, and they are more likely than those of earlier generations to give their lives for the cause. United States intelligence officials expect terrorist attacks to continue.[9]

Terrorism's war with America is not over.

Appendix 1

Major Terrorist Attacks on the United States and Its Interests, 1958–2001[1]

Date	Incident	Party Believed Responsible
November 1, 1958	An airliner hijacked on a flight from Miami to Varadero, Cuba, crashes, killing 17 people, and leaving only 3 survivors.	Supporters of Fidel Castro.
January 27, 1975	A bomb explodes in a Wall Street, New York, bar; 4 killed and 60 injured.	Puerto Rican nationalists.
December 29, 1975	A bomb exploded in the baggage claim area of New York's LaGuardia Airport, killing 11 and injuring 70 others.	Unknown.
April 18, 1983	Suicide car-bomb attack on U.S. embassy in Beirut; 63 dead including 16 Americans; 120 injured.	Hezbollah, a.k.a. Islamic Jihad, claimed responsibility.
October 23, 1983	Suicide truck-bomb attack on U.S. Marine barracks in Beirut; 241 marines killed. In simultaneous attack, 58 French troops killed.	Hezbollah, a.k.a. Islamic Jihad, claimed responsibility.
September 20, 1984	Truck-bomb attack on U.S. embassy annex in Beirut; 24 killed, 90 injured.	Hezbollah, a.k.a. Islamic Jihad, claimed responsibility.

April 12, 1985	Bomb attack on a restaurant near a U.S. Air Force base in Torrejon, Spain; 17 people killed, 82 people injured.	PFLP-SC claimed responsibility.
April 5, 1986	Bombing of discotheque in Berlin; 2 U.S. soldiers killed, 79 servicemen injured.	U.S. held Libya responsible.
December 21, 1988	Pan Am flight 103 destroyed by a bomb over Lockerbie, Scotland; all 259 people on board killed.	U.S. and Britain held Libya responsible.
February 26, 1993	A truck bomb is exploded in an underground garage at the World Trade Center in New York; 6 people killed and 1,000 injured.	Islamic terrorists led by Ramzi Yousef.
April 19, 1995	Bombing of the Alfred P. Murrah Federal Building in Oklahoma City; 168 killed, hundreds injured.	Right-wing extremists Timothy McVeigh and Terry Nichols.
November 13, 1995	A car bomb explodes at a U.S.-run training facility for the Saudi National Guard; kills 5 Americans and 2 Indians. Four Saudis confess on Saudi national television, saying they were inspired by Osama bin Laden. They are later beheaded.	The "Islamic Movement for Change" claimed responsibility.
June 25, 1996	A fuel truck carrying a bomb explodes outside the U.S. military's Khobar Towers housing facility in Dharan, Saudi Arabia; 19 U.S. military personnel are killed, 515 are injured, 240 of them American personnel.	Several groups claimed responsibility.
July 27, 1996	A bomb planted at Centennial Olympic Park during the summer Olympic Games in Atlanta, Georgia, kills one woman, causes a man to have a fatal heart attack, and injures 111 others.	Eric Robert Rudolph has been charged with this and other bombings.
August 7, 1998	A truck bomb explodes at the U.S. embassy in Dar es Salaam, Tanzania; 9 Tanzanians killed, 1 American injured, 76 Tanzanians injured.	Osama bin Laden and Al Qaeda network.

August 7, 1998	A truck bomb explodes at the U.S. embassy in Nairobi, Kenya; 12 Americans killed, 279 Kenyans killed, 6 Americans injured, thousands of Kenyans injured.	Osama bin Laden and Al Qaeda network.
October 12, 2000	A small boat loaded with explosives and controlled by two suicide bombers explodes as it rams the destroyer USS *Cole* in the port of Aden, Yemen; 17 sailors killed, 33 injured.	Osama bin Laden and Al Qaeda network suspected.
September 11, 2001	Two hijacked airliners crash into the World Trade Center in New York; approximately 3,000 killed, thousands more injured.	Osama bin Laden and Al Qaeda network.
September 11, 2001	A hijacked airliner crashes into the Pentagon, killing 125 people in the building and 65 persons aboard the airplane.	Osama bin Laden and Al Qaeda network.
September 11, 2001	A hijacked airliner crashes in western Pennsylvania. It is believed that passengers attacked the hijackers and prevented the hijacked plane from reaching its target in the Washington, D.C., area; 44 people aboard the airplane were killed.	Osama bin Laden and Al Qaeda network.

Appendix 2

The FBI's Most-Wanted Terrorists (October 10, 2001)[1]

Terrorist Attack, Date	Wanted Terrorist	Nationality
Hijacking of TWA flight 847, June 14, 1985	Imad Fayez Mugniyah	Lebanon
	Hassan Izz-Al-Din	Lebanon
	Ali Atwa	Lebanon
Bombing of the World Trade Center, February 26, 1993	Abdul Rahman Yasin	United States
Plot to bomb airliners flying from Southeast Asia to the United States, January 1995	Khalid Shaikh Mohammed (taken into U.S. custody, May 1, 2003)	Kuwait
Bombing of Khobar Towers, Dharan, Saudi Arabia, June 25, 1996	Ahmed Ibrahim Al-Mughassil	Saudi Arabia
	Ali Saed Bin Ali El-Houri	Saudi Arabia
	Ibrahim Salih Mohammed Al-Yacoub	Saudi Arabia
	Abdelkarim Hussein Mohamed Al-Nasser	Saudi Arabia
Bombing of U.S. embassies in Kenya and Tanzania, August 7, 1998	Osama bin Laden	Saudi Arabia
	Muhammad Atef (killed in Afghanistan, November 2001)	Egypt
	Ayman Al-Zawahiri	Egypt
	Fazul Abdullah Mohammed	Comoros

Mustafa Mohamed Fadhil	Egypt
Fahid Mohammed Ally Msalam	Kenya
Ahmed Khalfan Ghailani	Tanzania
Sheikh Ahmed Salim Swedan	Kenya
Abdullah Ahmed Abdullah	Egypt
Anas Al-Liby	Libya
Saif Al-Adel	Egypt
Ahmed Mohammed Hamed Ali	Egypt
Mushin Musa Matwalli Atwah	Egypt

Appendix 3

Foreign Terrorist Organizations[1]

In May 2003, the United States Department of State released *Patterns of Global Terrorism 2002*,[1] the most recent of its annual reviews of the subject. A section within the report titled "Background Information on Designated Foreign Terrorist Organizations" presents dossiers for thirty-six terrorist groups. This Appendix is an edited version of the State Department's document, in which entries have been excerpted to give the core information for these foreign terrorist organizations.

Abu Nidal Organization (ANO) a.k.a. Fatah Revolutionary Council, Arab Revolutionary Brigades, Black September, and Revolutionary Organization of Socialist Muslims

Description: International terrorist organization led by Sabri al-Banna. Split from PLO in 1974. Made up of various functional committees, including political, military, and financial.

Activities: Has carried out terrorist attacks in twenty countries, killing or injuring almost nine hundred persons. Targets include the United States, the United Kingdom, France, Israel, moderate Palestinians, the PLO, and various Arab countries. Has not attacked Western targets since the late 1980s.

Strength: Few hundred, plus limited overseas support structure.

Location/Area of Operation: Al-Banna relocated to Iraq in December 1998, where the ANO maintains a presence. Has operated over a wide area, including the Middle East, Asia, and Europe.

External Aid: Has received considerable support, including safe haven, training, logistic assistance, and financial aid from Iraq, Libya, and Syria (until 1987).

Abu Sayyaf Group (ASG)

Description: The ASG is the most violent of the Islamic separatist groups operating in the southern Philippines. Some ASG leaders have studied or worked in the Middle East and allegedly fought in Afghanistan during the Soviet war. The group split from the Moro National Liberation Front in the early 1990s. It is composed of several semiautonomous factions.

Activities: Engages in kidnappings for ransom, bombings, assassinations, and extortion. Although from time to time it claims that its motivation is to promote an independent Islamic state in western Mindanao and the Sulu Archipelago, areas in the southern Philippines heavily populated by Muslims, the ASG now appears to use terror mainly for financial profit.

Strength: Believed to have a few hundred core fighters.

Location/Area of Operation: Operates mainly in Basilan Province, in the neighboring provinces of Sulu and Tawi-Tawi in the Sulu Archipelago. The group expanded its operations to Malaysia in 2000 when it abducted foreigners from a tourist resort.

External Aid: Largely self-financing through ransom and extortion; may receive support from Islamic extremists in the Middle East and south Asia.

Al-Aqsa Martyrs Brigade

Description: The al-Aqsa Martyrs Brigade comprises an unknown number of small cells of Fatah-affiliated activists that emerged at the outset of the current *intifada* to attack Israeli targets. It aims to drive the Israeli military and settlers from the West Bank, Gaza Strip, and Jerusalem and to establish a Palestinian state.

Activities: Al-Aqsa Martyrs Brigade has carried out shootings and suicide operations against Israeli military personnel and civilians and has killed Palestinians who it believed were collaborating with Israel.

Strength: Unknown.

Location/Area of Operation: The West Bank, inside Israel, and the Gaza Strip.

External Aid: Unknown.

Armed Islamic Group (GIA)

Description: An Islamic extremist group, the GIA aims to overthrow the secular Algerian regime and replace it with an Islamic state. The GIA began its violent activity in 1992 after Algiers voided the victory of the Islamic Salvation Front (FIS), the largest Islamic opposition party, in the first round of legislative elections in December 1991.

Activities: Frequent attacks against civilians and government workers. Between 1992 and 1998, the GIA conducted a terrorist campaign of civilian massacres, sometimes wiping out entire villages in its area of operation. The group uses assassinations and bombings, including car bombs, and is known to favor kidnapping victims and slitting their throats.

Strength: Precise numbers unknown; probably around two hundred.

Location/Area of Operation: Algeria

External Aid: Algerian expatriates provide some financial and logistic support.

'Asbat al-Ansar

Description: 'Asbat al-Ansar, the League of the Followers, is a Lebanon-based, Sunni extremist group, composed primarily of Palestinians, which is associated with Osama bin Laden. Its goals include overthrowing the Lebanese government and thwarting perceived anti-Islamic influences in the country.

Activities: 'Asbat al-Ansar carried out assassinations of Lebanese religious leaders and several bombings in the mid-1990s. It raised its operational profile in 2000 with two dramatic attacks against Lebanese and international targets. The group was involved in clashes in northern Lebanon in late December 1999 and carried out a rocket-propelled grenade attack on the Russian embassy in Beirut in January 2000.

Strength: The group commands about three hundred fighters in Lebanon.

Location/Area of Operation: The group's primary base of operations is the 'Ayn al-Hilwah Palestinian refugee camp near Sidon in southern Lebanon.

External Aid: Probably receives money through international Sunni extremist networks and bin Laden's Al Qaeda network.

Aum Supreme Truth (Aum) a.k.a. Aum Shinrikyo, Aleph

Description: A cult established in 1987 by Shoko Asahara, the Aum aimed to take over Japan and then the world. Over time, the cult began to emphasize the imminence of the end of the world and stated that the United States would initiate Armageddon by starting World War III with Japan. Aum changed its name to Aleph in January 2000 and claimed to have rejected the violent and apocalyptic teachings of its founder.

Activities: On March 20, 1995, Aum members simultaneously released the chemical nerve agent sarin on several Tokyo subway trains, killing twelve persons and injuring up to six thousand. The group was responsible for other mysterious chemical accidents in Japan in 1994. Its efforts to conduct attacks using biological agents have been unsuccessful.

Strength: Current membership is estimated at fifteen hundred to two thousand persons.

Location/Area of Operation: Principal membership is located only in Japan, but a branch with an unknown number of followers has surfaced in Russia.

External Aid: None.

Basque Fatherland and Liberty (ETA) a.k.a. Euzkadi Ta Askatasuna

Description: Founded in 1959 with the aim of establishing an independent home-land based on Marxist principles in the northern Spanish provinces and the southwestern French departments.

Activities: Primarily involved in bombings and assassinations of Spanish govern-ment officials, security and military forces, politicians, and judicial figures. ETA finances its activities through kidnappings, robberies, and extortion. The group has killed more than eight hundred persons and injured hundreds of others since it began lethal attacks in the early 1960s. In November 1999, ETA broke its "unilateral and indefinite" cease-fire and began an assassination and bombing campaign that has killed thirty-eight individuals and wounded scores more by the end of 2001.

Strength: Unknown. May have hundreds of members, plus supporters.

Location/Area of Operation: Operates primarily in the Basque autonomous regions of northern Spain and southwestern France, but also has bombed Spanish and French interests elsewhere.

External Aid: Has received training in Libya, Lebanon, and Nicaragua.

Communist Party of Philippines/New People's Army (CPP/NPA)

Description: The military wing of the Communist Party of the Philippines (CPP), the NPA is a Maoist group formed in March 1969 with the aim of over-throwing the government through protracted guerrilla warfare. The chairman of the CPP's Central Committee and the NPA's founder, Jose Maria Sison, directs all CPP and NPA activity from the Netherlands, where he lives in self-imposed exile. Although primarily a rural-based guerrilla group, the NPA has an active urban terrorist infrastructure and assassination squads. It derives most of its funding from contributions of supporters in the Philippines, Europe, and elsewhere, and from so-called revolutionary taxes extorted from local businesses.

Activities: The NPA primarily targets Philippine security forces, politicians, judges, government informers, and alleged criminals. It opposes any U.S. mili-tary presence in the Philippines, and it targets U.S. troops participating in joint military exercises as well as U.S. Embassy personnel. The NPA has publicly expressed its intent to target U.S. personnel in the Philippines.

Strength: Slowly growing; estimated at more than 10,000.

Location/Area of Operations: Operates in rural Luzon, Visayas, and parts of Min-danao. Has cells in Manila and other metropolitan centers.

External Aid: Unknown.

Al-Gama'a al-Islamiyya (Islamic Group, IG)

Description: Egypt's largest militant group, active since the late 1970s. Its spiritual leader, Sheikh Omar Abdel-Rahman, was sentenced to life in prison in January 1996 for his participation in terrorist plots against New York landmarks. Senior member signed Osama bin Laden's *fatwa* in February 1998 calling for attacks against the United States. Primary goal is to overthrow the Egyptian government and replace it with an Islamic state, but disaffected IG members may be interested in carrying out attacks against U.S. and Israeli interests.

Activities: Group conducted armed attacks against Egyptian security and other government officials, Coptic Christians, and Egyptian opponents of Islamic extremism. From 1993, al-Gama'a launched attacks on tourists in Egypt, most notably the attack in November 1997 at Luxor that killed fifty-eight foreign tourists. Also claimed responsibility for the attempt in June 1995 to assassinate Egyptian president Hosni Mubarak in Addis Ababa, Ethiopia. The Gama'a has never specifically attacked a U.S. citizen or facility but has threatened U.S. interests.

Strength: Unknown. At its peak, the IG probably commanded several thousand hard-core members and a like number of sympathizers.

Location/Area of Operation: Operates mainly in southern Egypt, with support in Cairo and Alexandria. Has a presence in the United Kingdom, Afghanistan, Yemen, and Austria.

External Aid: The Egyptian government believes that Iran, bin Laden, and Afghan militant groups support the organization.

HAMAS (Islamic Resistance Movement)

Description: Formed in late 1987 to pursue the goal of establishing an Islamic Palestinian state in place of Israel. Loosely structured, with some elements working clandestinely and others working openly through mosques and social service institutions to recruit members, raise money, organize activities, and distribute propaganda.

Activities: HAMAS activists have conducted many attacks, including large-scale suicide bombings, against Israeli civilian and military targets. Increased operational activity in 2001 during the *intifada*, claiming numerous attacks against Israeli interests. Group has not targeted U.S. interests and continues to confine its attacks to Israelis inside Israel and the territories.

Strength: Unknown number of hardcore members; tens of thousands of supporters and sympathizers.

Location/Area of Operation: Primarily the West Bank, Gaza Strip, and Israel.

External Aid: Receives funding from Palestinian expatriates, Iran, and private benefactors in Saudi Arabia and other moderate Arab states.

Harakat ul-Mujahidin (HUM) (Movement of Holy Warriors)

Description: The HUM is an Islamic militant group based in Pakistan that operates primarily in Kashmir. HUM operated terrorist training camps in eastern Afghanistan until coalition air strikes destroyed them in fall 2001.

Activities: Has conducted operations against Indian troops and civilian targets in Kashmir. The HUM is also responsible for the hijacking of an Indian airliner on December 24, 1999, which resulted in the release of Ahmad Omar Sheikh, who was arrested for the abduction and murder in January–February 2001 of U.S. journalist Daniel Pearl.

Strength: Has several thousand armed supporters located in Kashmir, Pakistan, and India's southern Kashmir and Doda regions. Supporters are mostly Pakistanis and Kashmiris.

Location/Area of Operation: Based in Pakistan, but members conduct insurgent and terrorist activities primarily in Kashmir. The HUM trained its militants in Afghanistan and Pakistan.

External Aid: Collects donations from Saudi Arabia and other Gulf and Islamic states and from Pakistanis and Kashmiris.

Hezbollah (Party of God) a.k.a. Islamic Jihad, Revolutionary Justice Organization, Organization of the Oppressed on Earth, and Islamic Jihad for the Liberation of Palestine

Description: Formed in 1982 in response to the Israeli invasion of Lebanon, this Lebanon-based radical Shi'a group takes its ideological inspiration from the Iranian revolution and the teachings of the Ayatollah Khomeini. Hezbollah formally advocates ultimate establishment of Islamic rule in Lebanon and liberating all occupied Arab lands, including Jerusalem. It has expressed as a goal the elimination of Israel. Although closely allied with and often directed by Iran, the group may have conducted operations that were not approved by Tehran.

Activities: Known or suspected to have been involved in numerous anti-U.S. terrorist attacks, including the suicide truck bombings of the U.S. embassy in Beirut (April 1983), U.S. Marine barracks in Beirut (October 1983), and the U.S. embassy annex in Beirut (September 1984). Three members of Hezbollah, 'Imad Mugniyah, Hasan Izz-Al-Din, and Ali Atwa, are on the FBI's list of twenty-two most-wanted terrorists for the hijacking in 1985 of TWA flight 847 during which a U.S. Navy diver was murdered. Elements of the group were responsible for the kidnapping and detention of U.S. and other Western hostages in Lebanon.

Strength: Several thousand supporters and a few hundred terrorist operatives.

Location/Area of Operation: Operates primarily in Lebanon, but has cells in Europe, Africa, South America, North America, and Asia.

External Aid: Receives substantial amounts of financial, training, weapons, explosives, political, diplomatic, and organizational aid from Iran, and has received support from Syria.

Islamic Movement of Uzbekistan (IMU)

Description: Coalition of Islamic militants from Uzbekistan and other central Asian states opposed to Uzbekistani president Islom Karimov's secular regime. The IMU's primary goal has been the establishment of an Islamic state in Uzbekistan. The group's propaganda has always included anti-Western and anti-Israeli rhetoric.

Activities: The IMU primarily targeted Uzbekistani interests before October 2001 and is believed to have been responsible for car bombs and kidnappings.

Strength: Militants probably number under two thousand.

Location/Area of Operation: Area of operations includes Afghanistan, Iran, Kyrgyzstan, Pakistan, Tajikistan, and Uzbekistan.

External Aid: Support from other Islamic extremist groups and patrons in the Middle East and central and south Asia.

Jaish-e-Mohammed (JEM) (Army of Mohammed)

Description: The JEM is an Islamic extremist group based in Pakistan that was formed by Masood Azhar upon his release from prison in India in early 2000. The group's aim is to unite Kashmir with Pakistan. The group was banned and its assets were frozen by the Pakistani government in January 2002.

Activities: The JEM on October 1, 2001, claimed responsibility for a suicide attack on the Jammu and Kashmir legislative assembly building in Srinagar that killed at least thirty-one persons, but it later denied the claim. The Indian government has publicly implicated it, along with Lashkar-e-Tayyiba, for the December 13, 2001, attack on the Indian Parliament that killed nine and injured eighteen.

Strength: Has several hundred armed supporters located in Kashmir, Pakistan, and in India's southern Kashmir and Doda regions.

Location/Area of Operation: Based in Pakistan, but members conduct terrorist activities primarily in Kashmir. The JEM maintained training camps in Afghanistan until fall 2001.

External Aid: Most of the JEM's cadre and material resources have been drawn from other militant groups such as Harakat ul-Mujahedin (HUM). Osama bin Laden is suspected of giving funding to the JEM.

Jemaah Islamiya (JI)

Description: Jemaah Islamiya is a Southeast Asian terrorist network with links to Al Qaeda. The network plotted in secrecy through the late 1990s, following the stated goal of creating an idealized Islamic state comprising Indonesia, Malaysia, Singapore, the southern Philippines, and southern Thailand.

Activities: The JI was responsible for the Bali bombings on 12 October 2002, which killed nearly 200 and wounded 300 others. In December 2001, Singapore authorities uncovered a JI plot to attack the U.S. and Israeli Embassies and British and Australian diplomatic buildings in Singapore. Recent investigations also linked the JI to December 2000 bombings where dozens of bombs were detonated in Indonesia and the Philippines.

Strength: Singaporean officials have estimated total JI membership to be approximately 5,000. The number of operationally oriented JI members probably is several hundred.

Location/Area of Operation: The JI is believed to have cells spanning Indonesia, Malaysia, Singapore, the Philippines, and southern Thailand and may have some presence in neighboring countries.

External Aid: In addition to raising its own funds, the JI receives money and logistic assistance from Middle Eastern and South Asian contacts, NGOs, and other groups, including Al Qaeda.

Al-Jihad a.k.a. Egyptian Islamic Jihad, Jihad Group, Islamic Jihad

Description: Egyptian Islamic extremist group active since the late 1970s. Merged with bin Laden's Al Qaeda organization in June 2001, but may retain some capability to conduct independent operations. Primary goals are to overthrow the Egyptian government and replace it with an Islamic state and attack U.S. and Israeli interests in Egypt and abroad.

Activities: Armed attacks against high-level Egyptian government personnel, including cabinet ministers, and car bombings against official U.S. and Egyptian facilities. The original Jihad was responsible for the assassination in 1981 of Egyptian president Anwar Sadat. Has not conducted an attack inside Egypt since 1993. Responsible for bombing of Egyptian embassy in Islamabad in 1995. Its planned 1998 attack against the U.S. embassy in Albania was thwarted.

Strength: Unknown, but probably several hundred hardcore members.

Location/Area of Operation: Operates in the Cairo area, but most of its network is outside Egypt, including Yemen, Afghanistan, Pakistan, Lebanon, and the United Kingdom.

External Aid: Unknown. The Egyptian government claims that Iran supports the Jihad. Its merger with Al Qaeda also boosts bin Laden's support for the group.

Kahane Chai (Kach)

Description: Kach was founded by radical Israeli-American rabbi Meir Kahane, and its offshoot Kahane Chai ("Kahane Lives") was founded by Kahane's son Binyamin following his father's assassination. Kach's goal is to restore the biblical state of Israel. Both were declared to be terrorist organizations in March

1994 by the Israeli cabinet following the groups' statements in support of Dr. Baruch Goldstein's attack on the al-Ibrahimi Mosque and their verbal attacks on the Israeli government. Palestinian gunmen killed Binyamin Kahane and his wife in a drive-by shooting in December 2000 in the West Bank.

Activities: Organize protests against the Israeli government. Harass and threaten Palestinians in Hebron and the West Bank. Have threatened to attack Arabs, Palestinians, and Israeli government officials.

Strength: Unknown.

Location/Area of Operation: Israel and West Bank settlements.

External Aid: Receives support from sympathizers in the United States and Europe.

Kurdistan Workers' Party (PKK, KADAK)

Description: Founded in 1974 as a Marxist-Leninist insurgent group primarily composed of Turkish Kurds. The group's goal has been to establish an independent Kurdish state in southeastern Turkey, where the population is predominantly Kurdish. In the early 1990s, the PKK moved beyond rural-based insurgent activities to include urban terrorism.

Activities: Primary targets have been Turkish government security forces in Turkey. Conducted attacks on Turkish diplomatic and commercial facilities in dozens of western European cities in 1993 and again in spring 1995. In an attempt to damage Turkey's tourist industry, the PKK bombed tourist sites and hotels and kidnapped foreign tourists in the early to mid-1990s.

Strength: Approximately four to five thousand, most of whom currently are located in northern Iraq.

Location/Area of Operation: Operates in Turkey, Europe, and the Middle East.

External Aid: Has received safe haven and modest aid from Syria, Iraq, and Iran. In September 2000, Damascus reached an antiterror agreement with Ankara, pledging not to support the PKK.

Lashkar-e-Tayyiba (LT) (Army of the Righteous)

Description: The LT is the armed wing of the Pakistan-based religious organization Markaz-ud-Dawa-wal-Irshad (MDI), a Sunni anti-U.S. missionary organization formed in 1989. The LT is led by Abdul Wahid Kashmiri and is one of the three largest and best-trained groups fighting in Kashmir against India; it is not connected to a political party.

Activities: The LT has conducted a number of operations against Indian troops and civilian targets in Kashmir since 1993. It claimed responsibility for numerous attacks in 2001, including a January attack on Srinagar airport that killed five Indians along with six militants; an attack on a police station in Srinagar that killed at least eight officers and wounded several others; and an attack in

April against Indian border security forces that left at least four dead. The Indian government publicly implicated the LT along with JEM for the December 13, 2001, attack on the Indian parliament building.

Strength: Has several hundred members in Azad Kashmir, Pakistan, and in India's southern Kashmir and Doda regions. Almost all LT cadres are non-Kashmiris, mostly Pakistanis from madrassas across the country and Afghan veterans of the Afghan wars.

Location/Area of Operation: Based in Muridke (near Lahore) and Muzaffarabad. It trains its militants in camps across Pakistan-administered Kashmir and had trained in Afghanistan until fall 2001.

External Aid: Collects donations from the Pakistani community in the Persian Gulf and United Kingdom, Islamic nongovernment organizations, and Pakistani and Kashmiri businessmen.

Lashkar I Jhangvi (LJ) (Army of Jhangvi)

Description: Lashkar I Jhangvi (LJ) is the militant offshoot of the Sunni sectarian group Sipah-i-Sahaba Pakistan (SSP). The group focuses primarily on anti-Shia attacks and was banned by Pakistani President Musharraf in August 2001 as part of an effort to rein in sectarian violence. Many of its members then sought refuge with the Taliban in Afghanistan, with whom they had existing ties.

Activities: LJ specializes in armed attacks and bombings. The group attempted to assassinate former Prime Minister Nawaz Sharif and his brother Shabaz Sharif, Chief Minister of Punjab Province, in January 1999. Pakistani authorities have publicly linked LJ members to the kidnap and murder of U.S. journalist Daniel Pearl in early 2002. Police suspected LJ members were involved in two suicide car bombings in Karachi in 2002, one against a French shuttle bus in May and another against the U.S. Consulate in June. Press reports have linked LJ to attacks on Christian targets in Pakistan, including a grenade assault on the Protestant International Church in Islamabad in March 2002 that killed two U.S. citizens.

Strength: Probably fewer than 100.

Location/Area of Operation: LJ is active primarily in Punjab and Karachi. Some members travel between Pakistan and Afghanistan.

External Aid: Unknown.

Liberation Tigers of Tamil Eelam (LTTE)

Description: Founded in 1976, the LTTE is the most powerful Tamil group in Sri Lanka and uses overt and illegal methods to raise funds, acquire weapons, and publicize its cause of establishing an independent Tamil state. The LTTE began its armed conflict with the Sri Lankan government in 1983 and relies on a guerrilla strategy that includes the use of terrorist tactics.

Activities: The LTTE targets not only key personnel in the countryside but also senior Sri Lankan political and military leaders. It is notorious for its cadre of suicide bombers, the Black Tigers. Political assassinations and bombings are commonplace.

Strength: Exact strength is unknown, but the LTTE is estimated to have eight to ten thousand armed combatants in Sri Lanka, with a core of trained fighters of approximately three to six thousand.

Location/Area of Operations: The Tigers control most of the northern and eastern coastal areas of Sri Lanka but have conducted operations throughout the island.

External Aid: The LTTE exploits large Tamil communities in North America, Europe, and Asia to obtain funds and supplies for its fighters in Sri Lanka.

Mujahedin-e Khalq Organization (MKO or MEK) a.k.a. The National Liberation Army of Iran (NLA, the militant wing of the MKO), the People's Mujahideen of Iran (PMOI), National Council of Resistance (NCR), Muslim Iranian Student's Society (front organization used to garner financial support)

Description: The MKO philosophy mixes Marxism and Islam. Formed in the 1960s, the organization was expelled from Iran after the Islamic Revolution in 1979. Prior to the 2003 war, its primary support came from the Iraqi regime of Saddam Hussein. The MKO advocates a secular Iranian regime.

Activities: The MKO's worldwide campaign against the Iranian government stresses propaganda and occasionally uses terrorist violence. It supported the takeover in 1979 of the U.S. embassy in Tehran. In 1981, the MKO planted bombs in the head office of the Islamic Republic Party and the premier's office, killing some seventy high-ranking Iranian officials. In 1991, it assisted the government of Iraq in suppressing the Shia and Kurdish uprisings in northern and southern Iraq. In April 1992, it conducted attacks on Iranian embassies in thirteen different countries, demonstrating the group's ability to mount large-scale operations overseas. In recent years, the MKO has targeted key Iranian military and law enforcement units. MKO insurgent activities in Iran constitute the biggest security concern of the Iranian leadership.

Strength: Several thousand fighters on bases scattered throughout Iraq. Most fighters are organized in the MKO's National Liberation Army (NLA).

Location/Area of Operation: In the 1980s, the MKO's leaders were forced by Iranian security forces to flee to France. Since resettling in Iraq in 1987, the group has conducted internal security operations in support of the government of Iraq.

External Aid: Beyond support from Iraq, the MKO uses front organizations to solicit contributions from expatriate Iranian communities.

National Liberation Army (ELN)—Colombia

Description: Marxist insurgent group formed in 1965 by urban intellectuals inspired by Fidel Castro and Che Guevara.

Activities: Kidnapping, hijacking, bombing, extortion, and guerrilla war. Annually conducts hundreds of kidnappings for ransom, often targeting foreign employees of large corporations, especially in the petroleum industry. Frequently assaults energy infrastructure and has inflicted major damage on pipelines and the electric distribution network. Peace talks between Bogotá and the ELN, started in 1999, continued sporadically through 2001 until Bogota broke them off in August, but resumed in Havana, Cuba, by year's end.

Strength: Three to five thousand armed combatants and an unknown number of active supporters.

Location/Area of Operation: Mostly in rural and mountainous areas of north, northeast, and southwest Colombia and Venezuela border regions.

External Aid: Cuba provides some medical care and political consultation.

The Palestine Islamic Jihad (PIJ)

Description: Originated among militant Palestinians in the Gaza Strip during the 1970s. Committed to the creation of an Islamic Palestinian state and the destruction of Israel through holy war. Also opposes moderate Arab governments that it believes have been tainted by Western secularism.

Activities: PIJ activists have conducted many attacks, including large-scale suicide bombings against Israeli civilian and military targets. The group increased its operational activity in 2001 during the *intifada*. The group has not targeted U.S. interests.

Strength: Unknown.

Location/Area of Operation: Primarily Israel, the West Bank, and Gaza Strip, and other parts of the Middle East, including Lebanon and Syria, where the leadership is based.

External Aid: Receives financial assistance from Iran and limited logistic support from Syria.

Palestine Liberation Front (PLF)

Description: Broke away from the PFLP-GC in mid-1970s. Later split again into pro-PLO, pro-Syrian, and pro-Libyan factions. Pro-PLO faction led by Muhammad Abbas (Abu Abbas), who became a member of PLO Executive Committee in 1984 but left it in 1991.

Activities: The Abu Abbas–led faction is known for aerial attacks against Israel. Abbas's group also was responsible for the attack in 1985 on the cruise ship Achille Lauro and the murder of U.S. citizen Leon Klinghoffer.

Strength: Unknown.

Location/Area of Operation: PLO faction was based in Tunisia until the Achille Lauro attack. Prior to the 2003 war in Iraq, it was based in that country.

External Aid: Receives support mainly from Iraq. Has received support from Libya in the past.

Popular Front for the Liberation of Palestine (PFLP)

Description: Marxist-Leninist group founded in 1967 by George Habbash as a member of the PLO. Opposed the Declaration of Principles signed in 1993 and suspended its participation in the PLO. Took part in meetings with Fatah and PLO representatives in 1999 to discuss national unity and the reinvigoration of the PLO, but it continues to oppose negotiations with Israel.

Activities: The PFLP committed numerous international terrorist attacks during the 1970s. Since 1978, it has conducted attacks against Israeli or moderate Arab targets. Stepped up operational activity in 2001, highlighted by the shooting death of Israel's tourism minister in October in retaliation for Israel's killing of a PFLP leader in August.

Strength: Approximately eight hundred.

Location/Area of Operation: Syria, Lebanon, Israel, West Bank, and Gaza.

External Aid: Receives safe haven and some logistical assistance from Syria.

Popular Front for the Liberation of Palestine–General Command (PFLP-GC)

Description: Split from the PFLP in 1968, claiming it wanted to focus more on fighting and less on politics. Opposed to Arafat's PLO. Led by Ahmad Jabril, a former captain in the Syrian Army. Closely tied to both Syria and Iran.

Activities: Carried out dozens of attacks in Europe and the Middle East during 1970s and 1980s. Known for cross-border terrorist attacks into Israel using unusual means, such as hot-air balloons and motorized hang gliders. Primary focus now on guerrilla operations in southern Lebanon, small-scale attacks in Israel, West Bank, and Gaza.

Strength: Several hundred.

Location/Area of Operation: Headquartered in Damascus with bases in Lebanon.

External Aid: Receives support from Syria and financial support from Iran.

Al Qaeda (The Base)

Description: Established by Osama bin Laden in the late 1980s to bring together Arabs who fought in Afghanistan against the Soviet Union. Helped finance, recruit, transport, and train Sunni Islamic extremists for the Afghan resistance. Current goal is to establish a pan-Islamic caliphate throughout the world by working with allied groups to overthrow regimes it deems "non-Islamic" and expelling Westerners and non-Muslims from Muslim countries. Issued statement under banner of "The World Islamic Front for Jihad Against the Jews and Crusaders" in February 1998, saying it was the duty of all Muslims to kill U.S. citizens—civilian or military—and their allies everywhere. Merged with Egyptian Islamic Jihad (Al-Jihad) in June 2001.

Activities: On September 11, 2001, nineteen Al Qaeda suicide attackers hijacked and crashed four U.S. commercial jets, two into the World Trade Center in New York City, one into the Pentagon near Washington, D.C., and a fourth into a field in Shanksville, Pennsylvania, leaving about three thousand individuals dead or missing. Directed the October 12, 2000, attack on the *USS Cole* in the port of Aden, Yemen, killing seventeen U.S. Navy members and injuring another thirty-nine. Conducted the bombings in August 1998 of the U.S. embassies in Nairobi, Kenya, and Dar es Salaam, Tanzania, that killed at least three hundred individuals and injured more than five thousand others. Claims to have shot down U.S. helicopters and killed U.S. servicemen in Somalia in 1993 and to have conducted three bombings that targeted U.S. troops in Aden, Yemen, in December 1992. Al Qaeda is linked to the following plans that were not carried out: to assassinate Pope John Paul II during his visit to Manila in late 1994, to kill President Clinton during a visit to the Philippines in early 1995, the midair bombing of a dozen U.S. trans-Pacific flights in 1995, and to set off a bomb at Los Angeles International Airport in 1999. Also plotted to carry out terrorist operations against U.S. and Israeli tourists visiting Jordan for millennial celebrations in late 1999.

Strength: May have several thousand members and associates. Also serves as a focal point or umbrella organization for a worldwide network that includes many Sunni Islamic extremist groups.

Location/Area of Operation: Al Qaeda has cells worldwide and is reinforced by its ties to Sunni extremist networks. Coalition attacks on Afghanistan since October 2001 have led to the capture, death, or dispersal of Al Qaeda operatives. Some Al Qaeda members at large probably will attempt to carry out future attacks against U.S. interests.

External Aid: Osama bin Laden, member of a billionaire family, is said to have inherited tens of millions of dollars that he uses to help finance the group. Al Qaeda also maintains moneymaking front businesses, solicits donations from like-minded supporters, and illicitly siphons funds from donations to Muslim charitable organizations.

Real IRA (RIRA) a.k.a. True IRA

Description: Formed in early 1998 as a clandestine armed wing of the 32-County Sovereignty Movement, a "political pressure group" dedicated to removing British forces from Northern Ireland and unifying Ireland. The 32-County Sovereignty Movement opposed Sinn Fein's adoption in September 1997 of the Mitchell principles of democracy and nonviolence. Michael "Mickey" McKevitt, who left the IRA to protest its cease-fire, leads the group; Bernadette Sands-McKevitt, his wife, is a founder-member of the 32-County Sovereignty Movement, the political wing of the RIRA.

Activities: Bombings, assassinations, and robberies. Targets include British military and police in Northern Ireland and Northern Ireland Protestant communities. RIRA is believed to be responsible for the car-bomb attack in Omagh, Northern Ireland, on August 15, 1998, that killed 29 and injured 220 persons. In 2000 and 2001, conducted attacks in Northern Ireland and on the U.K. mainland against targets such as MI6 headquarters and the BBC.

Strength: One hundred to two hundred activists. British and Irish authorities arrested at least forty members in the spring and summer of 2001, including leader McKevitt, who is in prison in the Irish Republic awaiting trial for being a member of a terrorist organization and directing terrorist attacks.

Location/Area of Operation: Northern Ireland, Irish Republic, Great Britain.

External Aid: Suspected of receiving funds from sympathizers in the United States.

Revolutionary Armed Forces of Colombia (FARC)

Description: Established in 1964 as the military wing of the Colombian Communist Party, the FARC is Colombia's oldest, largest, most capable, and best-equipped Marxist insurgency. In 2001, the group continued a slow-moving peace negotiation process with the Pastrana administration that has gained the group several concessions, including a demilitarized zone used as a venue for negotiations.

Activities: Bombings, murder, kidnapping, extortion, and hijacking, as well as guerrilla and conventional military action against Colombian political, military, and economic targets. Foreign citizens often are targets of FARC kidnappings for ransom. Has well-documented ties to narcotics traffickers, principally through the provision of armed protection.

Strength: Approximately nine to twelve thousand armed combatants and an unknown number of supporters, mostly in rural areas.

Location/Area of Operation: Colombia, with some activities in Venezuela, Panama, and Ecuador.

External Aid: Cuba provides some medical care and political consultation.

Revolutionary Nuclei **a.k.a. Revolutionary Cells**

Description: Revolutionary Nuclei (RN) emerged from a broad range of anti-establishment and anti-US/NATO/EU leftist groups active in Greece between 1995 and 1998. The group is believed to be the successor to or offshoot of Greece's most prolific terrorist group, Revolutionary People's Struggle (ELA), which has not claimed an attack since January 1995.

Activities: Beginning operations in January 1995, the group has claimed responsibility for some two dozen arson attacks and bombings of a range of U.S., Greek, and other European targets in Greece. RN has not claimed an attack since November 2000.

Strength: Unknown. Group membership is believed to be small.

Location/Area of Operation: Primary area of operation is the Athens metropolitan area.

External Aid: Unknown, but believed to be self-sustaining.

Revolutionary Organization 17 November (17 November)

Description: Radical leftist group established in 1975 and named for the student uprising in Greece in November 1973 that protested the military regime. Anti-Greek establishment, anti-U.S., anti-Turkey, anti-NATO, and committed to the ouster of U.S. bases, removal of Turkish military from Cyprus, and severing of Greece's ties to NATO and the European Union (EU).

Activities: Initial attacks were assassinations of senior U.S. officials and Greek public figures. Added bombings in 1980s. Since 1990, has expanded targets to include EU facilities and foreign firms investing in Greece, and has added improvised rocket attacks to its methods.

Strength: Unknown, but presumed to be small.

Location/Area of Operation: Athens, Greece.

External Aid: Unknown.

Revolutionary People's Liberation Party/Front (DHKP/C) a.k.a. Devrimci So, Revolutionary Left, Dev Sol

Description: Originally formed in 1978 as Devrimci Sol, or Dev Sol, a splinter faction of the Turkish People's Liberation Party/Front. Renamed in 1994 after factional infighting, it espouses a Marxist ideology and is virulently anti-U.S. and anti-NATO.

Activities: Since the late 1980s, has concentrated attacks against current and retired Turkish security and military officials. Began a new campaign against foreign interests in 1990. Launched rockets at U.S. consulate in Istanbul in 1992. Turkish authorities thwarted DHKP/C attempt in June 1999 to fire antitank weapon at U.S. consulate in Istanbul. Conducted its first suicide bombings, targeting Turkish police, in January and September 2001. Series of safe-house raids and arrests by Turkish police over last three years have weakened group significantly.

Strength: Unknown.

Location/Area of Operation: Conducts attacks in Turkey, primarily in Istanbul.

External Aid: Unknown. Raises funds in western Europe. Finances its activities chiefly through armed robberies and extortion.

The Salafist Group for Call and Combat (GSPC)

Description: The Salafist Group for Call and Combat splinter faction that began in 1996 has eclipsed the GIA since approximately 1998 and currently is assessed to be the most effective remaining armed group inside Algeria. In contrast to the GIA, the GSPC has gained popular support through its pledge to avoid civilian attacks inside Algeria (although, in fact, civilians have been attacked). Its adherents abroad appear to have largely co-opted the external networks of the GIA, active particularly throughout Europe, Africa, and the Middle East.

Activities: The GSPC continues to conduct operations aimed at government and military targets, primarily in rural areas. Such operations include roadblocks and attacks against convoys transporting military, police, or other government personnel.

Strength: Unknown; probably several hundred to several thousand inside Algeria.

Location/Area of Operation: Algeria.

External Aid: Algerian expatriates and GSPC members abroad, many residing in western Europe, provide financial and logistics support.

Sendero Luminoso (Shining Path, or SL)

Description: Former university professor Abimael Guzman formed Sendero Luminoso in the late 1960s, and his teachings created the foundation of SL's militant Maoist doctrine. In the 1980s, SL became one of the most ruthless terrorist groups in the Western Hemisphere; approximately thirty thousand persons have died since Shining Path took up arms in 1980. Its stated goal is to destroy existing Peruvian institutions and replace them with a communist peasant revolutionary regime.

Activities: Conducted indiscriminate bombing campaigns and selective assassinations. Detonated explosives at diplomatic missions of several countries in Peru in 1990, including an attempt to car bomb the U.S. embassy in December. Peruvian authorities continued operations against the SL in 2001 in the countryside, where the SL conducted periodic raids on villages.

Strength: Membership is unknown but estimated to be two hundred armed militants. SL's strength has been vastly diminished by arrests and desertions.

Location/Area of Operation: Peru, with most activity in rural areas.

External Aid: None.

United Self-Defense Forces/Group of Colombia (AUC— Autodefensas Unidas de Colombia)

Description: The AUC, commonly referred to as the paramilitaries, is an umbrella organization formed in April 1997 to consolidate most local and regional paramilitary groups each with the mission to protect economic interests and combat insurgents locally. AUC political leader Carlos Castaño has claimed that 70 percent of the AUC's operational costs are financed with drug-related earnings, the rest from "donations" from its sponsors.

Activities: AUC operations vary from assassinating suspected insurgent supporters to engaging guerrilla combat units. The AUC generally avoids engagements with government security forces and actions against U.S. personnel or interests.

Strength: Estimated six thousand to more than eight thousand, including former military and insurgent personnel.

Location/Areas of Operation: AUC forces are strongest in northwest Columbia; since 1999, the group demonstrated a growing presence in other northern and southwestern departments. Clashes between the AUC and the FARC insurgents in Putumayo in 2000 demonstrated the range of the AUC to contest insurgents throughout Colombia.

External Aid: None.

Appendix 4

Overview of State-Sponsored Terrorism

On April 30, 2003, the United States Department of State released *Patterns of Global Terrorism 2002*,[1] the most recent in its annual reviews of the subject. The report included a completely revised and updated section titled "Overview of State-Sponsored Terrorism." Since this section gives a timely view of the subject by the U.S. government, it is reprinted here unedited and in its entirety. It gives a review of the U.S. government's assessment of the performance of the accused state sponsors, and it gives insight into government policies and actions against these states in the ongoing War on Terrorism.

Of particular interest is the discussion of Iraq as a state sponsor of terrorism, especially because this document was being written as U.S. forces were engaged in Operation Iraqi Freedom, the war against Iraq. The report accuses the Iraqi Intelligence service of planning attacks against unidentified Western targets. It accuses Iraq of providing safe haven and support for members of Al Qaeda. The U.S. government has yet to publish compelling evidence in support of either accusation. Surprisingly, the report makes no mention of weapons of mass destruction (WMD), the alleged threat of which was the primary justification for the war against Iraq and the regime of Saddam Hussein.

Despite significant pressure from the U.S. government, the seven designated state sponsors of terrorism—Cuba, Iran, Iraq, Libya, North Korea, Syria, and Sudan—did not take all the necessary actions to disassociate themselves fully from their ties to terrorism in 2002. While some of these countries have taken steps to cooperate in the global war on terrorism, most have also continued the very actions that led them to be declared state sponsors.

Although Cuba is a party to all twelve international counterterrorism conventions and protocols, and Sudan is a party to eleven, both nations continued to provide support to designated Foreign Terrorist Organizations. Likewise, Syria and Libya have continually indicated that they wish to aid the United States in the conflict against terrorism and have curtailed their sponsorship activities. Their cooperation remained deficient in other areas, however. Syria continued to provide safe haven and transit to some Palestinian rejectionist groups. Suspended UN sanctions against Libya remained in place, as Libya again failed to comply with UN requirements related to the bombing in 1988 of Pan Am flight 103 over Lockerbie, Scotland.

While some of the designated state sponsors have taken steps to accede to the international norms of combating terrorism, others—notably Iraq, Iran, and North Korea—have done little to comply. Iraq, through its intelligence service, prepared for possible attacks against Western targets and was a safe haven, transit point, and operational base for terrorist organizations that included members of Al Qaeda. Iran, for its part, remained the most active state sponsor of terrorism during 2002. It has provided funding, training, and weapons to Central Asian and anti-Israeli terrorist groups. In addition, some members of these groups, as well as Al Qaeda, have found safe haven in Iran.

State sponsors of terrorism impede the efforts of the United States and the international community to fight terrorism. These countries provide a critical foundation for terrorist groups. Without state sponsors, terrorist groups would have a much more difficult time obtaining the funds, weapons, materials, and secure areas they require to plan and conduct operations. The United States will continue to insist that these countries end the support they give to terrorist groups.

CUBA

Although Cuba signed and ratified all twelve international counterterrorism conventions in 2001, it has remained opposed to the U.S.-led Coalition prosecuting the war on global terrorism and has been actively critical of many associated U.S. policies and actions. On repeated occasions, for example, Cuba sent agents to U.S. missions around the world who provided false leads designed to subvert the post–September 11 investigation. Cuba did not protest the use of the Guantanamo Bay base to house enemy combatants from the conflict in Afghanistan.

In 2002, Cuba continued to host several terrorists and U.S. fugitives. Havana permitted up to 20 Basque Fatherland and Liberty members to reside in Cuba and provided some degree of safe haven and support to members of the Revolutionary Armed Forces of Colombia (FARC) and National Liberation Army (ELN) groups. Bogota was aware of the arrangement and apparently acquiesced; it has publicly indicated that it seeks Cuba's continued mediation with ELN agents in Cuba.

An accused Irish Republican Army (IRA) weapons expert and longtime resident of Havana went on trial in Colombia in 2002. He had been caught a year earlier in Colombia with two other IRA members and detained for allegedly training the FARC in advanced use of explosives. Some U.S. fugitives continued to live on the island.

IRAN

Iran remained the most active state sponsor of terrorism in 2002. Its Islamic Revolutionary Guard Corps and Ministry of Intelligence and Security were involved in the planning of and support for terrorist acts and continued to exhort a variety of groups that use terrorism to pursue their goals.

Iran's record against Al Qaeda has been mixed. While it has detained and turned over to foreign governments a number of Al Qaeda members, other Al Qaeda members have found virtual safe haven there and may even be receiving protection from elements of the Iranian Government. Iran's long, rugged borders are difficult to monitor, and the large number of Afghan refugees in Iran complicates efforts to locate and apprehend extremists. Nevertheless, it is unlikely that Al Qaeda elements could escape the attention of Iran's formidable security services.

During 2002, Iran maintained a high-profile role in encouraging anti-Israeli activity, both rhetorically and operationally. Supreme Leader Khamenei referred to Israel as a "cancerous tumor," a sentiment echoed by other Iranian leaders in speeches and sermons. Matching this rhetoric with action, Iran provided Lebanese Hezbollah and Palestinian rejectionist groups—notably HAMAS, the Palestine Islamic Jihad, and the Popular Front for the Liberation of Palestine-General Command—with funding, safe haven, training, and weapons. Tehran also encouraged Hezbollah and the Palestinian rejectionist groups to coordinate their planning and to escalate their terrorist activities against Israel.

Iran also provided support to extremist groups in Central Asia, Afghanistan, and Iraq with ties to Al Qaeda, though less than that provided to the groups opposed to Israel. In 2002, Iran became party to the 1988 Protocol on the Suppression of Unlawful Acts of Violence at Airports Serving International Civil Aviation. It is party to five of the twelve international conventions and protocols relating to terrorism.

IRAQ

Iraq planned and sponsored international terrorism in 2002. Throughout the year, the Iraqi Intelligence Services (IIS) laid the groundwork for possible attacks against civilian and military targets in the United States and other Western countries. The IIS reportedly instructed its agents in early 2001 that their main mission was to obtain information about U.S. and Israeli targets. The IIS also threatened dissidents in the Near East and Europe and stole records and computer files detailing anti-regime activity. In December 2002, the press claimed Iraqi intelligence killed Walid al-Mayahi, a Shi'a Iraqi refugee in Lebanon and member of the Iraqi National Congress.

Iraq was a safe haven, transit point, and operational base for groups and individuals who direct violence against the United States, Israel, and other countries. Baghdad overtly assisted two categories of Iraqi-based terrorist organizations—Iranian dissidents devoted to toppling the Iranian Government and a variety of Palestinian groups opposed to peace with Israel. The groups include the Iranian Mujahedin-e Khalq, the Abu Nidal organization (although Iraq reportedly killed its leader), the Palestine Liberation Front (PLF), and the Arab Liberation Front (ALF). In the past year, the PLF increased its operational activity against Israel and sent its members to Iraq for training for future terrorist attacks.

Baghdad provided material assistance to other Palestinian terrorist groups that are in the forefront of the *intifada*. The Popular Front for the Liberation of Palestine-General Command, HAMAS, and the Palestine Islamic Jihad are the three most important groups to whom Baghdad has extended outreach and support efforts.

Saddam paid the families of Palestinian suicide bombers to encourage Palestinian terrorism, channeling $25,000 since March through the ALF alone to families of suicide bombers in Gaza and the West Bank. Public testimonials by Palestinian civilians and officials and cancelled checks captured by Israel in the West Bank verify the transfer of a considerable amount of Iraqi money.

The presence of several hundred Al Qaeda operatives fighting with the small Kurdish Islamist group Ansar al-Islam in the northeastern corner of Iraqi Kurdistan—where the IIS operates—is well documented. Iraq has an agent in the most senior levels of Ansar al-Islam as well. In addition, small numbers of highly placed Al Qaeda militants were present in Baghdad and areas of Iraq that Saddam controls. It is inconceivable these groups were in Iraq without the knowledge and acquiescence of Saddam's regime. In the past year, Al Qaeda operatives in northern Iraq concocted suspect chemicals under the direction of senior Al Qaeda associate Abu Mus'ab al-Zarqawi and tried to smuggle them into Russia, Western Europe, and the United States for terrorist operations.

Iraq is a party to five of the twelve international conventions and proto-cols relating to terrorism.

LIBYA

In 2002, Libyan leader Muammar Qaddafi continued the efforts he undertook following the September 11, 2001, terrorist attacks to identify Libya with the war on terrorism and the struggle against Islamic extrem-ism. In August, Qaddafi told visiting British officials that he regards Osama bin Ladin and his Libyan followers a threat to Libya. In his Sep-tember 1 speech, he declared that Libya would combat members of Al Qaeda and "heretics"—a likely reference to Libyan extremists allied with Al Qaeda and opposed to his regime—as doggedly as the United States did. He further claimed that all political prisoners would be released and that the Libyan Government would henceforth only hold members of Al Qaeda. Libya appears to have curtailed its support for international ter-rorism, although it may maintain residual contacts with some of its former terrorist clients.

Libya's past record of terrorism continued to hinder Qaddafi's efforts to shed Libya's pariah status in 2002. In March, a Scottish appellate court upheld the conviction—originally returned in January 2001—of Libyan intelligence agent Abdel Basset Ali al-Megrahi for murder in connection with planting an explosive device on Pan Am flight 103 in December 1988. The explosion killed all 259 passengers and crew on board and 11 persons on the ground in Lockerbie, Scotland. There have been reports of a pro-posed out-of-court settlement of a suit brought by Pan Am 103 family members against Libya, but by year's end it had not been concluded.

Despite progress toward the payment of appropriate compensation, at year's end Libya had yet to comply with the remaining UN Security Council requirements related to Pan Am flight 103, necessary for the per-manent lifting of UN sanctions, including accepting responsibility for the actions of its officials.

In October, lawyers representing the seven U.S. citizens who died in the bombing of UTA flight 772 in 1989—for which a French court convicted six Libyans in absentia in 1999—filed a suit against Libya and Qaddafi, reportedly seeking $3 billion in compensation. The same month, Libya reportedly pledged to French authorities to increase payments already made to victims of the UTA bombing following the French court ruling in 1999.

In 2002, Libya became a party to the 1999 Convention for the Suppres-sion of the Financing of Terrorism and the 1991 Convention on the Mark-ing of Plastic Explosives for the Purpose of Detection. It is a party to all the twelve international conventions and protocols relating to terrorism.

NORTH KOREA

The Democratic People's Republic of Korea's (DPRK) response to international efforts to combat terrorism was disappointing throughout 2002, although in a statement released after the September 11 attacks, the DPRK had reiterated its public policy of opposing terrorism and any support for terrorism. In 2001, following the September 11 attacks, it also signed the UN Convention for the Suppression of the Financing of Terrorism and became a party to the Convention Against the Taking of Hostages.

Despite the urging of the international community, however, North Korea did not take substantial steps to cooperate in efforts to combat terrorism. Its initial and supplementary reports to the UN Counterterrorism Committee on actions it had undertaken to comply with its obligations under UNSCR 1373 were largely uninformative and nonresponsive. It did not respond to previous U.S. proposals for discussions on terrorism and did not report any efforts to freeze without delay funds and other financial assets or economic resources of persons who commit, or attempt to commit, terrorist acts that UNSCR 1373, among other things, requires all states to do.

North Korea is not known to have sponsored any terrorist acts since 1987. It has sold weapons to several terrorist groups, however, even as it reiterated its opposition to all forms of international terrorism. Pyongyang also has provided safe haven to several Japanese Red Army members who participated in the hijacking of a Japanese Airlines flight to North Korea in 1970.

Pyongyang continued to sell ballistic missile technology to countries designated by the United States as state sponsors of terrorism, including Syria and Libya.

North Korea is a party to six of the twelve international conventions and protocols relating to terrorism.

SUDAN

Sudan was cooperating with U.S. counterterrorism efforts before September 11, 2001, which included a close relationship with various U.S. government agencies to investigate and apprehend extremists suspected of involvement in terrorist activities. Sudan is a party to eleven of the twelve international conventions and protocols relating to terrorism. Sudan also has participated in regional efforts to end the civil war that has been ongoing since 1983—a U.S. policy priority that parallels the U.S. objective of having Sudan deny safe haven to terrorists.

While concerns remain regarding Sudanese government support for certain terrorist groups, such as HAMAS and the Palestine Islamic Jihad, the United States is pleased with Sudan's cooperation and the progress being made in their antiterrorist activities.

SYRIA

The Syrian government has continued to provide political and limited material support to a number of Palestinian groups, including allowing them to maintain headquarters or offices in Damascus. Some of these groups have committed terrorist acts, but the Syrian government insists that their Damascus offices undertake only political and informational activities. The most notable Palestinian rejectionist groups in Syria are the Popular Front for the Liberation of Palestine (PFLP), the Popular Front for the Liberation of Palestine-General Command (PFLP-GC), the Palestine Islamic Jihad (PIJ), and the Islamic Resistance Movement (HAMAS). Syria also continued to permit Iranian resupply, via Damascus, of Hezbollah in Lebanon. Nonetheless, the Syrian government has not been implicated directly in an act of terrorism since 1986.

At the UN Security Council and in other multilateral forums, Syria has taken a leading role in espousing the view that Palestinian and Lebanese terrorist groups fighting Israel are not terrorists; it also has used its voice in the UN Security Council to encourage international support for Palestinian national aspirations and denounce Israeli actions in the Palestinian territories as "state terrorism."

The Syrian government has repeatedly assured the United States that it will take every possible measure to protect U.S. citizens and facilities from terrorists in Syria. In times of increased threat, it has increased police protection around the U.S. Embassy. During the past five years, there have been no acts of terrorism against U.S. citizens in Syria. The government of Syria has cooperated significantly with the United States and other foreign governments against Al Qaeda, the Taliban, and other terrorist organizations and individuals. It also has discouraged any signs of public support for Al Qaeda, including in the media and at mosques.

In 2002, Syria became a party to the 1988 Protocol for the Suppression of Unlawful Acts of Violence at Airports Serving International Civil Aviation, making it party to five of the twelve international conventions and protocols relating to terrorism.

Notes

PREFACE

1. U.S. Department of State, "Preface and Introduction," in *Patterns of Global Terrorism: 2001,* May 21, 2002; www.state.gov/s/ct/rls/pgtrpt/html/10220.htm.

2. Libaw, Oliver, "Defining Terrorism: Little Agreement on Where to Draw the Line," Oct. 11, 2001; http://abcnews.go.com/sections/us/DailyNews/strike_011011definingterror.html.

3. Ross, Dave, "Nuclear," June 4, 2002; www.710kiro.com/daveross_commentary.view.jsp?commentary+21819.

CHAPTER 1: SKYJACKERS

1. "Captives from the Air," *Newsweek,* Nov. 10, 1958, 33.

2. Arey, James, *The Sky Pirates,* New York: Charles Scribner's Sons, 1972, 52–53.

3. Ibid., 49–52, 315–316.

4. "Miami-Cuba Plane Seized by Rebels," *New York Times,* Nov. 2, 1958.

5. "Flight 482 Is Missing," *Time,* Nov. 17, 1958, 38.

6. "Cuba: The Vengeful Visionary," *Time,* Jan. 26, 1959, 40–42, 47, 49.

7. "They Beat Batista," *Time,* Jan. 12, 1959, 33.

8. St. John, Peter, *Air Piracy, Airport Security, and International Terrorism: Winning the War against Hijackers,* Westport, Conn.: Quorum Books, 1991, 8.

9. Arey, *Sky Pirates,* 317.

10. St. John, *Air Piracy,* 1.

11. Arey, *Sky Pirates,* 54–55, 317.

12. Ibid., 317, 318, 319, 353.

13. St. John, *Air Piracy,* 1–2.

14. Senate Select Committee to Study Governmental Operations with Respect to Intelligence Activities, *Alleged Assassination Plots Involving Foreign Leaders: An Interim Report*, Washington, D.C.: U.S. Government Printing Office, Nov. 20, 1975, 71–180.

15. Ibid., 191–215.

16. Arey, *Sky Pirates*, 317–318.

17. Ibid., 315–354.

18. Ibid., 69–70.

19. St. John, *Air Piracy*, 11–12.

20. "Algerians Detain 21 Israelis on Jet," *New York Times*, July 24, 1968, 1, 16.

21. St. John, *Air Piracy*, 2.

22. Ibid., 48.

23. Ibid., 21.

24. Arey, *Sky Pirates*, 101–103.

25. St. John, *Air Piracy*, 43–49.

26. Ibid., 213.

27. Ibid., 220.

28. Ibid., 63.

29. "Skyjacking: An End of Sanity," *Newsweek*, Mar. 4, 1974, 21.

30. "Dead Hijacker's Goal Was White House," *Facts on File*, Mar. 30, 1974, 249.

31. Duersten, Matthew C., "9-11: Special Report—The Man in the Santa Claus Suit," *L.A. Weekly*, Sept. 14–20, 2001.

CHAPTER 2: WHO ARE THE TERRORISTS?

1. "Terrorism on the Left," *Newsweek*, Mar. 23, 1970, 26–30.

2. "Civil Rights: JFK Pledges Protection," *Facts on File*, 1962, 316.

3. "Civil Rights: Birmingham Bomb Kills 4," *Facts on File*, 1963, 326.

4. "Civil Rights: 3 Missing in Mississippi," *Facts on File*, 1964, 213.

5. "Racial Unrest: Bodies of 3 Found," *Facts on File*, 1964, 255.

6. Manchester, William, *The Glory and the Dream: A Narrative History of America 1932–1972*, Boston: Little Brown, 1974, 1166–1167.

7. "Rise of the Dynamite Radicals," *Time*, Sept. 7, 1970, 9–10.

8. Bigart, Homer, "Many Buildings Here Evacuated in Bomb Scares," *New York Times*, Mar. 13, 1970, 1, 6.

9. "Bombing: A Way of Protest and Death," *Time*, Mar. 23, 1970, 8–11.

10. "Man Dies in Wisconsin Blast," *Facts on File*, 1970, 646.

11. Federal Bureau of Investigation, "Most Wanted Terrorists," Oct. 10, 2001; www.fbi.gov/mostwant/terrorists/fugitives.htm.

12. Federal Bureau of Investigation, "The FBI's Ten Most Wanted Fugitives," Dec. 31, 2001; www.fbi.gov/mostwant/topten/fugitives/fugitives.htm.

13. U.S. Department of State, "Appendix B: Background Information on Designated Foreign Terrorist Organizations," in *Patterns of Global Terrorism: 2001*, May 21, 2002; www.state.gov/s/ct/rls/prtrpt/2001/html.

14. Reza, H.G., Halper, Evan, and Getter, Lisa, "Suspected Hijackers: 19 Quiet Lives That Shattered the World," *Los Angeles Times*, Sept. 15, 2001, A1, A22.

15. Associated Press, "15 of Sept. 11 Suspects Were Citizens, Saudis Say," *Los Angeles Times*, Feb. 6, 2002, A10.

CHAPTER 3: NATIONALISTS, COMMUNISTS, AND INSURGENTS

1. Rositzke, Harry, *The KGB: The Eyes of Russia*, Garden City, N.J.: Doubleday, 1981, 232–234.

2. Andrew, Christopher, and Mitrokhin, Vasili, *The Sword and the Shield: The Mitrokhin Archive and the Secret History of the KGB*, New York: Basic Books, 1999, 299.

3. Ibid., 377–385.

4. Senate Subcommittee to Investigate the Administration of the Internal Security Act and Other International Security Laws, Committee of the Judiciary, *The Tricontinental Conference of African, Asian, and Latin American Peoples*, Washington, D.C.: U.S. Government Printing Office, 1966; http://www.rose-hulman.edu/~delacova/tricontinental.htm.

5. Sterling, Claire, *The Terror Network: The Secret War of International Terrorism*, New York: Holt, Rinehart and Winston and Reader's Digest Press, 1981, 250.

6. Ibid., 14–15.

7. Fontaine, Roger W., *Terrorism: The Cuban Connection*, New York: Crane Russak, 1988, 36–39.

8. Sterling, *Terror Network*, 15, 16.

9. Guevara, Che, *Guerrilla Warfare*, New York: Vintage Books, 1969, 93.

10. Senate Select Committee to Study Governmental Operations with Respect to Intelligence Activities, *Alleged Assassination Plots Involving Foreign Leaders*, 71–180.

11. Guevara, Ernesto [Che], *Che Guevara Reader: Writings by Ernesto Che Guevara on Guerilla Strategy, Politics, and Revolution*, ed. David Deutschman, Melbourne and New York: Ocean Press, 1997, 313–328.

12. Rodriguez, Felix I., and Weisman, John, *Shadow Warrior: The CIA Hero of a Hundred Unknown Battles*, New York: Simon and Schuster, 1989, 129–162, 170–172.

13. Schlesinger, Stephen, and Kinzer, Stephen, *Bitter Fruit: The Untold Story of the American Coup in Guatemala*, New York: Doubleday, 1982.

14. Commission for Historical Clarification, *Guatemala, Memory of Silence: Report of the Commission for Historical Clarification, Conclusions and Recommendations*, 1999; http://shr.aaas.org/guatemala/ceh/report/english/toc.html.

15. "Guatemala: U.S. Envoy Slain," *Facts on File*, 1968, 372.

16. "U.S. Ambassador Kidnapped in Brazil," *Facts on File*, 1969, 570–571.

CHAPTER 4: THE PALESTINE LIBERATION ORGANIZATION AND THE POPULAR FRONT FOR THE LIBERATION OF PALESTINE

1. "Arafat, Yasir," *Current Biography Yearbook*, 1994, 29–33.

2. "Dr. Habbash's Strong Medicine," *Newsweek*, Sept. 21, 1970, 28.

3. Arey, *Sky Pirates*, 320–323.

4. "Algerians Detain 21 Israelis on Jet," *New York Times*, July 24, 1968, 1, 16.

5. "Israel and the Arabs: Israeli Plane Hijacked," *Facts on File*, 1968, 298.

6. "Israel and the Arabs: Algerians Free Israelis," *Facts on File*, 1968, 371.

7. Khaled, Leila, "My People Shall Live: Autobiography of a Revolutionary by Leila Khaled as told to George Hajjar," in St. John, Peter, *Air Piracy, Airport Security, and International Terrorism: Winning the War against Hijackers,* New York: Quorum Books, 1991, 221–250.

8. Ibid., 229, 231.

9. "The Lady Who Trained Tigers," *Newsweek,* Sept. 21, 1970, 25.

10. Reuters, "U.S. Jet with 113 Hijacked to Syria by 2 Young Arabs," *New York Times,* Aug. 30, 1969, 1, 2.

11. Khaled, "My People Shall Live," 226–227.

12. Ibid., 223–224.

13. Ibid., 227–229.

14. Ibid., 230.

15. "21 U.S. Aircraft Hijacked in Year," *New York Times,* Aug. 30, 1969, 2.

16. "Rogers Condemns Diversion of Plane as Act of Piracy," *New York Times,* Aug. 30, 1969, 2.

17. "Middle East: U.S. Jet Hijacked to Syria," *Facts on File,* 1969, 554–555.

18. Khaled, "My People Shall Live," 237.

19. "Middle East: Arab-Israeli Prisoner Exchanges," *Facts on File,* 1969, 787–788.

20. "The Hijack War," *Newsweek,* Sept 21, 1970, 20–21.

21. "Angry Men, Desperate Days," *Newsweek,* Sept. 21, 1970, 22–26.

22. Khaled, "My People Shall Live," 239.

23. Hudson, Rex A., *The Sociology and Psychology of Terrorism: Who Becomes a Terrorist and Why?* Washington, D.C.: Library of Congress, September 1999, 62–64.

24. Khaled, "My People Shall Live," 241–242.

25. Arey, *Sky Pirates,* 342–343.

26. "Arabs Destroy Hijacked Jets, Hold Some Hostages; Jordan Cabinet Out after New Clashes; Truce Deadlock," *Facts on File,* 1970, 653.

27. "Jordan Torn by Civil War," *Facts on File,* 1970, 669.

28. "The Commandos: Peace Is Their Greatest Fear," *Newsweek,* Sept. 21, 1970, 27–28.

29. "Fighting Ends in Cease-Fire Accord," *Facts on File,* 1970, 691.

30. "Hostages Freed," *Facts on File,* 1970, 691–692.

31. Khaled, "My People Shall Live," 249–250.

32. "Jordan: Postscript to Terror," *Time,* Oct. 12, 1970, 30.

33. Steven, Stewart, *The Spy Masters of Israel,* New York: Macmillan, 1980, 239–241.

34. Andrew and Mitrokhin, *Sword and the Shield,* 377–385.

35. Ibid., 385–386.

36. Rositzke, *The KGB,* 232–234.

37. Steven, *Spy Masters of Israel,* 259–261.

38. "Horror and Death at the Olympics," *Time,* Sept. 18, 1972, 22–24, 27–30.

39. Raviv, Dan, and Melman, Yossi, *Every Prince a Spy: The Complete History of Israel's Intelligence Community,* Boston: Houghton Mifflin, 1990, 183–184.

40. Steven, *Spy Masters of Israel,* 268–275.

41. Ibid., 267–268.

42. Ibid., 282–290.

43. Ibid., 292.

44. Raviv and Melman, *Every Prince a Spy*, 397–399.

45. "Palestinian Terrorists Take Over Saudi Embassy in Sudan; Kill U.S. Ambassador, 2 Other Diplomats," *Facts on File*, 1973, 177–178.

46. Central Intelligence Agency, "Lebanon," in *The World Factbook 2001*, Langley, Va.: Central Intelligence Agency, 2001; www.cia.gov/cia/publications/factbook/geos/le.html.

47. "U.S. Ambassador to Lebanon, Aide, Chauffeur, Kidnapped, Slain in Beirut; 3 Suspects Held," *Facts on File*, 1979, 425.

48. "U.S. Envoy Slain in Afghanistan: Shot after Kidnapping," *Facts on File*, 1979, 106.

CHAPTER 5: THE HOLY WAR

1. Wilber, Donald M., "Overthrow of Premier Mossadeq of Iran, November 1952–August 1953," Central Intelligence Agency, March 1954; www.gwu.edu/~nsarchiv.

2. McFadden, Robert, Treaster, Joseph B., and Carroll, Maurice, *No Hiding Place: Inside Report on the Hostage Crisis*, New York: Times Books, 1981, 183–184.

3. Ibid., 253–258.

4. Ibid., 3–5, 258.

5. Ibid., 176, 178, 258.

6. Ibid., 4–5.

7. Ibid., 182–183.

8. "Saudi Arabia's Grand Mosque in Mecca Seized by Militants," *Facts on File*, 1979, 898–899.

9. "U.S. Embassy in Pakistan Stormed: Two Americans Killed; Troops Help Embassy Staff Escape; Over 400 Evacuated," *Facts on File*, 1979, 893–894.

10. "U.S. Embassy in Libya Attacked," *Facts on File*, 1979, 914–915.

11. Central Intelligence Agency, "Libya," in *The World Factbook 2001*, Langley, Va.: Central Intelligence Agency, 2001; http://www.cia.gov/cia/publications/factbook/geos/ly.html.

12. Beckwith, Charlie A., with Knox, Donald, *Delta Force*, New York: Harcourt Brace Jovanovich, 1983, 1–10, 253–257.

13. Ibid., 267–283.

14. McFadden, Robert, Treaster, Joseph B., and Carroll, Maurice, *No Hiding Place*, 268, 271.

15. Ibid., 299–300.

16. Amanat, Abbas, "Empowered through Violence: The Reinventing of Islamic Extremism," in *The Age of Terror: America and the World after September 11*, ed. Strobe Talbott and Nayan Chanda, New York: Basic Books, 2001, 23–52.

17. Rashid, Ahmed, "They're Only Sleeping: Why Militant Islamicists in Central Asia Aren't Going to Go Away," *New Yorker*, Jan. 14, 2002, 34–41.

CHAPTER 6: REAGAN TAKES ON TERRORISM

1. Woodward, Bob, *Veil: The Secret Wars of the CIA 1981–1987*, New York: Simon and Schuster, 1987, 92–93.

2. Sterling, *Terror Network.*

3. Woodward, *Veil,* 124–126.

4. Persico, Joseph E., *Casey: The Lives and Secrets of William J Casey—From the OSS to the CIA,* New York: Penguin Books, 1990, 228.

5. Woodward, *Veil,* 160–161.

6. Persico, *Casey,* 236.

7. "International Terrorism in 1997: A Statistical View," Central Intelligence Agency, DCI Counterterrorist Center, March 1998; www.cia.gov/cia/di /products/terrorism/.

8. Kelly, James, "Searching for Hit Teams," *Time,* Dec. 21, 1981, 16–21.

9. "CIA International Terrorism Report," *Facts on File,* 1981, 470.

10. Andrew, Christopher, and Gordievsky, Oleg, *KGB: The Inside Story,* New York: HarperCollins, 1990, 550–551.

11. "A Plan to Overthrow Kaddafi," *Newsweek,* Aug. 3, 1981, 19.

12. Alpern, David M., Martin, David C., Lindsay, John J., and Hubbard, Henry W., "The CIA: Can Casey Survive?" *Newsweek,* Aug. 3, 1981, 18–20.

13. Brecher, John, Martin, David C., Walcott, John, DeFrank, Thomas M., and Moreau, Ron, "To the Shores of Tripoli," *Newsweek,* Aug. 31, 1981, 14–18.

14. Reagan, Ronald, *An American Life,* New York: Simon and Schuster, 1990, 291.

15. Ibid., 293.

16. Taubman, Philip, "U.S. Officials Say F.B.I. Is Hunting Terrorists Seeking to Kill President," *New York Times,* Dec. 4, 1981, A1, A27.

17. Kelly, "Searching for Hit Teams."

18. Woodward, *Veil,* 185.

19. Alpern, David M., Walcott, John, Martin, David C., DeFrank, Thomas M., and Sullivan, Scott, "Coping with a Plot to Kill the President," *Newsweek,* Dec. 21, 1981, 16–17, 19.

20. Chapman, William, "FBI Chief Unhappy over Publicity about Libyan Death Squad," *Washington Post,* Jan. 4, 1982, A11.

21. Hersh, Seymour M., "Target Qaddafi," *New York Times Magazine,* Feb. 22, 1987, 17, 19–22, 24, 26, 48, 71, 74, 84.

22. Lamb, David, "Israel's Invasions, 20 Years Apart, Look Eerily Alike," *Los Angeles Times,* Apr. 20, 2002, A5.

23. Ferrell, Robert H., ed., *The Twentieth Century: An Almanac,* New York: World Almanac Publications, 1985, 480.

24. Ibid., 483.

25. Smith, William E., Brew, Douglas, Talbott, Strobe, and Stewart, William, "Carnage in Lebanon," *Time,* Oct. 31, 1983, 14–18, 22, 25.

26. Marcinko, Richard, with Weisman, John, *Rogue Warrior,* New York: Pocket Books, 1992, 302–319.

27. Ibid., 304.

28. Ibid., 312.

29. Ibid., 318.

30. Deming, Angus, Jensen, Holger, Pringle, James, and Barnathan, Joyce, "Blood and Terror in Beirut," *Newsweek,* May 2, 1983, 22–25.

31. Kelly, James, "The Horror, the Horror!" *Time,* May 2, 1983, 28–31.

32. Beck, Melinda, Pringle, James, Horrock, Nicholas E., Foote, Donna, and Buckley, Jerry, "Inquest on a Massacre," *Newsweek,* Nov. 7, 1983, 85–87, 89.

33. Lawson, John R. III, "Barracks Bombing, 18 Years Ago," *Marines,* Oct. 18, 2001. www.usmc.mil/marinelink/mcn2000.nsf/lookupstoryref/200110189503.

34. Deming, Angus, Walcott, John, Willenson, Kim, Horrock, Nicholas M., and Stanger, Theodore, "How to Strike Back," *Newsweek,* Nov. 7, 1983, 90.

35. Smith, William E., Borrell, John, and Seaman, Barrett, "Again, the Nightmare," *Time,* Oct. 1, 1984, 30–32, 37.

36. Friedman, Thomas L., *From Beirut to Jerusalem,* New York: Farrar Straus Giroux, 1989, 505–506.

37. Woodward, *Veil,* 394–395.

38. Reagan, Ronald, "Executive Order 12333: United States Intelligence Activities," *Federal Register* 46 (Dec. 4, 1981), 200.

39. Persico, *Casey,* 428–430.

40. Woodward, *Veil,* 339–340.

41. Ibid., 339, 395.

42. Ibid., 395–398.

43. Nordland, Rod, "Beirut's Friday Bomber," *Newsweek,* Mar. 18, 1985, 34–35.

44. Smith, William E., "Aftershocks in Beirut," *Time,* Mar. 18, 1985, 30–32.

45. Persico, *Casey,* 428–430.

46. Ibid., 443.

47. Reuters, "Restaurant Blast in Spain Kills 17 near U.S. Air Base," *New York Times,* Apr. 13, 1985, 1, 4.

48. U.S. Department of State, "Terrorist Group Profiles," in *Patterns of Global Terrorism: 1995,* April 1996; http://web.nps.navy.mil/~library/tgp/pflpsc.htm/.

49. U.S. Department of State, "Appendix B: Background Information on Designated Foreign Terrorist Organizations," in *Patterns of Global Terrorism: 2001,* May 2002; http://www.state.gov/s/ct/rls/pgtrpt/2001/html.

50. "TWA Jet Hijacked by Lebanese Shiites; U.S. Vows Not to Yield on Hostages," *Facts on File,* 1985, 457–458.

51. Persico, *Casey,* 441.

52. "U.S. Lebanon Hostages Freed after 17 Days; Syria Plays Key Role in Ending Crisis," *Facts on File,* 1985, 489–490.

53. "Reagan Accuses 5 'Outlaw States' of Backing Terrorism," *Facts on File,* 1985, 506.

54. U.S. Department of State, "Overview of State-Sponsored Terrorism," in *Patterns of Global Terrorism: 2001,* May 2002; www.state.gov/s/ct/rls/pgtrpt/2001/html.

55. Bush, George W., "State of the Union Address," Jan. 29, 2002; www.whitehouse.gov/news/releases/2002/01/20020129-11.html.

56. " 'Other Hostages' Remain in Lebanon," *Facts on File,* 1985, 474.

57. Walsh, Lawrence E., "Executive Summary," *Final Report of the Independent Counsel for Iran/Contra Matters,* U.S. Court of Appeals for the District of Columbia Circuit, Aug. 4, 1993, xiii; http://www.fas.org/irp/offdocs/walsh.

58. Woodward, *Veil,* 412.

59. Kornbluth, Peter, and Byrne, Malcolm, ed., *The Iran-Contra Scandal: The Declassified History,* New York: New Press, 1993, xviii–xix.

60. Ibid., 441.

CHAPTER 7: MUAMMAR QADDAFI

1. Woodward, *Veil,* 409.

2. Ibid., 431.

3. Ibid., 452–443.

4. "Bomb Kills Four on TWA Jet Nearing Athens," *Facts on File,* Apr. 4, 1986, 217.

5. "TWA Suspect Denies Role," *Facts on File,* Apr. 11, 1986, 244.

6. Persico, *Casey,* 497–498.

7. Woodward, *Veil,* 444–445.

8. Hersh, "Target Qaddafi."

9. Whitaker, M., Walcott, J., and Underwood, A., "Getting Rid of Kaddafi," *Newsweek,* Apr. 28, 1986, 18–22, 25.

10. North, Oliver, with Novak, William, *Under Fire: An American Story,* New York: HarperCollins, 1991, 216.

11. Doerner, W.R., "In the Dead of the Night," *Time,* Apr. 28, 1986, 28–31.

12. Church, George C., "Hitting the Source," *Time,* Apr. 28, 1986, 16–20, 23–24, 27.

13. Watson, R., Barry, J., and Walcott, J., "Reagan's Raiders," *Newsweek,* Apr. 28, 1986, 26–31.

14. Marshall, Ruth, "A View from the Bull's-Eye," *Newsweek,* Apr. 28, 1986, 30.

15. Persico, *Casey,* 499.

16. "Transcript of President Reagan's Address on Libya," *Facts on File,* 1986, 258.

17. "Wanting It Both Ways," *Time,* Apr. 28, 1986, 20.

18. Reagan, *An American Life,* 519.

19. Ibid., 520.

20. Reagan, "Executive Order 12333."

21. Barry, John, and Charles, Roger, "The Inside Story of How an American Naval Vessel Blundered into an Attack on Iran Air Flight 655," *Newsweek,* July 13, 1992, 29–33, 36–39.

22. Miller, Judith, and Mylroie, Laurie, *Saddam Hussein and the Crisis in the Gulf,* New York: Times Books, 1990, 147.

23. "U.S. Navy Shoots Down Iranian Airliner over Persian Gulf, Killing 290; Reagan Regrets 'Tragedy,' " *Facts on File,* July 8, 1988, 489–492.

24. Miller, Marjorie, "Pan Am 103 Bombing Suspects Handed Over," *Los Angeles Times,* Apr. 6, 1999, A1, A14.

25. Miller, Marjorie, "Libyan Convicted in Lockerbie Blast," *Los Angeles Times,* Feb. 1, 2001, A1, A12.

CHAPTER 8: SADDAM HUSSEIN

1. Miller and Mylroie, *Saddam Hussein and the Crisis in the Gulf,* 24–41, 80.

2. Ibid., 43–46.

3. Ibid., 143–146.

4. Ibid., 143.

5. Ibid., 146–147.

6. "War Crimes," International Information Programs, U.S. Department of State, 1999; http://usinfo.state.gov/regional/nea/iraq/iraq99h.htm.

7. Sawchyn, Peter, "Scientist Details Effects of Chemical Attacks on Iraqi Kurds," USIA Washington File, Apr. 27, 1988; http://www.fas.org/news/iraq /1998/04/98042702_npo.html.

8. Miller and Mylroie, 124–127.

9. Ibid., 3–4.

10. U.S. News and World Report, *Triumph without Victory: The Unreported History of the Persian Gulf War*, New York: Times Books, 1992, 416.

11. Ibid., 123.

12. Broder, John M., "U.S. War Plan in Iraq: 'Decapitate Leadership,' " *Los Angeles Times*, Sept. 16, 1990, A1, A6–A7.

13. Beck, Melinda, and Barry, John, "For the Air Force, It's the Big One," *Newsweek*, Oct. 1, 1990, 23.

14. van Voorst, Bruce, "Ready, Aim, Fired," *Time*, Oct. 1, 1990, 55.

15. "Hussein to Be Target in War, Says Pentagon," *Minneapolis Star-Tribune*, Jan. 11, 1991, 7.

16. U.S. News and World Report, *Triumph without Victory*, 215–217.

17. Ibid., 409–410.

18. "The Last-Gasp Effort to Get Saddam," *U.S. News and World Report*, Jan. 20, 1992, 42–43.

19. U.S. News and World Report, *Triumph without Victory*, 272–274.

20. Ibid., 395.

21. Ibid., 397.

22. Powell, Colin, with Persico, Joseph E., *My American Journey*, New York: Random House, 1995, 491.

23. Schwarzkopf, H. Norman, *It Doesn't Take a Hero*, New York: Bantam Books, 1992, 318–319.

24. Bush, George, and Scowcroft, Brent, *A World Transformed*, New York: Alfred A. Knopf, 1998, 463–464.

25. Bush, George, *All the Best: My Life in Letters and Other Writings*, New York: Scribner, 1999, 610.

26. "Dressing Up for Bush's Arrival," *New York Times*, Apr. 14, 1993, A6.

27. "Former U.S. President Bush Visits," *Facts on File*, 1993, 316.

28. Ibrahin, Youssef M., "Trial of 14 in Plot Resumes, but U.S. Verdict Is Known," *New York Times*, June 27, 1993, 12; Turque, Bill, Waller, Douglas, Cohn, Bob, Warner, Margaret Garrard, and Barry, John, "Striking Saddam," *Newsweek*, July 5, 1993, 16–17.

29. Schmitt, Eric, "U.S. Says Strike Crippled Iraq's Capacity for Terror," *New York Times*, June 28, 1993, A1, A6.

30. Clinton, William J., "Clinton's Address: Message Is 'Don't Tread On Us,' " *New York Times*, June 27, 1993, 13.

31. Risen, James, "FBI Probed Alleged CIA Plot to Kill Hussein," *Los Angeles Times*, February 15, 1998, A1, A14.

32. U.S. Department of State, *Patterns of Global Terrorism: 1999*, April 2000; www.state.gov/www/global/terrorism/1999report/index.html.

33. U.S. Department of State, *Patterns of Global Terrorism: 2001*, May 2002; www.state.gov/s/ct/rls/pgtrpt/2001.

34. U.S. Department of State, *Patterns of Global Terrorism: 2000*, April 2001; www.state.gov/s/ct/rls/pgtrpt/2000.

35. Central Intelligence Agency, "Somalia," in *The World Factbook 2001*, Langley, Va.: Central Intelligence Agency, 2001; http://www.cia.gov/cia/publications/factbook/geos/so.html.

36. U.S. Department of State, *Patterns of Global Terrorism: 2002*, April 2003; http://www.state.gov/s/ct/rls/pgtrpt/2002.

CHAPTER 9: THE BLIND SHEIKH AND THE MASTERMIND OF TERROR

1. Hudson, *Sociology and Psychology of Terrorism*, 66–68.

2. Reeve, Simon, *The New Jackals: Ramzi Yousef, Osama bin Laden, and the Future of Terrorism*, Boston: Northeastern University Press, 1999, 60.

3. Bergen, Peter L., *Holy War, Inc.: Inside the Secret World of Osama bin Laden*, New York: Free Press, 2001, 66–67.

4. Mylroie, Laurie, *Study of Revenge: The First World Trade Center Attack and Saddam Hussein's War against America*, Washington, D.C.: AEI Press, 2001, 10–17.

5. Ibid., 24–28.

6. Ibid., 43–48, 52.

7. Reeve, *New Jackals*, 140–141.

8. Mylroie, *Study of Revenge*, 33–43.

9. Reeve, *New Jackals*, 149–151.

10. Ibid., 153–154.

11. Mylroie, *Study of Revenge*, 82.

12. Reeve, *New Jackals*, 146–147.

13. Ibid., 6–8, 10, 15.

14. Ibid., 10–15, 24–26.

15. Mylroie, *Study of Revenge*, 79–81.

16. Reeve, *New Jackals*, 29–36.

17. Ibid., 39–40.

18. Mylroie, *Study of Revenge*, 66, 76.

19. Ibid., 176.

20. Reeve, *New Jackals*, 62–63.

21. Ibid., 61–62.

22. "FBI Arrests Nine Men Linked to N.Y.C. Bombing Plot; United Nations, Tunnels among Reported Targets," *Facts on File*, 1993, 483–484.

23. "Cleric and Followers Convicted in U.N. Bomb Plot Trial," *Facts on File*, 1995, 734–735.

24. Mylroie, *Study of Revenge*, 183, 185.

25. Ibid., 191–192.

26. Hudson, *Sociology and Psychology of Terrorism*, 68–70.

27. Reeve, *New Jackals*, 50–54.

28. Ibid., 64–66.

29. Mylroie, *Study of Revenge*, 200–202.

30. Reeve, *New Jackals*, 71–72.

31. Ibid., 76–77.

32. Ibid., 79–80.

33. Ibid., 85.

34. Ibid., 87–90, 97.

35. Ibid., 90–91.

36. Ibid., 86–87.

37. Mylroie, *Study of Revenge*, 205.

38. Reeve, *New Jackals*, 97–101.

39. Hudson, *Sociology and Psychology of Terrorism*, 68–70.

40. Reeve, *New Jackals*, 103–106.

41. Wren, Christopher, "U.S. Jury Convicts 3 in a Conspiracy to Bomb Airliners," *New York Times*, Sept. 6, 1996, A1, B8.

42. Weiser, Benjamin, "The Trade Center Verdict: The Overview; 'Mastermind' and Driver Found Guilty in 1993 Plot to Blow Up Trade Center," *New York Times*, Nov. 13, 1997.

43. U.S. Department of State, "The Year in Review," in *Patterns of Global Terrorism: 1998*, 1998; www.state.gov/www/global/terrorism/1998Report /review.html.

44. Lumpkin, John J., "Kuwaiti Is Suspected as 9/11 Mastermind," *Washington Post*, June 5, 2002, A07.

45. Pincus, Walter, "Mueller Outlines Origin, Funding of Sept. 11 Plot," *Washington Post*, June 6, 2002, A01.

46. Paddock, Richard C., and Meyer, Josh, "Suspect's Role in '95 Plot Detailed," *Los Angeles Times*, June 7, 2002, A14.

47. Reeve, *New Jackals*, 112–121.

48. Ibid., 140.

49. Ibid., 243.

50. Mylroie, *Study of Revenge*, 61–62, 208–212.

51. Jones, Stephen, and Israel, Peter, *Others Unknown: The Oklahoma City Bombing Case and Conspiracy*, New York, Public Affairs, 1998, 4–7, 16.

52. Ibid., 7–9.

53. Ibid., 25.

54. Ibid., 299.

55. Ibid., 305, 311.

56. Ibid., 122–124, 144.

57. Ibid., 139–140.

58. Reeve, *New Jackals*, 83.

59. Jones and Israel, *Others Unknown*, 139–140.

60. Reeve, *New Jackals*, 83.

61. Ibid., 93.

62. "U.S. Executes Oklahoma City Bomber McVeigh," *Facts on File*, 2001, 445–446.

CHAPTER 10: AMERICA IN RETREAT

1. Bowden, Mark, *Black Hawk Down: A Story of Modern War*, New York: Atlantic Monthly Press, 331–334.

2. Reeve, *New Jackals,* 181–182.

3. Bowden, *Black Hawk Down: A Story of Modern War.*

4. Reeve, *New Jackals,* 198–201.

5. "U.S. Sets Somalia Pullout Deadline," *Facts on File,* 1993, 743–745.

6. "Clinton's Speech on Somalia," *Facts on File,* 1993, 744.

7. Pear, Norbert, "The Pilot: Friends Depict Loner with Unraveling Life," *New York Times,* Sept. 13, 1994, A20.

8. Dowd, Maureen, "Unimpeded, Intruder Crashes Plane into the White House," *New York Times,* Sept. 13, 1994, A1, A20.

9. Labaton, Stephen, "Pilot's Exploit Rattles White House Officials," *New York Times,* Sept. 13, 1994, A1, A20.

10. "Saudi Bombing Kills Seven at U.S.-Run Military Center," *Facts on File,* 1995, 851.

11. Mylroie, *Study of Revenge,* 216–217.

12. "Truck Bomb Kills 19 U.S. Troops in Saudi Arabia; Moslem Militants Suspected," *Facts on File,* 1996, 441–442.

13. Mylroie, *Study of Revenge,* 219–220.

14. Garamone, Jim, "19 Dead, 80 Hospitalized in Terror Attack in Saudi," *American Forces Information Service News Articles,* June 27, 1996; www .defenselink.mil/news/Jun1996/n06271996_9606271.html.

15. Cohen, William S., "Report: Personal Accountability for Force Protection at Khobar Towers," July 31, 1997; www.defenselink.mil/pubs/khobar/report.html.

16. Bergen, *Holy War, Inc.,* 88.

17. "Khobar Towers Indictments Returned," CNN.com; www.cnn .com/2001/LAW/06/21/khobar.indictments/index.html.

18. Clinton, William J., "Letter from the President to the Speaker of the House of Representatives and the President Pro Tempore of the Senate," December 18, 1998; http://www.whitehouse.gov/uri-res/I2R?urn:pdi://oma.eop.gov.us /1998/12/18/9.text.1.

19. "Pentagon Assessment of Desert Fox: 'Job Extremely Well Done,'" CNN.com, Dec. 19, 1998; http://cnn.com/US/9812/19/iraq.us.forces.02/.

20. Ratnesar, Romesh, "What Good Did It Do?" *Time,* Dec. 28, 1998–Jan. 4, 1999, 68–73.

21. Elliott, Michael, Contreras, Joseph, and Barry, John, "Back to Battle Stations," *Newsweek,* Dec. 28, 1998–Jan. 4. 1999, 44–48.

22. "General Anthony C. Zinni on Operation Desert Fox and Iraq," Department of Defense News Briefing, Jan. 8, 1999; www.defenselink.mil/news/jan1999.

23. Wilson, Admiral Thomas R., "Department of Defense News Briefing," Dec. 19, 1998; www.defenselink.mil/news/dec1998.

24. Wise, David, "The Thin Line between Diplomacy and Murder," *Los Angeles Times,* Apr. 25, 1999, M2.

25. Senate Select Committee to Study Governmental Operations with Respect to Intelligence Activities, *Alleged Assassination Plots Involving Foreign Leaders,* 71–181.

26. Gwynne, Sam C., "Spies Like Us," *Time,* Jan. 25, 1999, 48.

CHAPTER 11: OSAMA BIN LADEN

1. Barry, John, Dickey, Christopher, and LeVine, Steve, "Making a Symbol of Terror," *Newsweek,* March 1, 1999, 40–43.

2. Pike, John, "Al-Qa'ida (The Base)," FAS Intelligence Resource Program; www.fas.org/irp/world/para/ladin.htm.

3. Bergen, *Holy War, Inc.,* 78–82.

4. Ibid., 86.

5. Ibid., 92–93.

6. Central Intelligence Agency, "Afghanistan," in *The World Factbook 2001,* Langley, Va.: Central Intelligence Agency, 2001; www.cia.gov/cia/publications /factbook/geos/af.html.

7. Bergen, *Holy War, Inc.,* 13, 15.

8. Frantz, Douglas, and Rohde, David, "How bin Laden and Taliban Forged Jihad Ties," *New York Times,* Nov. 22, 2001.

9. Bergen, *Holy War, Inc.,* 64–69.

10. Bodansky, Yossef, *Bin Laden: The Man Who Declared War on America,* New York: Forum, 2001, 195–198.

11. Chivers, C.J., and Rohde, David, "Afghan Camps Turn Out Holy War Guerrillas and Terrorists," *New York Times,* March 18, 2002.

12. Finn, Peter, "Hijackers Depicted as Elite Group," *Washington Post,* Nov. 5, 2001, A01.

13. Shaykh Usamah Bin-Laden; Ayman al-Zawahiri, amir of the Jihad Group in Egypt; Abu-Yasir Rifa'i Ahmad Taha, Egyptian Islamic Group; Shayk Mir Hamzah, secretary of the Jamiat-ul-Ulema-e-Pakistan; and Fazlul, Rahman, amir of the Jihad Movement in Bangladesh, "Jihad against Jews and Crusaders," World Islamic Front Statement, Feb. 23, 1998; www.fas.org/irp/world/para/docs /980223-fatwa.htm.

14. Wright, Lawrence, "The Counter-Terrorist," *New Yorker,* Jan. 14, 2002, 50–56, 58–60.

15. Miller, Judith, Gerth, Jeff, and Van Natta, Jeff Jr., "Many Say U.S. Planned for Terror but Failed to Take Action," *New York Times,* Dec. 30, 2001.

16. Bergen, *Holy War, Inc.,* 17–23.

17. "Calls to Action," *Washington Post,* Aug. 23, 1998, A24.

CHAPTER 12: AL QAEDA'S WAR

1. McGeary, Johanna, "Sifting for Answers," *Time,* Aug. 24, 1998, 48–51, 54.

2. McGeary, Johanna, "Terror in Africa," *Time,* Aug. 17, 1998, 32–35.

3. Waller, Douglas, "A Pair of Quick Arrests," *Time,* Sept. 7, 1998, 45.

4. Watson, Russell, and Barry, John, "Our Target Was Terror," *Newsweek,* Aug. 24, 1998, 24–27.

5. Nelan, Bruce, "Our Target Was Terror," *Time.com Daily Magazine,* Aug. 31, 1998; www.time.com.

6. Cohen, William S., "Department of Defense News Briefing," Aug. 20, 1998; www.defenselink.mil.

7. Clinton, William J., "Statement by the President," Aug. 20, 1998; www.Clinton.nara.gov.

8. "Apologize," *New Republic,* Nov. 22, 1999, 9.

9. This is probably a version of the "memorandum of law" drafted in 1989, prior to the invasion of Panama. Wright, Robin, "U.S. OKs Covert Operations That May Kill Foreigners," *Los Angeles Times,* Oct. 14, 1989, A1, A16.

10. Richter, Paul, "White House Justifies Option of Lethal Force," *Los Angeles Times,* Oct. 29, 1998, A1, A10–A11.

11. Weisner, Benjamin, "Saudi Indicted in Bomb Attacks on U.S. Embassies," *New York Times,* Nov. 5, 1998.

12. Drogin, Bob, and Meyer, Josh, "Alleged 9/11 Mastermind Linked to Hamburg Cell," *Los Angeles Times,* June 6, 2002, A1, A18.

13. Interview with Osama bin Laden by Rahimullah Yusufai, "Conversation with Terror," *Time,* Jan. 11, 1999, 38–39.

14. Interview of Osama bin Laden by Jamal Ismail, "I Am Not Afraid of Death," *Newsweek,* Jan. 11 1999, 36–37.

15. Barry, Dickey, and LeVine, "Making a Symbol of Terror," 40–43.

16. Gellman, Barton, "Broad Effort Launched after '98 Attacks," *Washington Post,* Dec. 19, 2001, A01.

17. "Clinton Ordered bin Laden Killing," BBC News, Sept. 23, 2001; www.news.bbc.co.uk/hi/English/world/Americas/newsid_1558918/1558918.stm.

18. Risen, James, "U.S. Pursued Secret Efforts to Catch or Kill bin Laden," *New York Times,* Sept. 30, 2001.

19. Woodward, Bob, and Ricks, Thomas E., "U.S. Was Foiled Multiple Times in Efforts to Capture bin Laden or Have Him Killed," *Washington Post,* Oct. 3, 2001, A01.

20. Langewiesche, William, "The Crash of EgyptAir 990," *Atlantic Monthly,* November 2001, 41–52.

21. Hosenball, Mark, "The Last Word on EgyptAir 990?" *Newsweek,* July 2, 2001.

22. Klaidman, Daniel, and Hosenball, Mark, "I Put My Trust in God," *Newsweek,* Nov. 29, 1999, 30–37.

23. "Dead Hijacker's Goal Was White House," 249.

24. Hirschman, David, *Hijacked: The True Story of the Heroes of Flight 705,* New York: William Morrow, 1997.

25. Riding, Alan, "Police Say Hijackers Planned to Blow Up Jet over Paris," *New York Times,* Dec. 28, 1994, A3.

26. "The Lesson of Air France Flight 8969," MSNBC, Sept. 30, 2001; www.msnbc.com/news/635213.asp.

27. Bacon, Kenneth H., "Department of Defense News Briefing," Nov. 4, 1999; www.defenselink.mil/news/Nov1999/t11051999_t1104asd.html.

28. "Military Casualties: Egypt Allows Media to Report Egyptian Military Was on Crashed Jet," ABCNews.com, Nov. 2, 1999; www.abcnews.go.com/sections/world/DailyNews/egyptmilitary991102.html.

29. Associated Press, "Transportation Board Faults EgyptAir Pilot for Crash," *New York Times,* Mar. 21, 2002; www.nytimes.com.

30. Fainaru, Steve, and Whoriskey, Peter, "Hijack Suspects Tried Many Flight Schools," *Washington Post,* Sept. 19, 2001, A15.

31. Meyer, Josh, "Border Arrest Stirs Fear of Terrorist Cells in U.S.," *Los Angeles Times,* Mar. 11, 2001, A1, A30–A31.

32. Bergen, *Holy War, Inc.,* 140–141.

33. Miller, John, "The Connection: Yemen Probe Uncovers bin Laden Links and Missteps by Cole Bombers," ABCNEWS.com, Dec. 7, 2000; www.abcnews .com.go.com/sections/world/DailyNews/yemen001207b.html.

34. Associated Press, "Bin Laden's Plan: Cole Bombing Linked to Millenium Terror Plot," Dec. 24, 2000; www.abcnews.com.

35. Bartholet, Jeffrey, "A Sneak Attack," *Newsweek,* Oct. 23, 2000, 27–29.

36. Ratnesar, Romesh, "Sneak Attack," *Time,* Oct. 23, 2000, 42–44.

37. Clinton, William J., "Statement of the President on Middle East Situation and Incident on USS Cole in Yemen," Oct. 12, 2000; http://www.chinfo.navy.mil /navpalib/ships/destroyers/cole/prez-cole.txt.

38. Reuters, "Extradition Not Allowed," Dec. 10, 2000; http://abcnews.com .go.com/sections/world/DailyNews/cole001210.html.

39. "U.S. Finds Link between bin Laden and Cole Bombing," CNN.com, Dec. 7, 2000; www.cnn.com/2000/US/12/07/cole.suspect/index.html.

40. "Key Cole Suspects Fled to Afghanistan, Officials Say," CNN.com, Dec. 15, 2000; www.cnn.com/2000/US/12/15/cole.suspect/.

41. Elias, Diana, "Video Suggests bin Laden Men Perpetrated Cole Bombing," *Washington Post* (Associated Press), June 20, 2001, A24.

42. "FBI Searches Jersey City Apartment; 2nd Man Held as Witness," CNN.com, Sept. 16, 2001; www.cnn.com/2001/US/09/15/America.under .attack/.

43. Khan, Kamran, and Chandrasekaran, Rajiv, "Cole Suspect Turned Over by Pakistan," *Washington Post,* Oct. 28, 2001, A01.

44. Gellman, Barton, "Struggle inside the Government Defined Campaign," *Washington Post,* Dec. 20, 2001, A01.

45. Miller, Gerth, and Van Natta, "Many Say U.S. Planned for Terror."

CHAPTER 13: THE PAST AND THE FUTURE

1. Senate Subcommittee to Investigate the Administration of the Internal Security Act and Other International Security Laws, Committee of the Judiciary, *Tricontinental Conference of African, Asian, and Latin American Peoples.*

2. Guevara, *Che Guevara Reader,* 313–328.

3. Reuters, "U.S. Jet with 113 Hijacked to Syria by 2 Young Arabs."

4. "U.S. Embassy in Pakistan Stormed."

5. Reeve, *New Jackals,* 60.

6. Shaykh Usamah Bin-Laden; Ayman al-Zawahiri; Abu-Yasir Rifa'i Ahmad Taha; Shayk Mir Hamzah; and Fazlul, Rahman, "Jihad against Jews and Crusaders."

7. For more on this point of view, see Chomsky, Noam, *9-11,* New York: Seven Stories Press, 2002.

8. Bergen, *Holy War, Inc.,* 20–21.

9. Reeve, *New Jackals,* 261–262.

10. Sterling, *Terror Network.*

11. Ibid., 13–15, 192, 198–199, 286–297.

12. Persico, *Casey,* 286–288.

13. Woodward, *Veil,* 93, 124–126, 129.

14. Andrew and Mitrokhin, *Sword and the Shield,* 379–382, 384–385.

15. Wright, "The Counter-Terrorist," 50–56, 58–61.

16. Meyer, "Border Arrest Stirs Fear of Terrorist Cells in U.S."

17. Johnston, David, "Pre-Attack Memo Cited bin Laden," *New York Times,* May 15, 2002.

18. Priest, Dana, and Eggen, Dan, "9/11 Probers Say Agencies Failed to Heed Attack Signs," *Washington Post,* Sept. 19, 2002, A1.

19. Nordland, Rod, "Beirut's Friday Bomber."

20. "U.S. Navy Shoots Down Iranian Airliner over Persian Gulf, Killing 290; Reagan Regrets 'Tragedy.' "

21. Marshall, "A View from the Bull's-Eye," 30.

22. U.S. Department of State, "Overview of State Sponsored Terrorism," in *Patterns of Global Terrorism: 2001.*

23. Tucker, Jonathan B., "Historical Trends Related to Bioterrorism: An Empirical Analysis," *Emerging Infectious Diseases,* Vol. 5, No. 4, July–Aug., 2000; www.cdc.gov/ncidod/EID/vol5no4/tucker.htm.

24. Olson, Kyle B., "Aum Shinrikyo: Once and Future Threat?" *Emerging Infectious Diseases,* Vol. 5, No. 4, July–Aug., 2000; www.cdc.gov/ncidod/EID /vol5no4/olson.htm.

25. Sawchyn, "Scientist Details Effects of Chemical Attacks on Iraqi Kurds."

26. Barletta, Michael, Sands, Amy, and Tucker, Jonathan B., "Keeping Track of Anthrax: The Case for the Biosecurity Convention," *Bulletin of the Atomic Scientists,* Vol. 58, No. 3, May/June 2003, 57–62; www.bullatomicsci.cor/issues/2002 /mj02/mj02barletta.html.

27. Wohlstetter, Albert, "The Delicate Balance of Terror," *Foreign Affairs,* Vol. 37, Jan. 1959, 209–234; www.rand.org/publications/classics/wohlstetter /P1472/P1472.html.

28. St. John, *Air Piracy,* 21.

EPILOGUE

1. "Authorizing Use of United States Armed Forces against Those Responsible for Recent Attacks against the United States," *Congressional Record,* Sept. 14, 2001 (House), p. H5638.

2. U.S. Department of Homeland Security, "DHS Organization"; www .dhs.gov/dhspublic/display?theme+59&content409.

3. For an example, see: Hentoff, Nat, "Grassroots Patriots," *The Progressive,* July 2002; http://www.progressive.org/July%202002/hent0702.html.

4. Barletta, Michael, Sands, Amy, and Tucker, Jonathan B., "Keeping Track of Anthrax: The Case for the Biosecurity Convention," *Bulletin of the Atomic Scientists* 58, no. 3 (May/June 2003), 57–62; www.bullatomicsci.cor/issues/2002/mj02/ mj02barletta.html.

5. Associated Press, "Live in Prison: Shoe Bomber Unrepentant at His Sentencing for Trying to Blow Up Plane," *ABC News,* Jan. 30, 2003.

6. Associated Press, "Bali Bombers Targeted Americans," *CBS News.com,* Nov. 9, 2002.

7. Wright, Robin, Miller, Greg, and Meyer, Josh, "U.S. Fears 'Wave of Attacks'," *Los Angeles Times,* May 14, 2003.

8. Schmidt, Susan, "Trucker Pleads Guilty in Plot by Al Qaeda," *Washington Post,* June 20, 2003, A01.

9. Meyer, Josh, "A Resilient Al Qaeda Regroups and Plots," *Los Angeles Times,* June 1, 2003, A1, A10–A11.

APPENDIX 1: MAJOR TERRORIST ATTACKS ON THE UNITED STATES AND ITS INTERESTS, 1958–2001

1. This summary is based on information from "Significant Terrorist Incidents, 1961–2001" compiled by the Office of the Historian, U.S. Department of State (www.state.gov) and other sources cited in the text.

APPENDIX 2: THE FBI'S MOST-WANTED TERRORISTS (OCTOBER 10, 2001)

1. Federal Bureau of Investigations, "Most Wanted Terrorists."

APPENDIX 3: FOREIGN TERRORIST ORGANIZATIONS

1. Condensed and edited from U.S. Department of State, "Appendix B: Background Information on Designated Foreign Terrorist Organizations," in *Patterns of Global Terrorism: 2001 and 2002.*

APPENDIX 4: OVERVIEW OF STATE-SPONSORED TERRORISM

1. U.S. Department of State, "Overview of State-Sponsored Terrorism," *Patterns of Global Terrorism: 2002.*

Selected Bibliography

Andrew, Christopher, and Gordievsky, Oleg. *KGB: The Inside Story.* New York: HarperCollins, 1990.

Andrew, Christopher, and Mitrokhin, Vasili. *The Sword and the Shield: The Mitrokhin Archive and the Secret History of the KGB.* New York: Basic Books, 1999.

Arey, James A. *The Sky Pirates.* New York: Charles Scribner's Sons, 1972.

Beckwith, Charlie A., with Knox, Donald. *Delta Force.* San Diego, Calif.: Harcourt Brace Jovanovich, 1983.

Bergen, Peter L. *Holy War, Inc.: Inside the Secret World of Osama bin Laden.* New York: Free Press, 2001.

Bodansky, Yossef. *Bin Laden: The Man Who Declared War on America.* New York: Forum, 2001.

Bowden, Mark. *Black Hawk Down: A Story of Modern War.* New York: Atlantic Monthly Press, 1999.

Bush, George. *All the Best: My Life in Letters and Other Writings.* New York: Scribner, 1999.

Bush, George, and Scowcroft, Brent. *A World Transformed.* New York: Alfred A. Knopf, 1998.

Central Intelligence Agency. *The World Factbook 2001.* Langley: Central Intelligence Agency, 2001. www.cia.gov/cia/publications/factbook/index.html.

Fontaine, Roger W. *Terrorism: The Cuban Connection.* New York: Crane Russak, 1988.

Friedman, Thomas L. *From Beirut to Jerusalem.* New York: Farrar Straus Giroux, 1989.

Guevara, Ernesto [Che]. *Che Guevara Reader: Writings by Ernesto Che Guevara on Guerilla Strategy, Politics, and Revolution.* Edited by David Deutschman. Melbourne and New York: Ocean Press, 1997.

Guevara, Che. *Guerrilla Warfare.* New York: Vintage Books, 1969.

Hirschman, David. *Hijacked: The True Story of the Heroes of Flight 705.* New York: William Morrow, 1997.

Hudson, Rex A. *The Sociology and Psychology of Terrorism: Who Becomes a Terrorist and Why?* Washington, D.C.: Library of Congress, September 1999.

Jones, Stephen, and Israel, Peter. *Others Unknown: The Oklahoma City Bombing Case and Conspiracy.* New York: Public Affairs, 1998.

Manchester, William. *The Glory and the Dream: A Narrative History of America 1932–1972.* Boston: Little Brown, 1974.

Marcinko, Richard, with Weisman, John. *Rogue Warrior.* New York: Pocket Books, 1992.

McFadden, Robert, Treaster, Joseph B., and Carroll, Maurice. *No Hiding Place: Inside Report on the Hostage Crisis.* New York: Times Books, 1981.

Miller, Judith, and Mylroie, Laurie. *Saddam Hussein and the Crisis in the Gulf.* New York: Time Books, 1990.

Mylroie, Laurie. *Study of Revenge: The First World Trade Center Attack and Saddam Hussein's War against America.* Washington, D.C.: AEI Press, 2001.

North, Oliver, with Novak, William. *Under Fire: An American Story.* New York: HarperCollins, 1991.

Persico, Joseph E. *Casey: The Lives and Secrets of William J. Casey—From the OSS to the CIA.* New York: Penguin Books, 1990.

Powell, Colin, with Persico, Joseph E. *My American Journey.* New York: Random House, 1995.

Raviv, Dan, and Melman, Yossi. *Every Prince a Spy: The Complete History of Israel's Intelligence Community.* Boston: Houghton Mifflin, 1990.

Reagan, Ronald. *An American Life.* New York: Simon and Schuster, 1990.

Reeve, Simon. *The New Jackals: Ramzi Yousef, Osama bin Laden, and the Future of Terrorism.* Boston: Northeastern University Press, 1999.

Rodriguez, Felix I., and Weisman, John. *Shadow Warrior: The CIA Hero of a Hundred Unknown Battles.* New York: Simon and Schuster, 1989.

Rositzke, Harry. *The KGB: The Eyes of Russia.* Garden City, N.J.: Doubleday, 1981.

Schlesinger, Stephen, and Kinzer, Stephen. *Bitter Fruit: The Untold Story of the American Coup in Guatemala.* New York: Doubleday, 1982.

Schwarzkopf, H. Norman. *It Doesn't Take a Hero.* New York: Bantam Books, 1992.

Senate Select Committee to Study Governmental Operations with Respect to Intelligence Activities. *Alleged Assassination Plots Involving Foreign Leaders: An Interim Report.* Washington, D.C.: U.S. Government Printing Office, Nov. 20, 1975.

St. John, Peter. *Air Piracy, Airport Security, and International Terrorism: Winning the War against Hijackers.* Westport, Conn.: Quorum Books, 1991.

Sterling, Claire. *The Terror Network: The Secret War of International Terrorism.* New York: Holt, Rinehart and Winston and Reader's Digest Press, 1981.

Steven, Stewart. *The Spy Masters of Israel.* New York: Macmillan, 1980.

Talbott, Strobe, and Chanda, Nayan. *The Age of Terror: America and the World after September 11.* New York: Basic Books, 2001.

U.S. Department of State. *Patterns of Global Terrorism, 1995.* April 1996; http://web.nps.navy.mil/~library/tgp/pflpsc.htm.

———. *Patterns of Global Terrorism: 1998.* 1998; www.state.gov/www/global/terrorism/1998Report/review.html.

————. *Patterns of Global Terrorism: 1999.* April 2000; www.state.gov/www/global/terrorism/1999report/index.html.

————. *Patterns of Global Terrorism: 2000.* April 2001; www.state.gov/s/ct/rls/pgtrpt/2000.

————. *Patterns of Global Terrorism: 2001.* May 2002; www.state.gov/s/ct/rls/pgtrpt/2001.

————. *Patterns of Global Terrorism: 2002.* May 2003; www.state.gov/s/ct/rls/pgtrpt/2002.

U.S. News and World Report. *Triumph without Victory: The Unreported History of the Persian Gulf War.* New York: Times Books, 1992.

U.S. Senate. Subcommittee to Investigate the Administration of the Internal Security Act and Other International Security Laws, Committee of the Judiciary. *The Tricontinental Conference of African, Asian, and Latin American Peoples.* Washington, D.C.: U.S. Government Printing Office, 1966; http://www.rose-hulman.edu/~delacova/tricontinental.htm.

Walsh, Lawrence E. *Final Report of the Independent Counsel for Iran/Contra Matters.* U.S. Court of Appeals for the District of Columbia Circuit, Aug. 4, 1993; www.fas.org/irp/offdocs/walsh.

Woodward, Bob. *Veil: The Secret Wars of the CIA 1981–1987.* New York: Simon and Schuster, 1987.

Index

About the Author

DENNIS PISZKIEWICZ is the author of *Wernher von Braun: The Man Who Sold the Moon* (Praeger, 1998).